Tamburlaine

ARDEN EARLY MODERN DRAMA GUIDES

Series Editors:
Andrew Hiscock, University of Wales, Bangor, UK and
Lisa Hopkins, Sheffield Hallam University, UK

Arden Early Modern Drama Guides offer practical and accessible introductions to the critical and performative contexts of key Elizabethan and Jacobean plays. Each guide introduces the text's critical and performance history, but also provides students with an invaluable insight into the landscape of current scholarly research, through a keynote essay on the state of the art and newly commissioned essays of fresh research from different critical perspectives.

A Midsummer Night's Dream, edited by Regina Buccola
Doctor Faustus, edited by Sara Munson Deats
King Lear, edited by Andrew Hiscock and Lisa Hopkins
Henry IV, Part 1, edited by Stephen Longstaffe
'Tis Pity She's a Whore, edited by Lisa Hopkins
Women Beware Women, edited by Andrew Hiscock
Volpone, edited by Matthew Steggle
The Duchess of Malfi, edited by Christina Luckyj
The Alchemist, edited by Erin Julian and Helen Ostovich
The Jew of Malta, edited by Robert A. Logan
Macbeth, edited by John Drakakis and Dale Townshend
Richard III, edited by Annaliese Connolly
Twelfth Night, edited by Alison Findlay and Liz Oakley-Brown
The Tempest, edited by Alden T. Vaughan and
Virginia Mason Vaughan
Romeo and Juliet, edited by Julia Reinhard Lupton
Julius Caesar, edited by Andrew James Hartley
The Revenger's Tragedy, edited by Brian Walsh
The White Devil, edited by Paul Frazer and Adam Hansen
Edward II, edited by Kirk Melnikoff
Much Ado About Nothing, edited by Deborah Cartmell
and Peter J. Smith
King Henry V, edited by Karen Britland and Line Cottegnies
Troilus and Cressida, edited by Efterpi Mitsi

Further titles are in preparation.

Tamburlaine

A Critical Reader

Edited by
David McInnis

THE ARDEN SHAKESPEARE
LONDON • NEW YORK • OXFORD • NEW DELHI • SYDNEY

THE ARDEN SHAKESPEARE
Bloomsbury Publishing Plc
50 Bedford Square, London, WC1B 3DP, UK
1385 Broadway, New York, NY 10018, USA
29 Earlsfort Terrace, Dublin 2, Ireland

BLOOMSBURY, THE ARDEN SHAKESPEARE and the Arden Shakespeare logo
are trademarks of Bloomsbury Publishing Plc

First published in Great Britain 2020
This paperback edition published in 2022

Copyright © David McInnis and contributors, 2020

David McInnis and contributors have asserted their right under the Copyright, Designs
and Patents Act, 1988, to be identified as the authors of this work.

For legal purposes the Acknowledgements on pp. xiii–xiv constitute an extension
of this copyright page.

Cover design: Charlotte Daniels
Cover image taken from the 1615 title-page of *The Spanish Tragedy*, by Thomas Kyd

All rights reserved. No part of this publication may be reproduced or transmitted
in any form or by any means, electronic or mechanical, including photocopying,
recording, or any information storage or retrieval system, without prior
permission in writing from the publishers.

Bloomsbury Publishing Plc does not have any control over, or responsibility for,
any third-party websites referred to or in this book. All internet addresses given
in this book were correct at the time of going to press. The author and publisher
regret any inconvenience caused if addresses have changed or sites have
ceased to exist, but can accept no responsibility for any such changes.

A catalogue record for this book is available from the British Library.

A catalog record for this book is available from the Library of Congress.

ISBN:	HB:	978-1-3500-8271-7
	PB:	978-1-3502-4665-2
	ePDF:	978-1-3500-8273-1
	eBook:	978-1-3500-8272-4

Series: Arden Early Modern Drama Guides

Typeset by RefineCatch Limited, Bungay, Suffolk

To find out more about our authors and books visit www.bloomsbury.com
and sign up for our newsletters.

CONTENTS

List of Illustrations vii
Series Introduction viii
Notes on Contributors ix
Acknowledgements xiii

   Introduction 1
   David McInnis

1 The Critical Backstory: *Tamburlaine*, 1587–2000 – A Reception History 19
   M. L. Stapleton

2 The Performance History: 'High Astounding Terms' – Tamburlaine and *Tamburlaine* on Stage 43
   Peter Kirwan

3 The State of the Art: The Critical Landscape, 2000–Present 67
   Sarah Wall-Randell

4 New Directions: Mending *Tamburlaine* 85
   Claire M. L. Bourne

5 New Directions: Tamburlaine the Weather Man 107
   Tom Rutter

6 New Directions: Towards a Racialized
    Tamburlaine 129
    Sydnee Wagner

7 New Directions: Retooling Timür 147
    Matthew Dimmock

8 Three Tents for *Tamburlaine*: Resources and
    Approaches for Teaching the Play 167
    Liam E. Semler

Notes 193
Works Cited and Selected Further Reading 233
Index 251

ILLUSTRATIONS

1 *Tamburlaine the greate . . . The second part*
  (London: Edward White, 1606), sig. L2r, 1977 2594,
  Beinecke Rare Book and Manuscript Library.   87

2 *Tamburlaine the Great . . . The second part* (1606),
  sig. H4r, PR2669.A1 1606, Rare Books and
  Manuscripts, Eberly Family Special Collections
  Library, Penn State University Libraries.   99

3 *Tamburlaine the Great . . . The second part* (1606),
  sig. E3v, PR2669.A1 1606, Rare Books and
  Manuscripts, Eberly Family Special Collections
  Library, Penn State University Libraries.   100

4 *Tamburlaine the Great . . . The second part* (1606),
  sig. D4r, PR2669.A1 1606, Rare Books and
  Manuscripts, Eberly Family Special Collections
  Library, Penn State University Libraries.   102

5 *Tamburlaine the Great . . . The second part* (1606),
  sigs. D4v-Er1, PR2669.A1 1606, Rare Books and
  Manuscripts, Eberly Family Special Collections
  Library, Penn State University Libraries.   103

SERIES INTRODUCTION

The drama of Shakespeare and his contemporaries has remained at the very heart of English curricula internationally and the pedagogic needs surrounding this body of literature have grown increasingly complex as more sophisticated resources become available to scholars, tutors and students. This series aims to offer a clear picture of the critical and performative contexts of a range of chosen texts. In addition, each volume furnishes readers with invaluable insights into the landscape of current scholarly research as well as including new pieces of research by leading critics.

This series is designed to respond to the clearly identified needs of scholars, tutors and students for volumes which will bridge the gap between accounts of previous critical developments and performance history and an acquaintance with new research initiatives related to the chosen plays. Thus, our ambition is to offer innovative and challenging guides that will provide practical, accessible and thought-provoking analyses of early modern drama. Each volume is organized according to a progressive reading strategy involving introductory discussion, critical review and cutting-edge scholarly debate. It has been an enormous pleasure to work with so many dedicated scholars of early modern drama and we are sure that this series will encourage you to read 400-year-old play texts with fresh eyes.

Andrew Hiscock and Lisa Hopkins

NOTES ON CONTRIBUTORS

Claire M. L. Bourne is Assistant Professor of English at Pennsylvania State University, where she teaches Shakespeare, early modern drama and book history. Her first monograph, *Typographies of Performance in Early Modern England*, is forthcoming. Her work on typography and early modern reading practices has appeared in *English Literary Renaissance*, *Papers of the Bibliographical Society of America*, *Shakespeare*, and numerous edited collections. She is currently editing *Henry VI Part 1* for the Arden Shakespeare Fourth Series, and is the treasurer of the Marlowe Society of America.

Matthew Dimmock is Professor of Early Modern Studies at the University of Sussex. His work has focused on real and imagined engagements between early modern English and the wider world, particularly the world of Islam. He is author of *New Turkes: Dramatizing Islam and the Ottomans in Early Modern England* (2005) and *Mythologies of the Prophet Muhammad in Early Modern English Culture* (2013) plus a number of articles, and has edited collections and a play, *William Percy's Mahomet and His Heaven* (2006). He is editor on the Oxford Hakluyt and Thomas Nashe projects and his recently completed third monograph *Elizabethan Globalism* was published in 2019. He has been obsessed with the *Tamburlaine* plays for more than twenty years.

Peter Kirwan is Associate Professor of Early Modern Drama at the University of Nottingham. His books include *Shakespeare in the Theatre: Cheek by Jowl* (2019), *Shakespeare and the Idea of Apocrypha* (2015) and the co-edited volumes *Canonising Shakespeare* (2017) and *Shakespeare and the Digital World* (2014). His work on Marlowe includes an essay on *Tamburlaine* and *2 Henry VI* for *Christopher Marlowe, Theatrical Commerce and the Book Trade* (2018) and a new edition of *Doctor Faustus* for *The Routledge Anthology of Early Modern Drama* (2020). He has published extensively on performance history, including in nine volumes of the RSC Shakespeare and at his blog, *The Bardathon*, and is Performance Reviews Editor for *Shakespeare Bulletin*.

David McInnis is Associate Professor of Shakespeare and Early Modern Drama at the University of Melbourne. He is author of *Mind-Travelling and Voyage Drama in Early Modern England* (2013), co-editor (with Claire Jowitt) of *Travel and Drama in Early Modern England: The Journeying Play* (2018), and editor of Dekker's *Old Fortunatus* for the Revels Plays series (2020). He co-edited *Lost Plays in Shakespeare's England* (2014, with Matthew Steggle) and *Loss and the Literary Culture of Shakespeare's Time* (2020, with Roslyn Knutson and Steggle). He is currently preparing a monograph on Shakespeare and lost plays. With Knutson and Steggle, he is founder and co-editor of the *Lost Plays Database*. He serves on the editorial board of *The Journal of Marlowe Studies*, is Secretary of the Marlowe Society of America, and also created and maintains the *Marlowe Bibliography Online*.

Tom Rutter is Senior Lecturer in Shakespeare and Renaissance Drama at the University of Sheffield. He is the author of *Shakespeare and the Admiral's Men* (2017), *The Cambridge Introduction to Christopher Marlowe* (2012) and *Work and Play on the Shakespearean Stage* (2008), as well as numerous journal articles and book chapters on early modern drama. He has recently published on 'Hamlet, Pirates, and Purgatory' in *Renaissance and Reformation*, and on '*The Spanish Tragedy* and Virgil' in *The Spanish Tragedy: A Critical Reader*. He is a co-editor of the journal *Shakespeare*.

Liam E. Semler is Professor of Early Modern Literature at the University of Sydney and leader of the Better Strangers/

Shakespeare Reloaded project which is a collaboration between the school Barker College in Sydney and academics based at the University of Sydney, the Australian National University and James Cook University. He is author of *Teaching Shakespeare and Marlowe: Learning versus the System* (Bloomsbury, 2013) and various essays on early modern literary studies and education.

M. L. Stapleton has been Chapman Distinguished Professor of English at Purdue University, Fort Wayne, since 2004. He has authored seven books and over three dozen articles and reviews on various intersections between early modern English literature and classical culture transcribed through humanism. His publications have been on Seneca, Ovid, Vergil, Marvell, Shakespeare, Marlowe, Horace, Aphra Behn, Thomas Creech, Wynkyn de Worde, Thomas Heywood, Dante, Petrarch and Spenser. He is the founder of the only serial publication devoted to Marlowe, *Marlowe Studies: An Annual* (2011–16). He is the editor of the New Variorum Shakespeare *Julius Caesar*. His most recent book is *Marlowe's Ovid: The 'Elegies' in the Marlowe Canon* (2014). His most recent publication is his revision of his Christopher Marlowe entry for *Oxford Bibliographies Online* (2017).

Sydnee Wagner is an essayist, poet and PhD candidate in the English department of The Graduate Center at City University of New York. Her scholarship focuses on early modern literature and culture and the development of racial ideologies.

Sarah Wall-Randell is an associate professor of English at Wellesley College. Her first book, *The Immaterial Book: Reading and Romance in Early Modern England* (2013), examined scenes of reading in Spenser, Shakespeare, Wroth and Cervantes. Her articles about Renaissance literature and book studies have appeared in *Renaissance Quarterly*, *SEL* and *Marlowe Studies*, as well as in several edited collections, including *Christopher Marlowe, Theatrical Commerce, and the Book Trade* (2018). A 2014–17 Mellon/Rare Book School Fellow in Critical Bibliography, she is currently working on a project about prophetic Sibyls and the book as a vulnerable medium in the early modern period.

ACKNOWLEDGEMENTS

For Kit (McInnis)

Somewhat astonishingly, this appears to be the first edited collection devoted exclusively to Christopher Marlowe's *Tamburlaine* plays. A few monographs have focused on the plays, but this Critical Reader brings together some of the best Marlovians working on *Tamburlaine* to account for 430 years of critical thinking and audience responses since Richard Jones published the plays together in 1590. I am incredibly grateful to Andrew Hiscock and Lisa Hopkins, the series editors, for the chance to edit this book, and to the contributors – M. L. Stapleton, Peter Kirwan, Sarah Wall-Randell, Claire M. L. Bourne, Tom Rutter, Sydnee Wagner, Matthew Dimmock and Liam E. Semler – for producing such fine work and diverse perspectives. Thanks, too, to Pascale Aebischer for offering feedback on some of the chapters. I trust and I hope that this book will prove a valuable resource for anyone interested in *Tamburlaine*, for many years to come. It has been a pleasure to work with Lara Bateman, Katy Day, and Mark Dudgeon at Bloomsbury.

I would also like to thank my Honours students over the years, including the most recent class (with whom I explicitly tested ideas for this volume): Darcy Cornwallis, Jack Milgate, Jennifer Perkins, Lucy Turton, Sanjay Jeyakody and Victor Zhang. Julie Robarts provided research assistance at an important juncture in the project's development, which I appreciated greatly.

My greatest thanks is to the friends and colleagues who make up the Marlowe Society of America. I missed the registration deadline for the MSA conference in Canterbury in

2008, but Dympna Callaghan kindly introduced me to then-President Roslyn L. Knutson, who enthusiastically welcomed me into the fold, and there's been no looking back. The intellectual generosity of MSA members is evident in virtually every Marlowe-related publication of recent decades, including this present volume.

David McInnis,
Melbourne, Australia

Introduction

David McInnis

Christopher Marlowe's *Tamburlaine* plays (1587) are justly celebrated for their startling originality. The Prologue to *Part I* explicitly announces the playwright's intention to distance himself and his work from the dramatic conventions of the 1580s: the doggerel rhymes, the kind of clowning embodied by Richard Tarlton's famed jests, and the kind of protagonists who had dominated the London stages until then. The play introduced Londoners to what Ben Jonson would later praise as 'Marlowes *mighty line*' – the powerful and variable iambic pentameter that Shakespeare would go on to perfect.[1] The exotic subject matter of a Scythian shepherd-turned-conqueror cast such a long shadow over the plays written in imitation throughout the following decade that they came to be known (in Peter Berek's ungracious phrase) as the 'weak sons of Tamburlaine'.[2] Marlowe's ruthless protagonist was as novel as his metre and matter, sweeping a course of destruction across the known world and slaying the virgins of Damascus who had pleaded for mercy. The name 'Tamburlaine' soon became synonymous with moral ambivalence: in 1588, Marlowe's fellow playwright Robert Greene publicly distanced himself from those who were 'daring God out of heauen with that

Atheist *Tamburlan*' and in 1593, the pseudonymous author of the xenophobic libel pinned to the door of the Dutch Church in Broad Street, London, signed his diatribe '*per Tamburlaine*'.³ The plays style themselves as tragedies, yet in defiance of conventional tragic arcs, the protagonist enjoys a meteoric rise to power and appears to survive unpunished for his transgressions and immorality, succumbing finally not to any military enemy but to the common cold. No history of early modern English theatre is complete without appropriate acknowledgement of the *Tamburlaine* plays.

Modern readers and audiences experience the *Tamburlaine* plays as mediated by the editorial work of the plays' first printer, Richard Jones, and by the framework offered by the plays' prologues. When Jones published the plays together in octavo format in 1590, he took pains to alert his 'gentlemen readers' to the fact that he had '(purposely) omitted and left out some fond and frivolous gestures' that he deemed 'unmeet for the matter' and 'tedious unto the wise'.⁴ In other words, Jones took it upon himself to excise passages or scenes that were predominantly comic in nature, on the basis that they detracted from the artistic merits of the plays. Jones had, after all, designated the plays as 'two tragical discourses of the Scythian shepherd, Tamburlaine' whereas they had been described previously (on 14 August 1590) in the Stationers' Register as 'The twooe commicall discourses of Tomberlein the Cithian shepparde'.⁵ Frustratingly, we have very little sense of what Marlowe's comical style might entail: the texts of *Doctor Faustus* (1604 and 1616), with their comic subplot, are likely the product of posthumous revision by other playwrights; *The Jew of Malta*, with its black comedy and religious satire, exists in an edition of 1633 that was at least partially altered by Thomas Heywood. Quite what *Tamburlaine* would have looked like had Jones not intervened remains a mystery. The plays, for the most part, retain coherence even with the excision of the comic material, though, and certainly the prologues that frame our interpretation of the drama do not imply that the comedy would have affected the plays' reception radically. The prologue to *Part I* declares that the play's subject matter will be serious and new, pointedly in contrast with 'such conceits as clownage keeps in pay' (*Part I*, Pro.2). It also specifically shuns the 'jigging veins of rhyming mother wits' (*Part I*, Pro.1) – that is, the sing-song rhyme schemes of earlier drama, such as the fourteener: a metre favoured by Tudor interludes and such Queen's Men's plays as *Sir Clyomon and Clamydes* (1578).[6] Instead, the Prologue promises 'high astounding terms' (*Part I*, Pro.5) – a stately rhythm, an artful construction of language; in short, Marlowe's mighty line. The plays that follow certainly deliver on this promise, their language characterized by exotic place names, hyperbole, classical references and grandeur on an epic scale. The Prologue also hints at something remarkable: moral ambiguity. 'View but his picture in this tragic glass', the Prologue announces, implicitly likening the theatre to a prospective glass (somewhat analogous in principle to a crystal ball) that facilitates vicarious pleasure, 'And then applaud his fortunes as you please' (Pro.7–8).[7] The one concession to the comic mode that survives is the first play's ending: it concludes with the expectation of marriage to Zenocrate, and thus the promise of continuity, of reproduction, and of a new generation who will maintain Tamburlaine's legacy.

Jones's 'tragical' discourse and the Prologue's 'tragic' glass are potentially misleading classifications, however, at least for the student or scholar who encounters *Tamburlaine* (as none of Marlowe's first audiences did) after first experiencing Shakespeare's conception of tragedy. Tamburlaine, who rises from lowly beginnings as a 'sturdy Scythian thief' (*Part I*, 1.1.36) to a 'man or rather god of war' (*Part I*, 5.1.1), does not die at the end of *Part I*. An audience versed in the fickleness of Fortune and familiar with her wheel, which eventually completes a full revolution and sends to their doom those whom it once elevated in status, might expect Tamburlaine's rapid rise to power to be complemented by an ignoble demise.

Tamburlaine is a tragedy for almost everyone *except* the eponymous protagonist, whose fortunes are to be applauded (according to the Prologue). Rather than offering a didactic message, these plays encourage the audience to respond as they see fit.

It may be helpful to consider *Tamburlaine* in the context nominated by Jones: as a play to be read by those same 'gentlemen readers' who 'take pleasure in reading histories'. History plays formed a significant part of the 1580s theatrical landscape in London due to the pre-eminence of the Queen's Men, an all-star company assembled in 1583 by Elizabeth I's spymaster, Sir Francis Walsingham, in consultation with the Master of the Revels, Edmund Tilney. As Scott McMillin and Sally-Beth MacLean have observed, that company essentially 'invented' the English history play, though it was not their specific intention to do so:

> The Queen's Men were formed to spread Protestant and royalist propaganda through a divided realm and to close a breach within radical Protestantism. This resulted in a repertory based on English themes. The English history play came to prominence through this motive, and probably through the sheer fact of the company's size. They could do big plays, they ought to do English plays, and narrative sources for English history were being published.[8]

The regulation of the playing industry and the dissemination of Tudor Protestant propaganda may have been the impetus for the creation of the English history play but its invention at this point in time was also part of the broader development of the English nation state.[9] England, in the 1580s, experienced both the threat of invasion (from the Spanish Armada in 1588) and the thrill of imperial expansion (as they attempted to establish a foothold in the New World via the Roanoke Colony in 1585 and 1587). By offering propagandistic accounts of Tudor history that contributed to the public perception of the strength and stability of Elizabeth's rule, the Queen's Men were performing an essential role in the consolidation of national identity.

If the Queen's Men's unintentional invention of the English history play was 'one of the more predictable outcomes in literary history', the Admiral's Men's commercial response – to acquire Marlowe's *Tamburlaine* for inclusion in their repertory – was also in some ways a natural consequence.[10] The Queen's Men had developed a style of play that showcased large casts, complex choreography, elaborate battle scenes and historical subject matter; with *Tamburlaine*, the Admiral's Men could offer fare that emulated those successes but which introduced an exotic, foreign flavour and a moral ambivalence that contrasted with the didacticism of the Queen's company. Marlowe's plays are thus a kind of foreign history, but they have a potential purchase on the English present: does Tamburlaine represent a threat to the English or embody their expansionist rhetoric and mindset? Sydnee Wagner makes the parallels between Tamburlaine and the English more explicit when she observes in her chapter for this volume ('Towards a Racialized *Tamburlaine*') that Marlowe's plays can be seen to be 'imagining paleness as a type of barbarousness, suggesting unsettled racial similarities between white English and non-white barbarians'.[11] It is not entirely possible to condemn Tamburlaine's behaviour and actions outright. Those same playgoers who derive vicarious pleasure from revenge tragedies such as Thomas Kyd's *Spanish Tragedy* (1587), in which a protagonist pursues a kind of wild justice when failed by institutional mechanisms for righting a wrong, would surely notice that Tamburlaine – for all the atrocities he commits – also has his own clearly defined moral code that he abides by with integrity. One might be appalled by his slaughter of the virgins of Damascus after they finally plead for mercy, but one must also admire Tamburlaine's transparency and unswerving purpose. He clearly articulates his rules of engagement in warfare, explaining that:

> The first day when he pitcheth down his tents,
> White is their hue, and on his silver crest

> A snowy feather spangled white he bears,
> To signify the mildness of his mind
> That satiate with spoil refuseth blood;
> But when Aurora mounts the second time,
> As red as scarlet is his furniture –
> Then must his kindled wrath be quenched with blood,
> Not sparing any that can manage arms;
> But if these threats move not submission,
> Black are his colours, black pavilion,
> His spear, his shield, his horse, his armour, plumes,
> And jetty feathers menace death and hell;
> Without respect of sex, degree or age,
> He razeth all his foes with fire and sword.
>
> (*Part I*, 4.1.49–63)

We know from the lists of properties recorded by Philip Henslowe, manager of the Rose playhouse, that the Admiral's Men possessed 'Tamberlanes breches of crimson vellvet' and 'Tamberlynes cotte with coper lace'; the effect of the bright crimson breeches and the copper-laced coat glistening in the afternoon sun during the siege of Damascus episode must have inspired awe.[12] Tamburlaine's adversaries might not believe that he really will carry through with his threats, but just as a Hamlet or Hieronymo will take the law into their own hands, guided by a conviction of moral righteousness, so too Tamburlaine both announces and adheres to a moral code that he has developed. Unlike Shakespeare's ostensibly noble Henry V, who orders the murder of the captive luggage boys in an apparent war crime, Marlowe's military leader is consistent in his conduct.

In important ways, Marlowe's *Tamburlaine* plays thus form an important connective tissue between the Queen's Men's brand of providential Tudor history and the more fully psychologized and nuanced histories of the Chamberlain's Men, and of Shakespeare in particular:

> The history play which the Queen's Men came upon and which the Chamberlain's Men developed had a potential

which only one of those companies recognized, a potential that ran beyond the 'medley' style of writing. To imagine the crown politics of England as accessible to individualist aspiration, to recognize the national agony entailed by such will-to-power – these would be the ways to develop the potential of the history play. They are the spirit of *Tamburlaine* combined with the spirit of *Dr Faustus* and translated into historical terms.[13]

The form, too, of Marlowe's plays may be influential here, for Shakespeare's *Henry V* is somewhat unusual in the Shakespearean canon for exhibiting a very clear five-act structure (in the Folio text of 1623, at least; the quarto of 1600 is undivided and lacks the famous Choruses who mark the act divisions). From *c*.1590 until 1608 (when the King's Men began playing at their indoor Blackfriars playhouse), plays produced in the public amphitheatres tended not to observe act divisions (though the scenic unit held great importance). The five-act structure is a classical form, and Marlowe (being one of the 'university wits', alongside Greene, George Peele, John Lyly, Thomas Lodge and Thomas Nashe) demonstrably *did* conceive of his plays in this format. For example, *Part I* of *Tamburlaine* has a clear rhythm to the act-units, the first act introducing Tamburlaine and his aspirations, the second act charting the fall of the Persian empire and the crowning of Tamburlaine as its king, the third act documenting Tamburlaine's defeat of Bajazeth, the fourth act staging the siege of Damascus, and the fifth act culminating in the 'bloody spectacle' (5.2.277) of Bajazeth and Zabrina braining themselves, the Damascan virgins being slaughtered, and Tamburlaine defeating Zenocrate's father, the Soldan of Egypt.

To understand the juggernaut that was *Tamburlaine*, both in terms of the theatrical context from which it emerged and the legacy it left in the public theatres, it is helpful to consider the relationship between Marlowe's plays and the theatrical offerings, lost and extant, of the Admiral's Men and of the companies with which they competed for playgoer patronage.

Although the venue for early performances of Marlowe's *Tamburlaine* plays is unknown, their first printing advertised them as Admiral's Men's plays that had been 'sundrie times shewed vpon stages in the Citie of London' by 1590. One of these early performances of *Part II* seems to have occurred prior to 16 November 1587, the date at which Philip Gawdy related a tragic incident in which a pregnant woman and a child were killed, and a man injured, as the result of accidental gunfire at a performance.[14] Henslowe's diary tells us that *Part I* was performed nine times and *Part II* once at the Rose between August and December in 1594; both parts were performed there a further six times each in 1595.[15] The possibility of further performances can be inferred from the presence of not just Tamburlaine's copper-laced coat and crimson breeches but also his bridle (presumably for the 'pampered jades of Asia' scene, *Part II*, 4.3) in Henslowe's inventory lists of 10 and 13 March 1598 (or 1599, as Michael J. Hirrel has argued).[16]

The first repertorial response to *Tamburlaine, Part I* came from Marlowe himself in 1587, in the form of the urgent need to compose a sequel written in direct response to the 'General welcomes Tamburlaine received / When he arrived last upon our stage', which 'Hath made our poet pen his second part' (*II Tam.* Prol. 1–3). *Tamburlaine, Part I* is virtually unique amongst the surviving commercial drama in spawning a spontaneous sequel.[17] This very concept of a two-part play was influential. The unknown author (possibly Robert Greene) of *Selimus* (*c*.1591), a play about Bajazeth's son, advertised the play as being the first part and gestured to what will happen next ('Next shall you see him with triumphant sword . . .'), but no second part is known to have been written, and the Epilogue's forecasting of the contents of the next instalment appears to be Tamburlainean puffery.[18] Where the Prologue to *Tamburlaine, Part II* explains that the success of *Part I* necessitated a hasty sequel, the Epilogue to *Selimus* hopes that its first part will warrant a second: 'If this first part Gentles, do like you well, / The second part, shall greater murthers tell'.[19]

When Henslowe first records the title 'tamberlen' in his diary on 28 August 1594 it appears between performances by the Admiral's Men of lost plays about 'mahemet' ('Mahomet') and 'belendon' ('Belin Dun').[20] Roslyn L. Knutson has noted that '[t]he frequency with which Marlowe reruns appear in co-ordination with similar or counteractive plays suggests not mere coincidence but an industry-wide marketing strategy by which companies used the repertory both to promote their own offerings and to capitalize on each other's successful fare'.[21] Belin Dun was the first thief hanged in England, during the reign of Henry I; he has been described by Matthew Steggle as 'an evil twin' of Robin Hood.[22] The pairing of 'Belin Dun' with *Tamburlaine* may thus have provided playgoers with consecutive days' experiences of charismatic (if morally ambiguous) thieves who enjoy a steady rise in fortune, albeit with an important contrast in their fates. Little is known of the lost 'Mahomet' play, with scholarly discussion to date having focused almost exclusively on whether the play can be identified with George Peele's extant *Battle of Alcazar* or perhaps his lost 'The Turkish Mahomet and Hiren the Fair Greek'.[23] No doubt its eastern flavour stood it in good stead to attract those same playgoers who were intrigued by *Tamburlaine*, however. These plays were also in the same repertory as 'godfrey' ('Godfrey of Boulogne'), a play about the Crusades and the slaughter of Turks in Jerusalem by Christian soldiers – a complement to (or opposite of) *Tamburlaine*, in some ways. The pairing with 'Belin Dun' is repeated on 11 and 12 September 1594 and the pairing with 'Mahomet' reappears on 14 and 15 October that year. To the extent that the limited evidence permits, it seems that keeping these plays in repertory together was useful for the company. Marlowe's *Jew of Malta* and *Doctor Faustus*, plays interested in the east and in wide-ranging travel, respectively, also appear within the Admiral's repertory at this point in time, and on 4 November 1594 *Tamburlaine* precedes *Faustus* by a day.

Later that year, on 17 and 19 December 1594 (no performances took place on the intervening day), Henslowe records performances of 'tamberlen' followed by 'the 2 pte of 'tamberlen' in a schedule that was to set an important precedent.[24] Thereafter, the plays were frequently paired in consecutive performances (e.g. 11 and 12 March 1595, 21 and 22 May 1595); indeed, once *Part II* entered the Admiral's repertory the two were played together (or at most a day apart) on all but one known occasion. The influence of both *Tamburlaine* plays can of course be detected in the spate of 'conqueror' plays that featured in the repertories of commercial companies throughout the 1590s. These included *The Battle of Alcazar* and the aforementioned *Selimus*, but also such lost plays as the two-part 'Hercules' plays and the two-part 'Tamar Cham' plays, both of which emulated the Tamburlainean pattern of programming in concatenation. The 'Tamar Cham' plays appear to have taken over the role of the *Tamburlaine* plays in the repertory, offering a substitute for the eastern conqueror formula that had catapulted Marlowe (and the company) to success. Marlowe's pair of plays were last recorded together in Henslowe's diary on 12 and 13 November 1595, but the two 'Tamar Cham' plays (acquired from the Lord Strange's Men) premiered with the Admiral's on 6 May 1596 ('Part I', a day after a performance of *Faustus*) and 11 June 1596 ('Part II', following a performance of the first part the day before, and preceding *Faustus* on 12 June).[25] Their pairing was repeated shortly thereafter, on 26 and 27 June (when they preceded Marlowe's *Jew of Malta*).[26] The backstage plot for 'Part I' survived as late as 1803, when it was transcribed by George Steevens in his variorum edition of Shakespeare, but the original has subsequently disappeared or perished.[27] From the plot, it seems the play focused on a Mongolian warlord, Mango Cham (most famous for his conversion to Christianity) and his relationship to the Muslim world.[28] The play appears to have drawn on the exotic and Mandevillean fantasy, concluding with an elaborate procession of strange peoples, such as the 'Tartars', 'Canniballs', 'Hermaphrodites', 'Pigmies', 'Amozins' and the 'ollive cullord moores', though it also featured its share of violence (one scene calls for multiple severed heads) and the supernatural (an oracle speaks; satyrs and numerous spirits are allowed for in the plot).

Although Peter Berek has written disparagingly of such plays as the 'weak sons' of *Tamburlaine*, which he describes as capitalizing on Marlowe's successes but 'in a manner which tempered thrills with reassurances, and allowed the pleasures of style without many dangers of substance', recent scholarship has looked more kindly on this spate of plays.[29] Roslyn L. Knutson astutely observes that 'from a repertorial perspective, what matters is whether the so-called weak sons had success in the theatrical marketplace'.[30] Future research would do well to further investigate such lost plays as those about the Danish king Cutlack, the Albanian national hero Scanderbeg, or the Holy Roman Emperor Charlemagne – specifically in the sense that all of these eponymous protagonists are compared explicitly to Tamburlaine in non-dramatic texts of the period and as such warrant further attention as Tamburlainean intertexts.[31]

But there are other reference points for understanding the repertorial context of the *Tamburlaine* plays. Marlowe's plays did not arise from a vacuum, and attention to how the dramaturgy of such Queen's Men plays as *The Famous Victories of Henry the Fifth* influenced Marlowe is a topic that merits further investigation. One of the more conspicuous elements of that company's style is the theatrical literalism (the focus on key visual events and images) and the absence of 'poetry capable of expressing the pressures of realistic psychological experience'.[32] A notorious instance of this is the scene in which the prodigal Prince Henry character wears a cloak of needles (as 'a sign that I stand upon thorns 'til the crown be on my head') to see his father, the ailing King Henry IV.[33] His father interprets the symbolic garment's needles as 'a prick to my heart' and weeps (6.609); the Prince instantly recants his former behaviour, seeks redemption, and presently is transformed (for all intents and purposes) into the noble personage of King Henry V. The transformation is altogether more abrupt even than the unlikely development of Shakespeare's Hal into Henry V across three Shakespearean instalments of the same historical material, but playgoers attending the Queen's Men's play in performance would not expect psychological realism so much as a characterology driven by Christian theology: the prodigal son has recognized the errors of his ways and has repented; his salvation is instant and complete. Playgoers and readers who encounter *Tamburlaine* after *Famous Victories* are unlikely to be troubled when Tamburlaine literalizes his stated intention to rise in social status ('I am a lord, for so my deeds shall prove, / And yet a shepherd by my parentage') by shedding his shepherd's clothing and apparently revealing a soldier's amour underneath: 'Lie here ye weeds that I disdain to wear! / This complete armour and this curtle-axe / Are adjuncts more beseeming Tamburlaine' (*Part I*, 1.2.34–5, 41–3).[34] His transformation is both superficial (because sartorial) and genuine (because intrinsically related to his behaviour). In an explicit meditation on the Renaissance conception of Neoplatonic thought, Tamburlaine specifically reflects on the relationship between 'outward habit' and 'the inward man' later in that same scene (*Part I*, 1.2.163). Nor does the malleability of Tamburlaine's character end here in the transformation from pauper to king, for as Wagner notes, Tamburlaine undergoes a subsequent metamorphosis through sartorial display at the Siege of Damascus, when 'the use of black clothing and other material has the possibility to transform him ... into a racially black character' despite his physical paleness.[35] The dramaturgy of the Queen's Men lingers, but is itself transformed, in Marlowe's foreign history play. At the same time, Marlowe's version of this character transformation differs radically in its morality, for as Tom Rutter observes, Tamburlaine's meteoric rise 'is not only a threat to the power of existing monarchs: it represents a violation of hierarchy'.[36] Tamburlaine is not beholden to the grace of God for his new identity, but to Fortune and his own ruthless ambition.

Amongst the other notable elements of the Queen's Men's style that seem to have stimulated Marlowe's interests are their extravagant choreographies and their commitment to the visual over the verbal. Being such a large company, the Queen's Men were able to stage elaborate fight scenes (as well as processions and other crowded scenes), and they evidently did so very well: an entire scene in *Famous Victories* consists of a single stage direction cueing the battle to enter. No dialogue is included, only the prompt for an elaborate fight depicted through 'pantomime and wordlessness'.[37] At the climax of act three in *Part I* of *Tamburlaine*, Marlowe pulls the rug out from under the playgoers' feet by opting to have Tamburlaine's battle with Bajazeth take place offstage, with first Tamburlaine, then his adversary, departing with their followers for '*the battle within*' (*Part I*, 3.3.188 SD). The little glimpse the playgoer does get of the encounter is pantomime bordering on the slapstick comedy of silent cinema: 'BAJAZETH *flies [across the stage] and* [TAMBURLAINE] *pursues him [off]. The battle [is] short, and they [re-]enter.* BAJAZETH *is overcome*' (*Part I*, 3.3.211 SD). Instead of providing sophisticated fight choreography, Marlowe provides a glimpse of the effect of war on domestic life, opting to portray the exchange between Zabina and Zenocrate whilst the trumpets sound offstage as a reminder of the bloodshed taking place just out of view. There *are* plenty of examples of staged warfare elsewhere throughout Marlowe's two plays, but such devices are not the only weaponry in Marlowe's dramatic arsenal.

For all the spectacle and violence of the *Tamburlaine* plays, Marlowe is remarkably sensitive to the human costs of war, placing in the mouth of the humbled Persian king, Mycetes, one of the most eloquent examples of anti-war sentiment of the period:

> Accursed be he that first invented war!
> They knew not, ah, they knew not, simple men,
> How those were hit by pelting cannon shot
> Stand staggering like a quivering aspen leaf
> Fearing the force of Boreas' boisterous blasts.
>
> (*Part I*, 2.4.1–5)

The defeat of Mycetes early in *Part I* is an excellent example of Marlowe's reimagining of the symbolic significance of the visual: where the Queen's Men subordinated language to visual elements such as props (crowns, thrones) and costumes (Prince Henry's cloak of needles), Marlowe imbues Mycetes' crown with emblematic importance. The king enters furtively, '*his crown in his hand, offering to hide it*' (2.4.0), and decides to bury it in a hole in the ground to prevent Tamburlaine from seizing it – and by extension, power – from him. When Tamburlaine appears unexpectedly and catches Mycetes in the act, there follows an amusing yet pathetic exchange in which the crown passes from Persian king to Scythian shepherd and back again. The debasement of Mycetes, whose lack of verbal proficiency had earlier marked him as an impotent ruler,[38] is completed here through the exchange of words as well as the highly charged stage property: Tamburlaine mockingly offers to buy the crown from Mycetes, then deftly snatches it, causing the Persian king to ridiculously claim that he had *let* Tamburlaine take it. Mycetes fails to save face, but Tamburlaine nevertheless returns the crown in a portentous gesture:

> Here, take it for a while, I lend it thee
> Till I may see thee hemmed with armed men:
> Then shalt thou see me pull it from thy head.
> Thou art no match for mighty Tamburlaine.
>
> (2.4.37–40)

Tamburlaine's rhetoric is devastating, but all eyes are on the symbolic passing back and forth of the Persian crown, just as in *Famous Victories* the English crown is more than just a 'useful' property; it carries 'a visual significance which is the hallmark of the style and dramatic ideology of the company'.[39] Mycetes is left to ponder why a 'thief' had not simply stolen away the crown (2.4.41), but the playgoers recognize that although the crown has been returned to Mycetes, the power has emphatically shifted to Tamburlaine. Marlowe seems to be asking here, as Shakespeare later would in *King Lear*, what residue of kingship adheres when title, but not authority, remains?

But far from simply divesting the visual of its symbolic importance through such bathetic exchanges, Marlowe remains true to the Queen's Men's investment in ocular signifiers but – typically – hyperbolically exceeds them on every count. The concept of a large or important stage prop such as a throne or crown in a play by the Queen's Men is amplified into what Marlowe describes as 'sights of power' (*Part I*, 5.2.412). Although few of Marlowe's gloriously excessive lines are quoted in other contexts,[40] the iconic moments of Tamburlaine debasing mighty emperors by using them as footstools (*Part I*, 4.2) or as 'pampered jades' to pull his chariot (*Part II*, 4.3.1); besieging Damascus in white, red and black; and burning the Qur'an on stage (*Part II*, 5.1.176–200) have become etched into the popular imaginary.

The *Tamburlaine* plays were performed and printed often in their own time, but by 1609 Ben Jonson could snidely deride 'the *Tamerlanes* and *Tamer-Chams* of the late age' for having 'nothing in them but the scenical strutting and furious vociferation to warrant them to the ignorant gapers' (recalling, perhaps, Richard Jones's dismissal of the excised comic portions of *Tamburlaine* as having been 'greatly gaped at' by 'some vain conceited fondlings').[41] Indeed, the plays were less successful in the Restoration, making it possible for Charles Saunders to perhaps implausibly claim that his *Tamerlaine the Great* (1681) owed nothing to Marlowe's plays, which he had never heard of and which ought to be judged by their 'obscurity' and by the inability of booksellers or players to 'call [them] to Remembrance'.[42] However, since the plays' apparent first modern revival in 1919 at Yale University, the military exploits of Marlowe's eastern conqueror have proved more relevant to the twentieth century (in an age of world wars) and the twenty-first century (an age obsessed with the threat of terrorism in the wake of the World Trade Center attacks on 11 September 2001), as Richard Wilson has reminded us.[43] The religious radicalism and scepticism of the plays, their depiction of war and violence, their exploration of the conquest of exotic geographies, and their construction of gender (and masculinity more specifically) have all made them resonate strongly with contemporary critics' concerns. Since the mid-twentieth century, the plays have been performed at the Old Vic (dir. Tyrone Guthrie, 1951), the National Theatre (dir. Peter Hall and Albert Finney, 1976), the RSC (dir. Terry Hands and Antony Sher, 1992), the Blackfriars Theatre in Staunton, VA (2011), The Theatre for a New Audience in NYC (2014), and by Lazarus Theatre Co, London (2015) amongst others. In the most rigorous and comprehensive stage history of *Tamburlaine* available, Peter Kirwan here charts such trends and challenges in performance, which he notes are frequently 'inextricable from narratives of disaster and celebration, topicality and brinkmanship'.[44] '[F]ew plays have inaugurated so many theatres', Kirwan notes, yet the challenges of the provocative subject matter, the risk of monotony, and the tendency to turn to textual editing to conflate the two parts into a single performance, have combined to make a new production of *Tamburlaine* an 'event'.

The chapters by M. L. Stapleton and Sarah Wall-Randell complement Kirwan's by offering erudite overviews of the *Tamburlaine* plays' critical heritage from 1587–2000 and 2000–present respectively, including landmark critical editions, venerable opinions, and shifting cultural responses. They track key moments in the development of the plays' reputations, from the tacit queering of *Tamburlaine* by the future sexologist, Havelock Ellis, in an edition of 1887 to the romanticizing of Marlowe, the philological and fantastical readings of his plays in the twentieth century, and the mid-century burst of critical energy that coincided with the quatercentenary of Marlowe's birth. The publications surveyed question Marlowe's moral purpose, his sexuality, his politics, and his theatrical history; they show that Marlowe has played pivotal roles in the development of later-twentieth-century criticism including cultural materialism and new historicism, queer theory, gender studies, feminism and more.

The central section of this critical reader consists of four new contributions to knowledge of *Tamburlaine*, each showcasing promising new avenues of inquiry for future researchers to pursue.

In the forty-odd years since Robert Darnton published his 'What is the History of Books?', the field of book history has grown exponentially and Darnton's seemingly comprehensive schematic diagram of 'the communications circuit' (a holistic view of book production) has been complicated by the work of new generations of scholars.[45] When Darnton revisited his thoughts in 2007, he nominated a handful of key concerns that he regretted not having attended to in 1982, including a key topic raised by Thomas R. Adams and Nicholas Barker in their proposed revision of Darnton's original chart: Survival.[46] Claire M. L. Bourne's contribution to this volume represents some of the exciting work now being done in book history; treating the surviving early editions of *Tamburlaine* as physical objects, Bourne demonstrates how they 'preserve traces of reading that both affirm and dispute elements of the plays' fictional world, sometimes simultaneously'.[47] Bourne examines the physical changes that early readers made to their copies of the printed plays, from editorial to physical alterations, in bids to 'mend' *Tamburlaine* through 'small acts of interpretation and preservation'.

A different form of historical inquiry underpins Matthew Dimmock's chapter, which addresses the neglected topic of the historical Tamburlaine, Amir Timür Gurgan (1336–1405), and how 'Timür is distanced and made strange, blurred into the "first heir" of Marlowe's invention, and thereby becomes a creature of the London playhouses rather than a historical actor and vital cultural presence in his own right.'[48] By tracking the early modern English knowledge of Timür and foreign history, Dimmock shows how Marlowe's plays 'contribute to the ways the English actually and imaginatively integrated themselves into established narratives and iconography that made that wider world more knowable'.[49]

Sydnee Wagner's chapter, 'Towards a Racialized *Tamburlaine*', begins the important work of expanding the exciting developments in early modern race studies by Kim F. Hall, Arthur L. Little, Jr, Ian Smith, and others – which has so far focused mostly on Shakespeare, and is yet to fully embrace Marlowe and other early modern dramatists – and applying that framework and critical energy to a new reading of the construction of Tamburlaine's racial identity in Marlowe's plays. For, as Wagner notes, '[w]hile scholars have made tangential gestures to race in *Tamburlaine* in the form of geography, foreignness, or vagabonds, they have done so without explicitly naming these formations as "race".'[50] She engages with the 'technologies of race-making in the period to demonstrate the reproductions (and new formations) of racial ideologies at work in Marlowe's play' and the Othering of Tamburlaine in particular.[51]

The intersection of science and literature interests Tom Rutter, whose chapter on meteorology in *Tamburlaine* addresses the construction of scientific knowledge in society, building on diverse work by Mary Thomas Crane, Chloe Kathleen Preedy, and others, to argue that 'in his treatment of the causes of meteorological phenomena, Marlowe is as much concerned with theological questions as with the physical nature of the universe'.[52] Rather than using an ecocritical approach, Rutter offers 'an account of the sceptical, subversive uses to which Marlowe put his depictions of meteorology'.

In the final chapter, Liam E. Semler, whose book *Teaching Shakespeare and Marlowe* will be familiar to most teachers who pick up this volume, offers an entertaining and lucidly written guide to teaching the *Tamburlaine* plays. Appropriating the progressive stages of white, red and black tents from Tamburlaine's own approach to war, Semler here prepares the reader for a tactical engagement with Marlowe's work. His 'white tent' equips the reader for their campaign through an overview of Marlovian biographies, critical editions, and source material; his 'red tent' details the valiant efforts of those scholars and teachers who have gone before (the guides to teaching early modern drama, the edited collections, the websites and resources); and his 'black tent' identifies current or recent critical conflicts over *Tamburlaine* (focusing on language and genre; stagecraft; gender and sexuality; empire, race and religion; and adaptation and performance).

1

The Critical Backstory: *Tamburlaine*, 1587–2000 – A Reception History

M. L. Stapleton

I. Beginnings to 1900

As with most medieval and early modern literary texts, the reception of *Tamburlaine* begins with an amalgam of anecdotes, allusions, play references, and offhand comments. Though little of this material amounts to criticism, virtually all editions and commentary have used it and cemented its importance in the play's history. Its first mention seems to have been in Robert Greene's preface to *Perimedes* (1588): 'latelye two Gentlemen Poets . . . had it in derision, for that I could not make my verses iet vpon the stage in tragicall buskins, euerie worde filling the mouthe like the faburden of Bo-Bell, daring God out of heauen with that Atheist Tamburlan'. Richard Jones's preface to the initial publication of the two parts (1590) comprised another type of commentary in his admission that he removed comic scenes from the text: 'I haue (purposely) omitted and left out some fond and friuolous Iestures, digressing (and in my poor opinion) far vnmeet for the matter'. Philip Henslowe lists performances of Marlowe's plays at the Rose in 1594–95, along with inventory (in 1598) for items such as a 'Tamberlyne brydell', perhaps for the 'pampered jades' of Part II, along with 'Tamberlynes cotte [i.e. coat] with coper lace' and 'Tamberlanes breches of crymson vellvet' for son-in-law Edward Alleyn's costume. Elsewhere in his diary, the entrepreneur mentioned buying the script for 40 shillings from Alleyn on 2 October 1602.[1] In spite of this seemingly fortuitous purchase, no records of a post-1595 early modern performance survive.

However, this subsequent dearth of theatrical exposure does not signify that *Tamburlaine* had been entirely forgotten, given the number of allusions, many satirical, in plays and other texts of the time, such as the references to a 'stalking *Tamberlaine*' in Thomas Dekker's *Wonderful Year* (1603) and a 'warlike Tamburlaine' in his *Old Fortunatus* (1600); Shakespeare's parody in *2 Henry IV*, courtesy of Pistol (1598); and the injunction to 'play the *Tamburlaine*' in *Histriomastix* (1598).[2] The satirist Joseph Hall (1597) imagined a drunk in the theatre swaggering about as 'the Turkish Tamburlaine', fuelled by 'huf-cap termes, and thundring threats'.[3] Thomas Heywood's prologue to *The Jew of Malta* (1633), performed at the Cockpit before Charles and Henrietta Maria, mentions Marlowe and Alleyn in context with *Tamburlaine*:

>   by the best of Poets, in that age,
> The Malta Jew had being, and was made;
> And He, then by the best of Actors play'd:
> In *Hero and Leander*, one did gain
> A lasting memorie: in *Tamberlaine*,
> This *Jew*, with others many.[4]

Those in the seventeenth and eighteenth centuries who interested themselves in 'Mr. Marloe' and his conqueror read this piece of evidence differently from one another, and thus created a different controversy: authorship. Based on these couplets, John Milton's nephew Edward Phillips attributed 'the first and second parts of *Tamerlane*, the Great *Scythian* Emperour' not to Marlowe but to Thomas Newton, who had edited and contributed to *Seneca His Tenne Tragedies* (1581).[5] Francis Kirkman (1671) and Gerard Langbaine (1691), reading the same Heywoodian lines, together settled on Marlowe as the author. Edmond Malone (1790) concurred but vacillated, under the influence of Richard Farmer, who could not believe that the playwright had written *Tamburlaine*. The writer of the preface to the plays in the landmark Pickering edition of Marlowe (1826) suggested that the aforementioned passage should be read without punctuation of any kind after 'Tamburlaine', so that 'In the words of the poet one "made" and the other "played" the Jew; and therefore as far as relates to this play the latter part of the sentence may be applied to either Marlowe or Alleyn, and in like manner what is said of Tamburlaine, may independently of other evidence, be applied to the author or the actor'. For the record, this commentator did not think Marlowe to be the author. There is, of course, more to the story of the early reception of *Tamburlaine*, with other play references, parodic or otherwise.[6]

Though the *Tamburlaine* plays eventually disappeared from the public theatres, references to them or to the historical figure continued from the mid-seventeenth to the early nineteenth centuries. In *Timber* (1640), Ben Jonson, who learned much of his craft from watching and reading Marlowe, nonetheless famously observed that the 'true Artificer' of the theatre should eschew fustian and bombast and 'speake to the capacity of his hearers' so that his language 'shall not fly from all humanity, with the *Tamerlanes* and *Tamer-Chams* of the late Age, which had nothing in them but the scenical strutting, and furious vociferation, to warrant them to the ignorant gapers'. Sage as Ben was considered to be, it is difficult to ascertain how influential this pronouncement actually was. The seventeenth century featured no shortage of heroes furiously vociferating to gapers who did not consider themselves to be ignorant. Sir John Suckling mentions *Tamburlaine* in his play *The Goblins* (1648), as does Sir William Davenant in *A Playhouse to Be Let*

(1663), and Thomas Shadwell's *The Humourists* (1670), whose Drybob exclaims, 'I have been beaten more severely, than ever *Turk* was by *Tamerlain*; which by the way, is no ill Comparison; hah?'. Edmund Gayton (1654) reported that at various 'festivals', groups of players would put on *Tamburlaine*, *The Jew of Malta*, and other allegedly forgotten old works.[7]

Though Marlowe's authorship of *Tamburlaine* was hardly assured in the eighteenth century or the first quarter of the nineteenth, interest in his oeuvre did not abate, taken up by a pair of influential critics in their editions. Charles Lamb (1808), exuberant as always, exclaimed: 'The lunes of Tamburlaine are perfect "midsummer madness"'. Furthermore, 'Nebuchadnezzar's are mere modest pretensions compared with the thundering vaunts of this Scythian Shepherd'. He spoke derisively and humorously, as one might expect, about the 'pampered jades' passage in Part II. Yet he then made an amalgam of erotic Marlowe verses, combining a sexy passage from *Lust's Dominion* – not thought apocryphal then – with Gaveston's opening speech from *Edward II*, and then the 'Of stature tall, and straightly fashioned' (*1 Tam* 2.1.7–30) description of Tamburlaine's manly beauty. John Payne Collier (1820), disdainful of Lamb's tone and perceived amateurism, countered that though the language may seem 'extravagant, perhaps bombastic', the careful reader should note that 'Marlow was obliged to make his language correspond with the nature of the clime ... in the utmost gorgeousness of oriental splendor: what was wanting in the scenery and dresses, he was, in a manner, bound to make up for in the glitter and glare of description'. Tamburlaine's speeches 'are not half so exaggerated and wind-swollen' as those of John Dryden's Almanzor in *The Conquest of Granada*. Collier accomplished much for Marlowe's benefit here, legitimately and otherwise. At about the same time, he had created one of his forgeries in Henslowe's diary that established Marlowe as the author of the two plays. By this device, and by crediting him as a master innovator of dramatic blank verse with links to Shakespeare, he created a fairly accurate literary history that scholars have accepted ever since.[8]

Alexander Dyce produced an edition of Marlowe (1850) seven years before the first of his three Shakespeares (1857, 1864–5, 1875–6) and two decades after the landmark Pickering publication (1826), which had been the first competently edited text of Marlowe's works. Dyce's textual scholarship was relatively accurate, his commentary and introductions providing useful information on *Tamburlaine* and the rest of the dramatic corpus. Along with the problematic Pickering, Oxberry, and anonymous Regency-era volumes, some expansive and colourful remarks about Marlowe's works might have struck Dyce as amateurish. This necessitated a learned alternative, a solid text with a named editor whose work followed the philology of the time. James A. Broughton (1830) had implied that he was responsible for at least one of the pair of editions preceding Dyce's. His handwritten note in his copy of the Pickering (1826) reads: 'In an edition of Tamburlaine printed (but not published) 1818, I enumerated various circumstances which had occasioned me to be sceptical as to Marlowe's property in the play'. Broughton thereby continued the authorship issue regarding the twinned works from the previous century. But others thought differently. Arthur Hallam (1839) admired the *Tamburlaine* technique, credited the plays to Marlowe, yet thought them a 'failure'. Granted, in *Tamburlaine*, 'a better kind of blank verse is first employed; the lines are interwoven, the occasional hemistich and redundant syllables break the monotony of the measure, and give more of a colloquial spirit to the dialogue'. The 'inflated style' and 'bombast' are 'not so excessive as has been alleged', and besides, were 'thought appropriate to such oriental tyrants. This play has more spirit and poetry than any which, upon clear grounds, can be shown to have preceded it. We find also more action on the stage, a shorter and more dramatic dialogue, a more figurative style, with a far more varied and skilful versification'. Leigh Hunt (1844) admired Marlowe as a romantic radical. His hero's glorious speeches apparently outweighed any atrocities, and to this old friend of John Keats, Marlowe's blank verse in the plays bore comparison to Milton: 'It has latterly been thought, that a genius like Marlowe could have had no hand in a play so bombastic as this huffing tragedy. But besides the weighty and dignified, though monotonous tone of his versification in many places, . . . there are passages in it of force and feeling, of which I doubt whether any of his contemporaries were capable in so sustained a degree'. Dyce seemed aware of the issues of decorum, attribution, and morality regarding *Tamburlaine*, and attempted to appear neutral by tempering his considerable enthusiasm, which approached that of Hallam and Hunt.[9]

These opinions outlined the reception of *Tamburlaine* for the rest of the nineteenth century. Another Shakespeare commentator, Edward Dowden (1870), believed the construction of Marlowe's paired plays to be arbitrary, their scenes resembling 'the fiery-hearted blossoms of some inexhaustible tropical plant, blown with sudden and strong vitality, fading and dropping away at night, and replaced next morning by others as sanguine and heavy with perfume', the action 'ending only 'from sheer exhaustion of resources'. Despite such condescension disguised in proto-Aubrey-Beardsley prose, Dowden considered the plays 'the work of a master-hand, untrained', as if 'from some painting ill-composed, full of crude and violent colour, containing abundant proofs of weakness and inexperience, and having half its canvas crowded with extravagant grotesques which the artist took for sublime'. At the same time, readers should not judge the conqueror by their 'little lives' that 'run on with few great ambitions', since 'this gross kind of ambition is peculiarly out of relation to our habits of desire. But Marlowe, the son of the Canterbury shoemaker, realized in imagination this ambition as if it were his very own, and gave it most living expression'.[10]

Though Thomas Dabbs (1991) argued that Victorian educators and critics created the concept of the 'romantic' Marlowe, clearly some palimpsest of this construction preceded the era, the only difference perhaps the deployment of the adjective. Additionally, the playwright's Scythian hero was his surrogate. A. C. Bradley (1880) objected to passages 'full of horror and glare' that were merely 'the rising passion of a single character'. Yet, he admitted, 'there is that incommunicable gift which means almost everything, *style*; a manner perfectly individual yet, at its best, free from eccentricity'. A. H. Bullen, who produced the major three-volume edition of Marlowe (1884) that followed Dyce's, echoed his predecessors' comments: 'That the play is stuffed with bombast, that exaggeration is carried sometimes to the verge of burlesque, no sensible critic will venture to deny. But the characters, with all their stiffness, have life and movement. ... There is nothing mean or trivial in the invention. The young poet threw into his work all the energy of his passionate nature'.[11]

In their Mermaids edition of selected Marlowe plays including *Tamburlaine* (1887), Havelock Ellis and John Addington Symonds were the first commentators who 'queered' the hero and his creator, albeit tacitly. Ellis, the future author of the seven-volume *Studies in the Psychology of Sex* (1897–1928), closely attended to the physical description of the naked Leander from the epyllion in which he swims, and quoted his colleague Symonds's theory that 'l'amour de l'impossible', a code phrase for homosexuality, animated Marlowe as his 'characteristic note', along with his heroes. This 'young god of undaunted verse set free' conceived the *Tamburlaine* plays as a 'series of scenes held together by the poetic energy of his own dominating personality. He is his own hero, and the sanguinary Scythian utters the deepest secrets of the artist's heart'. Ellis's language imagining Tamburlaine as a surrogate for a Marlowe who needed to express himself as an artist and aesthete clearly echoes that of Dyce, Dowden, Bradley, and Bullen. Yet it would not be too much to say that the epistemology of the closet informs his analysis and distinguishes it from theirs. Symonds, who had previously published *Male Love: A Problem in Greek Ethics* (1883), used a code much like Ellis's. He admired *Tamburlaine*, in which Marlowe 'interwove the double strings of this Impossible Amour'. He read the early encounter between the hero and Theridamas as romantic, in which each 'favours the manly bearing of his foe' (*I Tam* 1.2.155–60; 165–209). Probably evoking and countering earlier comments by Lamb, he concludes: 'this hyperbolical monster moves admiration rather than loathing. Marlowe has succeeded in saving his hero, amid all his "lunes" from caricature, by the inbreathed spirituality with which he sustains his madness at its height'.[12]

II. 1900–1964

The first part of the twentieth century inaugurated the true professionalization of Marlowe studies, with *Tamburlaine* an essential component, though the fanciful, romantic variety of interpretation continued. C. F. Tucker Brooke inaugurated this genuine scholarly movement with his one-volume Oxford edition (1910), the first with an accurate critical apparatus for the entire known opus printed sequentially, running at the bottom of the page for the reader's convenience. He published his commentary separately, in a brief essay on the canon (1911) and another, longer piece on the playwright's reputation (1922), the latter invaluable for its comprehensive account of Marlowe's publication history and of references to him and his works. The two parts of *Tamburlaine*, Brooke wrote, provided 'the classic instance of chivalrous romance turned drama' and 'the source and original of the Elizabethan history play'. Like Collier, he accounted for their 'bombast and violence' as the impetus for the formation of an authorial personality, entities 'transmuted into legitimate dramatic material by the fervency with which the poet expressed his own high aspiring soul in the terms of world-conquest and warlike ruthlessness'. Yet Brooke tempered this idealistic reading by accounting for Marlowe's source materials, which informed 'the picture which the entire work paints of warlike ambition and royal magnificence' and influenced its successors.[13]

With perhaps as much influence on subsequent readers as Brooke's precise scholarship, A. C. Swinburne's brief passages on *Tamburlaine* (1908) represented simultaneous apotheoses of the conqueror as bard and of the Byronic Marlowe, 'the first English poet whose powers can be called sublime'. Tamburlaine's 'majestic and exquisite excellence' tempers 'the stormy monotony of Titanic truculence which blusters like a simoom through the noisy course of its ten fierce acts'.[14]

Fantastical, subjective readings, then, oddly complemented philological research on *Tamburlaine*, forming a systole and diastole of interpretative communities. Charles Crawford produced and published his Marlowe concordance in Louvain (1911–33), a hotbed of scholarly production of early modern literary editions and commentary, its presses unfortunately destroyed by German bombs in 1915. This remarkable publication was created, of course, minus the aid of databases and computers, without which modern scholars would likely be quite helpless if they attempted the same feat. Crawford included not only the canonical works, but also *The Tragedy of Locrine*, *Lust's Dominion*, and Shakespeare's *Henry VI* trilogy, which even then some readers believed to be a Marlovian collaboration. Most significantly, for the first time, it would be possible to see individual lines of *Tamburlaine* in tandem with the rest of the plays and poetry, arranged alphabetically by individual words. Ethel Seaton (1924, 1929) offered proof that Abraham Ortelius's *Theatrum Orbis Terrarum* (1570) furnished the map of the world to which Tamburlaine memorably applied his finger, and along with Leslie Spence (1926, 1927), located the *Übermensch* conception of the hero in the writings of Thomas Fortescue and others. Carrol Camden (1929) investigated the idea that humoral theory informed Tamburlaine's sensibilities. Willard Thorp (1930), in some ways foretelling the scholarship of Battenhouse in the following decade, contested the truism that Marlowe was unorthodox or a rebel who wanted to shock his audiences by presenting the Scythian as a nonpareil of unorthodoxy. As the Scourge of God, according to Richard Jones's 1590 title-page, Thorp wrote that the audience expected the blasphemies and atrocities that would prove Tamburlaine the bad example that Marlowe surely intended him to be.[15]

Tamburlaine benefited from other types of attention during this period. T. S. Eliot, for one, took the plays up in his essay on Marlowe (1918) and defined their 'verse accomplishments' as 'notably two'. The playwright 'gets into blank verse the melody of Spenser, and he gets a new driving power by reinforcing the sentence period against the line period'. E. K. Chambers (1923) happened on what remains the most explosive modern discovery about the plays, the letter from one Philip Gawdy to his father (16 November 1587) that describes a terrible playhouse accident with a prop gun that resembles the shooting of the Governor of Babylon in *II Tamburlaine* (5.1), though some doubt the identification. Una Ellis-Fermor's study of Marlowe (1927) and her edition of *Tamburlaine* (1930) in the R. H. Case multi-volume *Works and Life* devoted to the poet-playwright partook of the two aforementioned perspectives on the author and his Scythian spectacle, romanticism and philological rigour. She wrote a masterful introduction to the work as a whole and its issues and sources. Her modern-spelling text, based almost completely on the 1590 octavo, cannot be easily faulted. Yet the Swinburnean impulse in her general interpretation defined Tamburlaine and his creator as twin individualists, heroic rebels, as some of her predecessors had done. She argued that this conception dictated the alleged formlessness and plotlessness of the plays, appropriate for the portrayal of the whims of a single, unbalanced protagonist. The plays' imagery tells us 'that the highest inspiration lies elsewhere and that the great poetry of these early plays is not poetry of imagery at all, but poetry of ideas'.[16]

In the wake of R. H. Case's multi-volume Methuen edition of Marlowe came seven book-length publications that devoted significant attention to *Tamburlaine*. With the attribution question long settled, the main controversy for critics was the matter of personality and morality. Is the protagonist a subversive, amoral hero whom Marlowe celebrates, or a blasphemous tyrant? Was the playwright venting his cherished heretical opinions, crafting a morality tale, or coldly disinterested, content to let readers and playgoers decide for themselves? Roy

Battenhouse's *Marlowe's 'Tamburlaine': A Study in Renaissance Moral Philosophy* (1941) strove to locate the work and the man in his intellectual milieu. Its two interlocking theses held that the two plays should be read as a unified ten-act work. The protagonist should be seen as a tragic figure whose decline the playwright intended as a warning to his audiences in this Elizabethan reanimation of a morality, the Almighty scourging his Scourge for pride and ambition. The book strongly challenged all prevailing views, most polemically against those who had asserted that Marlowe's conqueror served as mouthpiece for his ingrained unorthodoxy and heresy. Like Seaton and Camden, Battenhouse sought to root *Tamburlaine* in its early modern intellectual milieu. His final sentence exemplifies his work: 'Certainly these ten acts of *Tamburlaine* offer one of the most grandly moral spectacles in the whole realm of English drama'. In the following year, John Bakeless's *The Tragicall History of Christopher Marlowe* (1942) read the canon biographically. He made *Tamburlaine* a crucial component in his interpretation, advancing the idea of theatre history after a fashion, proclaiming it 'the first blank verse play of permanent literary value' as his nineteenth-century predecessors had so heralded it, and contributed a list of dramatic references to the two works, complementing the earlier study by Brooke (1922).[17]

The Battenhouse thesis tended to dominate the site that critics had built for the play, an intellectual formulation that some scholars strongly challenged. In an article, Paul H. Kocher (1942) documented not Marlowe's fondness for moral philosophy but his close reading and appropriation of sources such as Paul Ive's *Practice of Fortification* (1589) and other military manuals. He intended his *Christopher Marlowe: A Study of His Thought, Learning and Character* (1946) as a corrective to Battenhouse and Bakeless. For Kocher, *Tamburlaine*, hardly a study in aesthetics or a tragedy, instead advances the concept that the individual needs his own will only, not divine aid. Marlowe the subjectivist sought merely to express himself, not paraphrase classical wisdom, and the plays were 'a new interpretation of phenomena selected from the common knowledge of the time', a truly new regime of literary drama. F. P. Wilson (1953) strongly disagreed with this triumvirate of American Marlovians. Battenhouse's 'desperate argument' and Kocher's subjectivist approach made Tamburlaine into a clownish mouthpiece and puppet for his creator's burgeoning spirituality: 'The danger of reading private allusions into Marlowe's plays is that we do injury to his dramatic gifts. We are tempted to see him as a frustrated lyric poet instead of the very considerable dramatic poet that he was'.[18]

The title of Harry Levin's *The Overreacher* (1952) provided an epithet that many readers have applied to the poet-playwright and Tamburlaine. The critic thought Marlowe an ironist in his initial effort because Part II demolishes Part I. At the same time, the playwright infused his protagonist with heroic leanings because he reached for more than he could hold, as Levin's motif implies. Tamburlaine demonstrates his heroism in rhetoric for the simple reason that the limitations of the dramatic form in which he appeared necessitated that he must express his emotions externally. The critic suggested that the two plays resembled *A Mirror for Magistrates* dramatized, but with the structural complication that Tamburlaine's 'step by step' rise 'is predicated upon a succession of falls from higher and higher places'. Marlowe's 'audacity lay in taking a metaphor and acting it out, in turning a manner of speaking into a mode of action, in concretely realizing what had theretofore subsisted on the plane of precept and fantasy'.[19]

Irving Ribner was probably the most influential mid-century commentator on *Tamburlaine*. In three essential articles (1953, 1954, 1955), he strove to place the plays in their theatrical context. Robert Greene's notorious jibe seemed odd to the critic because that playwright's *Alphonsus of Arragon* and *The Tragicall Raigne of Selimus* so completely imitated the diction and bombast and even plagiarized character names from Marlowe's production. Ribner theorized that Greene sought to answer his colleague's 'humanistic philosophy of history' without entirely comprehending what it entailed. Actually,

Marlowe sought to subvert such conceptions by denying the role of Providence and presenting a hero who could rise from humble origins and dominate his environment without dependence on supernatural aid, thus glorifying 'ruthless self-sufficiency'.[20]

The year 1962 featured a trifecta of influential book-length studies focused on Marlowe or featuring him as a catalyst, with emphasis on *Tamburlaine*. Eugene Waith's *The Herculean Hero* considered the protagonist heroic, like Hercules; one we must admire, and be awed by, even when he falls. Douglas Cole took the opposite stance. In *Suffering and Evil in the Plays of Christopher Marlowe*, he argued that figures such as Tamburlaine rise from strife rather than harmony, 'and it can only be fulfilled in terms of destructive physical violence'. Such conflict animates a moral framework whose architecture was predicated on the *de casibus* tradition in medieval literature and the moralities. Hence the 'major structural pattern: the parading of character with a morally shocking nature through a series of incidents which demonstrate dramatically his destructive or evil quality'. However, David Bevington's *From 'Mankind' to Marlowe* was the most significant and influential of the three. His reading of *Tamburlaine* was that Marlowe's sources conflicted with the dramatic conventions he had inherited from the moral plays. Therefore, 'contrary impressions of divinity and bestiality are never reconciled, and their interplay creates the basic interest of the drama'. In spite of the 'primitive form' of *Tamburlaine*, its inner logic and consistency cannot be faulted.[21]

III. 1964–2000

The quatercentenary of Marlowe's birth (along with his contemporary from Stratford-on-Avon) occasioned three essay collections and a monograph devoted to his canon. These are Clifford Leech's *Marlowe: A Collection of Critical Essays* (1964); a special issue of *Tulane Studies in Drama* under the supervision of Irving Ribner (1964); Brian Morris's critical anthology *Christopher Marlowe* (1968); and J. B. Steane's idiosyncratic survey, *Marlowe: A Critical Study* (1964), along with his widely-used Penguin edition of the plays (1969). These scholars detonated the explosion of scholarship that enabled and informed the achievements of the succeeding era that have continued into this century. It could even be said that to the careful observer, traces of twenty-first-century critical approaches are visible in some of these materials.[22] *Tamburlaine*, naturally, was a primary concern.

Patrick Cheney (2004) credited Leech's introductory essay to his 1964 collection for demarcating areas of Marlowe criticism and predicting their future influence in the field.[23] Leech saw these sub-fields related to the playwright as threefold: the intellectual, his creative forces struggling between tradition and iconoclasm, exemplified by the work of Kocher; the ironist, sceptic, and sabotager of his heroes, as in the approach of Ellis-Fermor and Battenhouse; and his theatrical achievements and their future possibilities, an area that Leech claimed for himself. Of course, there turned out to be something more than this, and *Tamburlaine* proved essential to this scholarship in every way.

The Kocherian vein of *Tamburlaine* criticism expressed itself in debates about Marlowe's moral purpose in his creation. C. L. Barber (1966) maintained that nothing matters except what 'aggrandizes the hero's identity. Otherness is a challenge which must either be incorporated or destroyed'. Wilbur Sanders (1968) found the intellectual ambiguity about ethos in the plays troubling, even intolerable, and wondered if they should be interpreted 'as a Christian fable against presumption, or as a humanist manifesto of the free spirit?' Christopher Fanta (1970) concluded that the hero's doings 'give expression to a duality of outlook, and equally to a gradually developed pessimism, that characterized Marlowe's mind'. Roma Gill (1971) observed that Tamburlaine was intended to be 'superhuman in his relentless ambition, and this sets him beyond considerations of ordinary morality'.[24]

The Ellis-Fermor *cum* Battenhouse ironist strain that Leech identified was certainly evident in studies of *Tamburlaine* over the quarter-century under discussion and continues today. In an essay that unintentionally foretold the idea of queerness that might have informed Marlowe's conception of his conqueror, John Cutts (1967) noted with considerable scorn as well as accuracy that the protagonist rarely engages in battle, the author lovingly delineates his mien and appearance as feminine, and many of his deeds are simply revolting. He is, in short, a blowhard: 'The show must go on, pampered and jaded as it has become.... this is the only way a Tamburlaine can operate, and fortunately for him the world is so easily won with words and looks that his manly prowess in mighty deeds of military valor is never called in question'. William A. Armstrong (1966) similarly observed of the plays, 'Flyting, not fighting, is Marlowe's chosen way of indicating battles'. With similar scepticism, Robert Cockcroft (1968) interpreted the notorious chariot scene in Part II to which Cutts alluded as Marlowe's way of sabotaging his hero: 'What if the very manner and matter of "taming" ironically suggest how Tamburlaine himself remains perverse and uncontrolled?'[25]

Some critics have sensed Machiavelli's presence in *Tamburlaine*, if ironically. W. Moelwyn Merchant (1968) contended that Marlowe infused his protagonist with the formulation from *Il principe* (1532) that *fortuna* and *gloria* underlie *virtù*. Conflict arises because the Scythian asserts himself as the prince should, but his rise violates the natural order because of his striving and low birth. Michael Hattaway (1968) made a similar point. Tamburlaine's existential absurdity, more like Bertolt Brecht's than Albert Camus's, creates ridiculous ironies. Surely early audiences noted that the hero's quasi-Machiavellian *virtù* provides in its arrogance the exact opposite of the Beatitudes, with whose homely eloquence they must have been familiar.[26]

Serious performance study and, to a much lesser extent, the idea of theatre history inaugurated themselves in mid-sixties *Tamburlaine* criticism, a trend that Leech, again, strongly encouraged. Though the reviewers were unkind to the point of savagery toward the post-war revival of the plays at the Old Vic (1951), this production and others allowed Marlowe's chronicle to rise from the page to the stage (where it was intended to be heard) once again, after 350 years of silence. Therefore, scholars and playgoers could listen to the music of the poetry and enjoy the gestures and movement that the action warranted. This inability to experience *Tamburlaine* in performance, Harry Morris (1964) argued, hopelessly compromised the judgement of even the greatest critics, such as T. S. Eliot, whose praise was vague to the point of uselessness. He failed to notice 'the rage and torrent' of Tamburlaine's speech, which 'gathers its true mightiness from the rhetoric of sound, the juxtaposition of vowels and consonants in rolling cataracts of harmonies from the lower registers of verbal music', and 'in spuming rhetorics of foam and eddy: in sibilants, gutturals, dentals, and explosives; in long vowels, double vowels, and especially *o* and *u* vowels'. In an overlooked essay on performing the plays, John Russell Brown (1964) historicized the idea of acting style, arguing that it would be anachronistic to object to the probable declamatory method that Edward Alleyn employed as the hero or to decry it as bombast. Indeed, 'An actor must not expect to live on the fat of Marlowe's words; they are "working" words, witty as well as brave, energetic like Marlowe's skeptical thought', comprising speeches created 'to give an impression of a lively, self-contained mind' built with 'large-spanned verbal architecture'. For reasons such as these, Leech proposed that examining the oft-maligned Part II reveals the dramatic chronicle's deep structure and patterning that interconnects its two parts. In a complementary argument, Susan Richards (1965) maintained that the sequel leans toward tragedy. Powell's aforementioned essay underscored the importance of the sequel and provided one of the first indispensable accounts of Zenocrate, one that foretold the feminist readings of Marlowe to come. For Powell, Zenocrate is 'not only the hero's wife, but an extension of himself, too – a part of his soul, as well as a part of his life', and 'represents his ambition'. Her appearances 'gain much of their power from the resonances created by her personality as a woman, and her significance as a symbol'.[27]

Two book-length interpretations devoted exclusively to the Marlowe canon accounted for the importance of *Tamburlaine* in literary history. J. B. Steane's immensely readable *Marlowe: A Critical Study* (1964) was a throwback to the romantic Victorian conception of the playwright as a rebel who fashioned protagonists as his surrogates. Hence, in spite of the conqueror's 'growing extremism and an obsessive megalomaniacal destructiveness', there is 'so little evidence of the author disassociating himself from it' that 'there is an utter disregard of any possible moral criticism'. His 'magnanimity, magnificence, and magniloquence are dazzling', and his proto-Fascism 'can appear less monstrous than it is only because of the stardust in the eyes of author and audience alike'. W. L. Godshalk's *The Marlovian World Picture* (1974) depicted Marlowe as disinterested, surely not a moralist or a cheerleader, one 'whose feelings are not engaged one way or the other by the dramatic characters he has created'. The audience for *Tamburlaine*, then, is on its own, the spectacle reflecting early modern society and its focus on acquisitiveness, its concern with the disruptions that an 'aspiring mind' such as his could cause.[28]

C. L. Barber (1966) and Constance Brown Kuriyama (1980) provided Freudian interpretations of the plays. Barber posited that Tamburlaine's language describing Zenocrate is 'literally frigid', making her the stuff of a mother-figure, 'chastely and worshipfully cherished', with whom, once honoured with conquests, he can consummate their marriage 'in his titanic struggle for manhood'. Kuriyama depicted the hero's milieu in starkly opposite terms: 'One is in general either kingly, strong, intelligent, masculine, and warlike or is slavish, weak, stupid, feminine, and amorous'. Tamburlaine, in search of a father and in his fear of the feminine, deploys hypermasculinity to compensate for this state of mind. His developmental conflicts mirror Marlowe's, which hint at the fear of oral and anal rape, the detritus of his repressed homosexuality, which the critic unfortunately saw as a sickness, an ahistorical view with which several reviewers naturally took issue.[29]

Marlowe's prominence and the importance of *Tamburlaine* ensured that both would be present at the dawn of the new historicist enterprise promulgated most notably by Stephen Greenblatt in *Renaissance Self-Fashioning* (1980). The hero, a model for the critic's paradigm of literature as a discourse of subversion and containment, becomes a comment on Tudor society, creating himself through the cultivation of violence as the play interrogates various types of orthodoxy. According to Greenblatt, for 'the analogue to Tamburlaine's restlessness, aesthetic sensibility, appetite, and violence, we might look not at the playwright's literary sources, not even at the restless power-hunger of Tudor absolutism, but at the acquisitive energies of English merchants, entrepreneurs, and adventurers'. Marjorie Garber's anthropological-semiotic interpretation (1984) presented the conqueror as a type of author, a surrogate for Marlowe, continually 'writing and unwriting' in his destruction of the Qur'an and in his examination of the map of the world, undercut by boasting he cannot fulfil, yet 'adept in the language of signs' and a 'master of speech acts'. Jonathan Dollimore (1984), writing of Tamburlaine's 'indomitable will to power', saw the plays as transgressive expressions of 'transcendent autonomy' for both hero and playwright so that the enterprise 'liberates from its Christian and ethical framework the humanist conception of man as essentially free, dynamic and aspiring'. Simon Shepherd's *Marlowe and the Politics of Elizabethan Theatre* (1986) argued that Marlowe's texts such as *Tamburlaine* 'work to make knowledge of the ideological language of the state'.[30]

Four editions, a concordance, and excellent traditional scholarship and criticism widened previous perspectives of the *Tamburlaine* plays. John D. Jump's single-volume text was a conservative modern-spelling version featuring one of the finest short introductions to Parts I and II in existence. In fifteen pages, he addresses topics that contemporary readers would do well to know: publication, textual, and stage history; reception;

sources; Machiavelli; and criticism from the first half of the century. Like Godshalk, Jump usefully reminds students of the play that the Gawdy letter unearthed by E. K. Chambers thirty years earlier might not concern Part II after all. He seems to have been the first commentator to note that both episodes of *Tamburlaine* must have been produced in different types of theatres, thus contributing to the play's performance history. A platform stage could have accommodated the first, but the second needed more ingenuity: for example, commanders on city walls arguing with attacking armies below, and the dying Zenocrate requires an arras. Fredson Bowers's two-volume edition of the Marlowe canon (1973) prepared what remains the most exhaustive critical apparatus for the *Tamburlaine* plays, informed by the principles of the New Bibliography. J. W. Harper (1971) and J. S. Cunningham (1981, 1986) edited New Mermaids versions.[31]

In the tradition of Bevington, Harold F. Brooks (1968) and Joel Altman (1978) read *Tamburlaine* in light of the late medieval and early modern traditions that it embodies. Brooks argued that Marlowe understood the moralities' fondness for stage tableaux. The endings of the conqueror and his consort in Part II would seem to invoke God's messenger, Death, in works such as *Everyman*, just as the 'Scourge of God' epithet on Jones's title-page was designed to invoke Tudor homiletic about the Lord's coming Judgement. Tamburlaine's hubris seems to be 'provoking the Deity whose Scourge he is, as it was characteristic of a Scourge to do'. In *The Tudor Play of Mind*, Altman located the genesis of Marlowe's hero in the humanist schoolroom, his thesis that drama grew from the rhetorical tradition of posing questions and arguing them *in utramque partem*, which accounts for the development of conflicts and paradoxes therein. Tamburlaine has no moral compass except irregularity, and the phrase in the Prologue, 'applaud his fortunes as you please', runs counter to the homiletics of earlier plays. Altman found paradox in *Tamburlaine*, which 'represents not the tragic fall but the tragic *rise* of a great man. Ultimately, that is, we must locate the tragic in the hero's success'.[32]

Irving Ribner's 'Marlowe and the Critics' (1964) and Kenneth Friedenreich's 'Directions in *Tamburlaine* Criticism' (1974) remain invaluable guides to commentary on the plays. Millar MacLure's *Christopher Marlowe: The Critical Heritage, 1588-1896* (1979) provided a one-volume source for early remarks and references. Robert J. Fehrenbach's massive concordance to the Marlowe canon (1974) was the first since Crawford's multi-volume effort, with the advantage of computer assistance, and without including spurious or contested texts.[33]

Cultural materialist and new historicist interpretations of *Tamburlaine* continued to be produced. Mary Beth Rose's *The Expense of Spirit* (1988) argued that Marlowe's plays featuring the Scythian conqueror constructed sex and sexuality dualistically, a viewpoint that 'either idealizes or degrades women and eros and regards marriage as a necessary evil'. Alan Sinfield (1992) widened this line of inquiry to include what scholars would now term 'queer theory' in his investigation of Tamburlaine's anxiety over his self-admitted tendency to 'reclaim the feminine' when he enjoys the zenith of his power at the end of Part I: 'how unseemly is it for my Sex . . . To harbour thoughts effeminate and faint?' (*I Tam* 5.1.174, 177). Such gender trouble informs the hero's role in line with Marlowe's tendency to 'tease an audience with the prospect of ethical and political closure, thereby calling into question the patterns to which they allude'. Emily Bartels (1992, 1993), Lisa Hopkins (1996), and Alan Shepard (1993) contributed influential studies of *Tamburlaine* that historicized conceptions of gender and explored the gendering of history. To explore how Marlowe's plays reflect English engagement with the East, Bartels began with a traditional subject, the playwright's deployment of his sources. His Scourge of God emanated from Petrus Perondinus's *Vita magni Tamerlanis* (1551), which depicted him as a barbarian, along with George Whetstone's *English Mirrour* (1586) and its more benevolent view. Yet Bartels transcended conventional approaches and analysed Marlowe's reworking of his source materials so that his conception of his hero might interrogate English notions of Eastern inferiority. He knew that his home country had become a world 'in which gods and fiends were being made of men, all in the name of power', a land no less barbaric than the Scythians, Turks, and Tamburlaine himself, to whom it considered itself superior. Hopkins wrote that in most respects, England was an insignificant island on the periphery of the Ottoman Empire, and that as a result, 'The Scythian is in the mirror; however widely Marlowe's explorations of the world may range, they show us, in the end, only ourselves'. Alan Shepard wrote that the plays critique notions of masculinity by sexualizing competition and combat. In this formulation, soldiers 'consider murder more regenerative than heterosexual intercourse', thinking of their male conquests as sexual partners with whom they will remake the worlds they have conquered, the sword symbolic of an iron phallus.[34]

Feminist and psychoanalytic commentators such as Sara Munson Deats (1997), Lisa Starks (1999), and Sarah Emsley (2000) wrote about the complex female roles in *Tamburlaine*. Deats argued that the two works are dialogic and open-ended about matters of gender to the point of normalizing androgyny. Her Lacanian analysis explored Marlowe's development of fully realized psyches and personalities in his characters, his portrait of the hero and his troubled sense of masculinity exemplifying this achievement most of all. Starks explained the playwright's exploitation of the 'economy of desire, along with that of masochism' to imagine his protagonist as 'a god-like tyrant who dominates the play as spectacle and object of the masochistic gaze'. Emsley argued that Zenocrate, Zabina, and Olympia act with Machiavellian *virtù*, a blend of 'shrewdness, strength, and power' to survive and prosper, and should not be reduced to mere emblems of 'sweetness and light' as earlier critics had claimed.[35]

Patrick Cheney (1997) and Mark Thornton Burnett (1999) made the greatest impact on Marlowe studies in this time period, including commentary on *Tamburlaine*. In *Marlowe's Counterfeit Profession*, Cheney advanced the novel and influential thesis that the playwright consciously designed an emulative counter-Vergilian *cum* Spenserian *cursus*, or career path, with the plays devoted to the Eastern conqueror crucial to his plan. By etymology, the aforementioned Latin noun, *cursus*, connects itself to the idea of the chariot, and thus to *Tamburlaine*, which Marlowe dramatized in the 'pampered jades' scene in Part II. To Cheney, this scene symbolized the playwright 'making the "ultima meta" from Ovidian amatory poetry to the "area maior" of Senecan tragedy'. Further, the famous prologue to Part I emulates Spenser's 'October' eclogue, an 'Ovidian' improvisation on the turn from pastoral to epic poetry. Burnett's essays on *Tamburlaine* (1987–91), along with his edition of Marlowe's opus (1999) and the critical collection *Marlowe, History, and Sexuality* (1999), were equally vital contributions to knowledge on the subject.[36]

More traditionally-oriented criticism provided other useful perspectives. Richard Wilson's introduction to his edited collection on Marlowe, along with his essay within, 'Visible Bullets' (1999), implicitly criticized the practice of cultural materialism, and concluded that in *Tamburlaine* and elsewhere, 'the power of speech, violence and virility is juxtaposed to the impotence of literacy, culture and criticism itself. Marlowe's aggression savagely defies the world of art. In fact, this studiously academic writer seems driven by a detestation of everything that his critical readers represent'.[37] In this formulation, the playwright's hero would seem to confute the poststructuralist ideologies applied to the plays in which he thrives, even excels, sword in hand. David Fuller's old-spelling edition of the *Tamburlaine* plays (1998) provided an accurate and scholarly text with a first-rate apparatus rivalling Bowers's, along with a comprehensive introduction that goes beyond textual scholarship to lay out critical and stage history. Thomas Dabbs's illuminating inquiry into the 'creation' of Marlowe by nineteenth-century scholarship explained how the two plays were essential to this foundational conception.

The contours of *Tamburlaine* criticism in the last two decades of the twentieth century should seem familiar to students of the two-part spectacle in the twenty-first. Indeed, most current ways of reading those plays and other early modern literary texts were birthed in these years before the turn of the millennium. These include the schools of interpretation that have implemented new historicism and cultural materialism, queer theory, feminism, memory, performance and print, book history, theatre history, otherness, 'orientalism', and Englishness, and related topics that have continued to proliferate.

2

The Performance History: 'High Astounding Terms' – Tamburlaine and *Tamburlaine* on Stage

Peter Kirwan

> Tamburlaine *is as monotonous a play as one is likely to find tucked away in the dustier archives of the British theatre. There is, admittedly, a sort of grandeur in that iambic surge, billowing down and over you with unerring regularity – but who wants to spend four-odd hours feeling like a battered mussel?*[1]
>
> *The effect is of one damned thing after another.*[2]

Benedict Nightingale and Lyn Gardner are not alone among modern critics in dreading as much as anticipating a production of *Tamburlaine*. For all of the play's apparent early modern popularity, the sheer scale of the *Tamburlaine* plays, and their repetitive, cyclical structure of victory after victory on the part of the Scythian shepherd, often leave reviewers looking at their metaphorical watches before the production has even begun. Complaints such as Nightingale's about the monotony and repetitiveness of the plays characterize the responses of a wide range of commentators across decades of production, and the capacity of *Tamburlaine* to overwhelm its audiences with as much force as Tamburlaine himself does his victims is too much for some.

Yet the challenge of mounting *Tamburlaine* keeps producers returning to it. Michael Boyd remarks that 'At any time it remains one of the great plays of the English Renaissance and I don't know why it is rarely produced'.[3] Boyd's remark is perhaps a little disingenuous; he himself notes the tight editing needed 'to bring them down to one evening of no more than three hours' playing time', and the sheer amount of labour required to work the plays into a form that fits contemporary commercial models (especially for smaller companies with fewer financial and infrastructural resources) means that putting on *Tamburlaine* is not a venture on which companies embark lightly. The allure for theatremakers is thus balanced by the logistical challenges, leading to a great deal of justification and ingenuity when a theatre does take on the play.

The result of this is that productions of *Tamburlaine* are an event. Where *Edward II*, *Doctor Faustus* and *The Jew of Malta* have a regular recurring presence in the classical repertoire, productions of *Tamburlaine* are inextricable from narratives of disaster and celebration, topicality and brinkmanship. The endeavour to stage *Tamburlaine* evokes the hubris of Tamburlaine himself in seeking to pull off the unexpected; Nightingale may find the play monotonous, but its performance history is anything but. In this chapter, I trace the play from the long shadow cast by Edward Alleyn's late sixteenth-century performances, across centuries of adaptation (in which Tamburlaine and *Tamburlaine* become briefly separated), to the re-emergence of the play in the twentieth and twenty-first centuries when, with the return of the figure of the vaunting strongman to positions of global authority, the play has found itself increasingly (and depressingly) timely.

Tamburlaine at the Rose

Thomas Heywood's prologue for *The Jew of Malta* at the Cockpit, published in the preliminaries to Nicholas Vavasour's edition of *The Jew of Malta* (1633), identifies Edward Alleyn as key to the early success of Marlowe's early plays. Barabas, specifically, was '*by the best of Actors play'd*', with an asterisk and marginal note clarifying that this refers to 'Allin'.[4] The prologue aligns praise of Marlowe with praise of Alleyn:

> *In* Tamberlaine,
> *This* Jew, *with others many: th'other man* [Alleyn]
> *The Attribute of peerelesse, being a man*
> *Whom we may ranke with (doing no one wrong)*
> Proteus *for shapes, and* Roscius *for a tongue*,
> So could he speake, so vary ...

The prologue does take a small swipe at Alleyn, though, with the note that the present actor of Tamburlaine does not seek '*To exceed, or equall*' Alleyn's performance, '*being of condition / More modest*' and aiming merely '*To prove his best*'.[5] Amusingly, then, Tamburlaine was associated with (Alleyn's) hubris from the start.

Tamburlaine was presumably first performed at the Rose around 1587; in 1588, Robert Greene spoke of having 'had it in derision, for that I could not make my verses jet upon the stage in tragicall buskins ... daring God out of heaven with that Atheist *Tamburlan*'.[6] Tom Rutter argues that Greene's remarks suggest something of the 'aesthetically and intellectually controversial' nature of the play in its early performances, Greene distinguishing himself from the 'Atheist'.[7] While Holger Schott Syme rightly urges caution around narratives that risk overstating the immediacy and totality of *Tamburlaine*'s influence on the early modern stage, the early references suggest it made an impact.[8] At a performance in November 1587, during the execution of the governor of Babylon, a 'player's hand swerved, his calliver being charged with bullets, missed the fellow he aimed at, and killed a child and a woman great with child, and hurt another man very sore in the head'.[9] Quite what the player *was* attempting to hit with real bullets is unclear, but the play's danger in this anecdote becomes lethal.

Allusions were not always complimentary. *Tamburlaine* appears in garbled quotation in Pistol's overblown 'hollow pampered jades of Asia' (*2 Henry IV*, 2.4.141), and Ben Jonson criticized 'the *Tamerlanes* and *Tamer-Chams* of the late age, which had nothing in them but the scenical strutting and furious vociferation to warrant them to the ignorant gapers'.[10] Christopher Matusiak argues that 'the poet's propulsive rhetoric and the actor's high-set stride shocked and awed the public', drawing on Joseph Hall's references to 'stalking steps' and 'thundring threates' in *Virgidemiarum* (1597).[11] The emphasis on Alleyn's mobility is perhaps supported by the unusually sequential nature of the stage directions in the 1590 edition, which emphasize the processional order of entries and action.[12] Anthony Dawson notes that *Part II* makes particular use of the Rose stage, including a trapdoor for the cremation of Olympia's husband and son (3.4), an upper playing area for the scaling of Babylon's walls (5.1), and a discovery space for Zenocrate's bedchamber (2.4) and Calyphas's tent (5.1); *Part I* makes few such demands and may not have had a specific theatre in mind.[13] Henslowe's inventory suggests that the play made spectacular use of costumes, including Tamburlaine's 'breches of crymson vellvet' and the transformation from shepherd's weeds to armour in 1.2 of *Part I*.[14] The play received twenty-two performances in the 1594–5 year, fifteen of *Part I* and seven of *Part II*, the latter usually the day after *Part I*. Yet while it appears to have been commercially popular, references such as Jonson's suggest that the play also dated quickly.

When the Rose Theatre site was reopened to the public in 1999, the historical associations of the space were an immediate draw to performers, and it was *Tamburlaine*'s lot to be the first play to receive a full production on the site in almost 400 years, with Ben Naylor directing Ben Power's adaptation for Cannon's Mouth in 2003 and rounding out the association of that space with the play. Confined primarily to the viewing platform next to the outlines of the Rose's foundations (marked by glowing red lines in the damp, cave-like space), the production offered a ritualistic tribute to the play's earliest performances:

> The show began and ended with a ritual encompassing the entire Rose. At the opening, the actors stood apart from the audience, amidst the ruins of the Rose itself. Facing the outermost wall, they chanted Islamic prayers. Their voices gradually rose in volume, until one actor began to strike a drum and led the others in a procession to the playing area. This ritual was repeated at the conclusion, when the actors marched away from the stage back to the ruins.[15]

The emergence of the actors from the shadows of the cavernous void imagined the spirits of Alleyn and company returning from the dead, Tamburlaine continuing to stalk his stage. Although Lyn Gardner felt that the spatial restrictions of the viewing platform hampered the performance, she commended the production on its verse-speaking and inventive staging.[16] In its all-male company and extensive doubling and cutting to squeeze the production into two hours, the company alluded to certain early modern practices, but Heather Violanti drew more attention to bravura pieces of action such as the throwing of lit flash paper towards the audience to symbolize the burning of Larissa, and the stylized slow-motion dances of the battle sequences.[17]

Perhaps surprisingly, especially given its spectacular staging possibilities, the play has not at the time of writing been staged at any reconstructions of an early modern amphitheatre, though the American Shakespeare Center performed *Part 1* at the Blackfriars in Staunton, VA, in 2011. Paul Menzer writes of the 'proxemic challenge of staging such a free-ranging, peripatetic play' in a relatively intimate space, drawing attention to the central sequence of the siege in which the entire *frons* was covered by massive banners, cloaking the entrances and closing off the space. 'The effect was immediately stifling, like we were all bedfellows in a massive canopied bed with the curtains drawn. In diegetic terms, it conveyed the sealed-off quality of a city (and a stage) that quite literally had "no exit" . . . In this case, the illusion was that no one gets out, or on, alive'.[18] The potential for *Tamburlaine* to become claustrophobic in a confined space is intriguing, and hopefully the play's increased interest to twenty-first century producers suggests that further explorations in reconstructions of early modern playhouses will be forthcoming.

Tamburlaine's afterlives before the twentieth century

Introducing his play *Tamerlane the Great* in the 1681 edition, Charles Saunders confesses

> *that I never heard of any Play on the same Subject, until my own was Acted, neither have I since seen it, though it hath been told me, there is a Cock-Pit Play, going under the name of the* Scythian Shepherd, *or* Tamberlain the Great, *which how good it is, any one may Judge by its obscurity, being a thing, not a Bookseller in* London, *or scarce the Players themselves, who Acted it formerly, cou'd call to Remembrance.*[19]

If Saunders is to be believed, *Tamburlaine* had completely disappeared from the minds of London's theatre scene in the Restoration, and Marlowe's association with the play forgotten. The 1681 play, avowedly written with no intention of performance, inaugurates the tradition of Marlowe-adjacent adaptations of the Timür story that lasted until the twentieth century. Although Nancy Leslie argues that these are 'completely independent' of Marlowe's play, their choices remain revealing.[20] Saunders's somewhat melodramatic tragedy focuses on Tamerlane's relationship with his sons, the heroic Arsanes – banished owing to the influence of flatterers on Tamerlane – and the scheming Mandricard. Linda McJannet argues that in Mandricard's plot to have Tamerlane turn against Arsanes, the play resembles the Gloucester plot of William Shakespeare's *King Lear*.[21] Yet the plot is somewhat more sensational than that implies, especially the climactic revelation that Mandricard in fact died twenty years earlier, replaced by the son of the treacherous courtier Odmar. Tamerlane is a relatively passive figure, manipulated by courtiers and ultimately reunited with Arsanes in a tragicomic conclusion. The most Marlovian element is Tamerlane's scorn for Bajaset, newly captured at the start of the play, whose daughter both Arsanes and Mandricard ask for permission to marry. Tamerlane's fury at the request, and at Bajaset's refusal to submit to him, leads to the placement of Bajaset in the iron cage after 'mounting / His Shoulders to his Chariot'.[22]

Nicholas Rowe's *Tamerlane, A Tragedy* was published in thirty-five editions between 1701 and 1835, and was Rowe's favourite of his own plays.[23] Here, too, there was no reference to Marlowe. Rowe's Tamerlane 'is so perfect a monarch that he was immediately read as an image of the king [William III], who died the year that the play was published'.[24] Donald B. Clark notes the deliberate analogies adapted from Richard Knowles's Elizabethan history of the Turks, in which Tamerlane (whom Rowe figured as William III) sends an ambassador to Bajazet (Louis XIV) to dissuade him from further attacks on Greece (the Spanish Netherlands), which the latter had laid waste to in violation of treaty. McJannet notes that the play was mounted on the 4th and 5th of November regularly – respectively, William's birthday and the anniversary of his arrival in England in 1688.[25] In a distinctly un-Marlovian move, Tamerlane is tolerant of all diversities of religion, and his subjugation of Bajazet is a display of the victory of a tolerant God over Bajazet's irreligious pride.[26]

While Rowe's version had a life until the mid-nineteenth century, the Tamburlaine story also found its way to the stage in operatic form, in George Frideric Handel's English-language *Tamerlano* (first performed 31 October 1724, just before the annual performance of Rowe's play) and Antonio Vivaldi's Italian *Bajazet* (which premiered in Verona in 1735). As with Saunders, both operas begin with the capture of Bajazet, but here it is Tamerlano who wants to marry Asteria, jilting his fiancée, Irene. Handel's version in particular 'deepened sympathy for Bajazet' with an extended on-stage death scene, but in both operas Bajazet's death (along with the pleas of the women) ultimately helps convert the selfish Tamerlano, and both end in a celebration of the power of love.[27] The romantic image of the Tamburlaine figure lingered in the cultural memory when Marlowe's play was finally revived in the twentieth century.

Reviving *Tamburlaine* in the twentieth century

The modern performance history of *Tamburlaine* starts in America, with a 1919 production at Yale University that 'emphasized pageantry over poetry'.[28] Leslie offers an extensive analysis of the script of this adaptation by Edgar Montillion Woolley and Vincent Benét. The compression cut the more brutal violence (including the slaughter of the Virgins of Damascus and the shooting of the Governor of Babylon), and 'reinforced a sympathetic portrait of a conqueror whose abilities are rewarded and whose questionable ethics are rarely, if ever, subjected to irony'.[29] Particularly of note in Leslie's analysis are the decision to have Tamburlaine enter already in his armour, removing the dramatic image of the discarding of the shepherd's clothes, and a reduction in the role of Bajazeth (though even here, student reviewers apparently noted the effectiveness of the cage scenes).[30] The burning of Islamic books was also removed, and Tamburlaine's death was natural; he was, in Leslie's terms, a 'Tartarian Robin Hood-turned-Napoleon', a reading of the character that evoked the heroism of Rowe's Tamerlane, but (perhaps unsurprisingly) has been repeated onstage rarely since.[31]

Tyrone Guthrie's *Tamburlaine* of 1951 and 1956 was the first known professional revival of the play since the seventeenth century, and established many conventions of the play's modern performance history. It was heavily abridged to compress the two plays into the conventional running time of a single performance; Ervin Beck, working with the now out-of-print acting version, estimates that about 59 per cent of *Part I* and 52 per cent of *Part II* remain.[32] It served as a star vehicle for a leading actor of the day: Donald Wolfit at the Old Vic in 1951 and Anthony Quayle at Stratford, Ontario and New York in 1956, and, in its violent spectacle, it seems to have been overwhelming for many audience members.

One of the unusual aspects of Guthrie's adaptation was the relative side-lining of Bajazeth and Zabina, whose material was brought earlier in the first half, before the Damascus sequences begin; their long speeches were severely cut and they were taken from the stage unmourned.[33] In subsequent productions, Bajazeth and Zabina would tend to form a more climactic and structural role, their ongoing onstage presence in Tamburlaine's cage counterbalancing the vaunting tyrant. Another unusual decision was the excision of Olympia, the only named female character in the second half of *Part II*, whose ultimately suicidal resistance to Theridamas has been a powerful part of many productions. Beck's evaluation was that Guthrie's production was 'anti-romantic', insofar as the very decision to compress the two plays into a single performance defied the 'heroic' interpretations scholars have offered for *Part I* by insisting that Tamburlaine's actions be read in the light of his eventual death.[34] Guthrie's own introduction to the printed version argued that to an epoch familiar with the pictures of Belsen and of Dachau; to the epoch that wrought the destruction of Warsaw and Hiroshima, whose sky echoes to the wild music of the jet-plane; when once again the idea of Absolute Power in the hands of a single Dynast or a group of Oligarchs, begins to be not only familiar but attractive; to such an age may there not likewise be something attractive and contemporary in Marlowe's orgy of sadism by the light of meteors.[35]

As such, the production evoked what Leslie refers to as 'Grand Guignol', quoting T. S. Eliot's report that the production 'makes *King Lear* look as if it might have been written by Sir James Barrie'.[36] With a cast size reported to be anywhere between sixty and ninety-two across the different productions, and a spectacular set that decorated Tamburlaine's chariot and throne with skulls and dead bodies, the effect appears to have rather overwhelmed reviewers, with Richard Hayes complaining of 'a montage of images of barbarism, with the verse swallowed in incoherence, and no imposition anywhere of an attitude: merely the exploitation of sensation'.[37] The production closed in New York after only twenty performances, suggesting that the production had finally exhausted its energies.

The Glasgow Citizens' Company staged a somewhat radical version in 1972–3, directed by Keith Hack with an outstanding cast including Jonathan Kent as Callapine, Paola Dionisotti as Zenocrate, Ian McDiarmid as Bajazeth, and three actors – Rupert Frazer, Jeffery Kissoon and Mike Gwilym – playing Tamburlaine. These three men each took the role of Tamburlaine in turn; Jane Stedman characterizes Frazer as the young Tamburlaine, 'most successful in speaking Marlowe's verse', Kissoon as 'the matured conqueror ... embodying the character's vicious grace' and Gwilym as specializing in 'psychological effects' as Tamburlaine approached death.[38] David Bevington notes that 'generous amounts of stage blood spilled down into the audience. Skeletons hung from posts on stage and in the auditorium'.[39] The tendency towards bloody spectacle seemed, in the mind of reviewers, to trump the production's attempts to establish a more clearly delineated arc for the central character.

Perhaps the most significant and spectacular production of *Tamburlaine* of the twentieth century was Peter Hall's for the National Theatre in 1976, which had the distinction of being the first production to play on the Olivier stage. Assistant Director John Heilpern referred to it as 'the most rehearsed play in the history of the British theatre', with a cast of fifty rehearsing over six months.[40] The production's arrival was inextricable from the prolonged wait for the theatre itself to be ready, and anecdotes from the rehearsal period include Hall finding himself padlocked out of his own theatre when he went to check on the work, and the company finally in exasperation staging stagger-through rough performances on the South Bank itself, free to passers-by.

The archival photographs of the outdoor performances capture the structural principles of blocking that underpinned the production, from the symmetrical staging of Zabina and Zenocrate on opposing thrones to the sight of Albert Finney's Tamburlaine standing, gesturing to the heavens, surrounded by a crowd arranged in the semi-circular pattern of the new Olivier Theatre. When the production made it into the auditorium, the primary focus was a circle of white sand in the centre of the stage, a space dominated by the central figure of each scene. In the opening few scenes, control of this space passed from Mycetes to Cosroe, then to Tamburlaine, and so forth.[41] A hole in the circle, in which Mycetes hid his crown (2.4) and into which Cosroe's corpse was thrown (2.7), was labelled as the 'death hole' in the production materials.[42] The patterning of the set, however, was seen by some as a hindrance; while Tamburlaine himself came alive, 'the other characters, as if trapped by the geometrical set, stand or sit around with very little to do'.[43]

A large pair of upstage doors opened to allow figures to enter (amusingly, the rehearsal notes dictate that the doors should only open a little way for Mycetes (*Part I*, 2.4), whereas they opened fully for Tamburlaine and other more powerful figures).⁴⁴ The use of these central doors to 'reveal' characters shaped the power relations; for example, in 2.5, the doors opened to reveal the crowned Cosroe while Tamburlaine entered from the left vomitorium, a very rare side entrance for the title figure. However, from this appearance in glory to receive Tamburlaine, the doors then traced his quick downfall, as he appeared again through them with his armies in 2.6, and finally alone and dying at the start of 2.7, in a brilliant up-ending of the trope of the doors revealing the most powerful figure. Tamburlaine thereafter almost always entered from these upstage doors, at one point appearing as 'a smoke-wreathed Tamburlaine riding his huge chariot through what might be the corridors of hell'.⁴⁵ A notable exception was 4.2, for which Tamburlaine entered on his chair from one side of the stage while Bajazeth's cage was brought in from the other. The sequence of Denis Quilley's Bajazeth bashing his brains out was one of the few violent moments of the first half, and there was much praise for Quilley's ability to 'bring major tragic force to a secondary role, [making] Bajazeth's fall far more impressive than Tamburlaine's rise'.⁴⁶

Part II was treated to some significant reordering. Zenocrate's death was moved earlier, making the brutal wars against the European alliance of *Part II* an act of vengeance on her behalf. The coronation of Callapine, by contrast, was moved later, making that moment more climactic as an introduction to the final sequence. And the final Callapine scene (5.2) was moved to interrupt Tamburlaine's death scene at 5.3.115, in order to give a stronger sense of the armies closing in. Hall rewrote 5.2.57–9 as a promise:

> And now we know him absent from his camp
> Sick in his substance and consum'd with choler
> Assail it and be sure of victory.

In juxtaposing Callapine and Tamburlaine one final time, Hall's production emphasized the extent to which Tamburlaine goes out swinging.

Heilpern describes something of Hall's approach in the rehearsal room, in which he told Finney to

> play it with chutzpah ... that untranslatable Yiddish word which has been defined as that quality enshrined in a man who, having killed his mother and father, throws himself on the mercy of the court because he's an orphan. It was the one word that Hall never stopped using throughout the entire production, and in many ways chutzpah became the key to Finney's interpretation of the massive role of Tamburlaine.[47]

The temptation to align the chutzpah of Finney's Tamburlaine with the ambition of the new theatre was more than many reviewers could resist; Irving Wardle commented that 'for those who have viewed the theatre as the victim of some more malignant spell, there could be no more fitting first play than Marlowe's chronicle of insatiable atheistic conquest'.[48] But despite the fascination with the Olivier, Finney's performance commanded the most attention. 'What he communicates most strongly is the sense of an invulnerable being; one relishes the early triumphs simply for the reversals in status'.[49] Michael Billington found 'a promising vein of ironic comedy' in Hall and Finney's choices: 'whether threading captured crowns on his sword like wedding-rings or inviting the audience to share the pleasures of kingship, Finney gave one a sense of a real human being'.[50] The difficult balance between humanity and inhumanity in playing Tamburlaine remained, in this production, crucial to the reviewers' perception of success.

Reviewers were ultimately caught up in the spectacle of this 'medieval Hitler' (a phrase that recurred in several reviews), as 'great gouts of blood gush from throats and heads and drip from daggers' and 'the drums roll, the lights turn blood-red and screams echo from the loudspeakers'.[51] The scale of the spectacle didn't remove concerns about monotony, but the production filled the Olivier Theatre in a way that productions ever since have often struggled to do.

The balance between spectacle and humanity characterized the RSC's only twentieth-century production of the play, for which Terry Hands directed Antony Sher as Tamburlaine in the Swan Theatre in 1992. Irving Wardle celebrated the production as 'Marlowe's Rambo triumphant', praising Sher's depiction of an 'under-sized nonentity who becomes the terror of the earth'.[52] That terror extended to the audience-performer relationship:

> Beginning with a threatening, foot-stomping Zulu wardance, played direct to the audience by Tamburlaine's army before their battle with the Persians, we are subjected to periodic intimidation and assault: rope-climbing, stilt-walking, powder-flashing, blood-splashing, this is *dangerous* theatre, and for the spectator there is the recurrent fear that an actor may lose his balance and fall into the stalls, or that the front row will be splattered with the blood which is poured so liberally about the stage.[53]

The 'danger' noted by Martin Wiggins continued the twentieth-century interest in bloody spectacle, but here with a more iconoclastic edge. J. S. Cunningham and Eithne Henson suggest that Hands 'heightened the elements of exoticism, barbarity, and horror, all oppressively close at hand in the intimate Swan'.[54] The horror was not empty spectacle; David Bevington argues that Tamburlaine's 'cannibalistic feasting to celebrate his conquest of the Turkish Emperor (Malcolm Storry), now confined to a cage and fed morsels from a gigantic tureen, became a fantasy on the theme of conquest as its chief and only reward', especially as Tamburlaine's men urinated on the human flesh they offered Bajazeth.[55] But McJannet felt that the production's emphasis on animal barbarism concealed uglier resonances, particularly as the white South African Sher 'leads his troops in foot-stamping chants and lethal high kicks'[56] choreographed by Welcome Msomi. The alignment of hallmarks of Zulu dance with a production in which Hands showed actors 'tapes of the African hunting dog' drew a problematically racialized set of associations between black African culture and barbarism that included cannibalism.[57]

Yet while Sher's performance was explicitly animalistic, other reviewers noted a humanizing element of his depiction. Margaret Loftus Ranald thought that 'Sher's eyes were his most frightening feature, and his decline into age by way of grief was signified by the lessening of his dominating gaze and the increasing heaviness, even clumsiness of his movement'.[58] Wardle singled out Sher's delivery of 'the great speech [*Part II*, 4.3.97–133] forecasting his homecoming and death. Sher delivers it lyrically until he gets to the last four words – "and meet him there" (meaning the Almighty, should he exist); at which point his voice turns to thunder and he stabs a challenging finger at the sky'.[59] At the end of the twentieth century, Wardle felt that Tamburlaine's contradictions were resolved in the explicit, furious challenge to God.

Tamburlaine in the twenty-first century

If Sher challenged God, Greg Hicks's Tamburlaine 'sticks two fingers up at the heavens and looks for a long time as if he will get away with it'.[60] David Farr's production for Young Genius, which played at Bristol Old Vic and London's Barbican in 2003, was the first major professional production of the new century, and in contrast to the spectacle of the preceding century's tendencies, Lyn Gardner noted the 'spare and clear' nature of the production, with an 'icy . . . puritan' performance from Hicks that 'makes this blankness – the void at Tamburlaine's heart – totally compelling'.[61]

The most remarked-upon element of Farr's production was the decision, in the wake of the 9/11 terrorist attacks, to cut the cursing of Mohammed and have Tamburlaine torch 'a collection of harmlessly unidentified "holy books" just before the first traces of his final illness appeared'.[62] Skip Shand noted it would have been 'foolhardy' to stage this, though David Farr himself reacted angrily to accusations that the choice was 'to avoid upsetting Muslims'. In a piece entitled 'Tamburlaine wasn't censored', Farr outlined his views:

> I believe one reason my production of Tamburlaine became so successful was that it eschewed the normal shields-and-shouting masquerade in favour of a philosophically purer and harsher reading of the text. Greg Hicks' Tamburlaine was an existential free spirit encountering the inevitable nihilism of his own godless ambition ... I wanted to make it very clear that his act was a giant two fingers to the entire theological system, not an [sic] piece of Christian triumphalism over the barbarous Turk. So, in our production, Marlowe's 'heap of superstitious books' were the books of all religions.[63]

The typography of the article title makes it fascinatingly ambiguous whether 'Tamburlaine' or *'Tamburlaine'* wasn't censored, and Farr aligns the defence of the production's own freedom of expression with Tamburlaine's self-assertion of an individual belief system. While the production still deployed gore for the onstage murders, and even visualized images such as Olympia setting fire to the corpses of her son and husband's bodies with the aid of a jerry-can, the stripped-down aesthetic (wooden boxes for set, costumes hanging from rails at the side and rear of stage for onstage costume changes, minimal props) emphasized a more thoughtful approach.[64] Sam Marlowe argued that the 'violent imagery has all the more impact for its economy', and Shand found the production 'understated, rather than gloriously hyperbolic', with Tamburlaine 'compellingly smart and ruthlessly confident, but frozen in his class origins, his worldwide acts of conquest never lifting him to the heights that one might imagine'.[65]

Across the Atlantic, the Shakespeare Theatre Company in Washington DC staged *Tamburlaine* in Michael Kahn's spectacular production of 2007–8 which, as with Peter Hall and Ben Naylor's productions, once again christened a new theatre: the spectacular Sidney Harman Hall. This was the first major production to cast a black actor (here, Avery Brooks) in the title role, a decision which Linda McJannet demonstrates has become increasingly common in the twenty-first century.[66] However, what could have been a landmark production received lacklustre reviews, perhaps best summed up in Laura G. Godwin's judgement of the production's interest in 'simplicity over intricacy' and a disjointed approach to dramaturgy that lacked continuity.[67]

The production generated responses of confusion and concern in relation to its spectacle. McJannet notes that the 'eclectically designed' production drew on a range of influences from across Asia, including suspended taiko drums and an antique Chinese canopy bed, but that 'the play's Islamic milieu was not emphasized', despite the burning of an oversized Qur'an.[68] Anita M. Hagerman pushes this further:

> The production simplistically – and problematically – conflates Oriental cultures. From Arabic tunics to Indian turbans, Persian shoes to Japanese sleeves, ad nauseam, cultures are intermingled in each costume. Only colour-coding the cloth differentiates the cities Tamburlaine conquers ... but the colours themselves seem to signify nothing ... Furthermore, there is little effort made to challenge or explore our traditional, received notions of 'Orientalism': the Oriental Other is opulent, strange, sexualized and dangerous.[69]

While other critics enjoyed the 'extended pageantry ... [and] incessant drumbeat of violence', this pageantry appears to have manifested as Orientalist spectacle, a display of otherness that remained non-specifically foreign and avoided political commentary, rendering the spectacle empty.[70] Godwin further argued that the production 'lowered the stakes' by weakening all of Tamburlaine's adversaries, including portraying Bajazeth as 'an English pantomime emperor straight out of a West End production of *Aladdin*'.[71]

Brooks's performance prompted conflicting responses. McJannet remarks on Godwin's characterization of Brooks's delivery as 'animalistic growls', noting the 'historical sting' of applying this to an actor of colour.[72] Hagerman's review, however, suggests that this 'bestial interpretation' was a deliberate choice of the performance rather than Godwin's projection.[73] She notes that at the production's end, 'Tamburlaine is majestic, haughty, presenting a sheathed sword that he drops disdainfully at the audience before exiting with a scowl', but that this contrasted markedly with Brooks's Tamburlaine elsewhere: 'That Tamburlaine is subhuman, an animal who by turns backs, growls, grunts, and whinnies his way through scenes'. The subhuman appears again in Charles Isherwood's view that Brooks had a 'rich, booming baritone of seductive beauty', but that 'the gorgeous rhetoric never coalesces around a persuasively human character, leaving a void of hot air at the center of the play'.[74] Yet even if the reviewers are accurately reporting Brooks's choices, McJannet's historical overview – especially in relation to the 1992 RSC production – is an important reminder of the ease with which critics and productions of this play have associated blackness and animal-ness, a racist characterization of both Tamburlaine and *Tamburlaine*. Ultimately, both in its treatment of the title character and in its particular mode of spectacle, the production was out of keeping with the more thoughtful approaches of the new century.

Surprisingly, in the second decade of the century, *Tamburlaine* became suddenly popular on the London fringe circuit. A rare repertory staging of the two parts of *Tamburlaine* on alternating nights (with a final all-day back-to-back event) was staged by the Fourth Monkey actor training company in London in March 2015. Directed by Steve Green and Sarah Case, the peculiar invention of this production was to switch the genders of the characters for *Part II*, so that Tamburlaine and his associates were referred to as 'girls'.[75] Where *Part II* usually suffers in compressed versions, Maryam Philpott felt that this play offered 'much more for the character to do' as both tyrant and parent, with Amy Mills balancing the emotional side of the role with the violence. Later the same year, Ricky Dukes and Gavin Harrington-Odedra directed a stripped-down modern dress version for Lazarus Theatre at the Tristan Bates studio. The blank studio backdrop focused attention on the energetic ensemble performances. Neil Cheesman commented that Prince Plockey's 'physique du rôle and his permanent sneer perfectly convey the brutality and powerful fascination with evil which will guide his actions and transform him from shepherd into king'.[76] The transformation was traced through costume: Tamburlaine's armies began in loose sportswear, but over time took on the trappings of power of the Persian Emperor – 'sharp suits and not a hair out of place'.[77] Where the production fell down was in its storytelling, with several reviewers remarking on the odd cuts (including Tamburlaine's sons), severely shortened second half and rushed conclusion.

Yellow Earth's 2017 touring production for six actors and a taiko drummer was more successful, and also finally cast an actor of Asian descent in the lead role. The advance publicity suggested a specifically political angle: 'In an age when Trump can become leader of the Free World, conflict rages across the Middle East, Europe is increasingly divided and a new power from the East asserts its growing dominance, Marlowe's classic takes on a new urgency and relevance for our time'.[78] In fact, its primary target was toxic masculinity. The only male actor in the cast, Leo Wan, played the least obviously 'masculine' characters – the feeble Mycetes and the pacifist Calyphas, a doubling choice used also by Cannon's Mouth at the Rose in 2003 – while Lourdes Faberes played a Tamburlaine whose performance of masculinity 'serve[d] to highlight the absurdities and dangers of all this excessive testosterone'.[79] Her performance stressed the character's interest in the emasculation of others, taking great pleasure in bridling Orcanes, dangling food through the bars of Bajazeth's cage, and holding Mycetes' crown tauntingly out of reach. Faberes' swaggering self-assurance was the closest the production got to a specific political commentary, imagining (and satirizing in the body of the female actor) the braggadocio of a new generation of world-leading 'strongmen'.

Yellow Earth's dramaturgy found intelligent ways of compressing the play into a single performance. Peter Malin notes the conflation of Bajazeth and Cosroe into a single role, and the survival of Bajazeth and Zabina far into the second half, 'so that they had apparently spent sixteen years in captivity and could therefore coexist with their grown-up son, Callapine'.[80] Similarly, the relationship between Zenocrate and Tamburlaine was elongated to provide a larger structural arc, and Zenocrate's death scene was a climactic point, with Tamburlaine promising the whole of Asia as her face contorted in agony. The choice to have only Faberes play a single role throughout placed a greater emphasis on Tamburlaine's personal arc, the despot standing centrally on the stage driving the action as others came and went.

The political point made by the production was about the power of words. Violence was almost entirely eschewed – the 'braining' of Zabina and Bajazeth saw the two simply exhale and allow their bodies to slump, and there was no onstage fighting. Where stage blood was used, it was usually in moments that focused on character, such as a grief-stricken Tamburlaine biting a chunk out of his own arm. Instead, the wars were rhetorical, Tamburlaine talking his enemies to death. One of the most impressive visual sequences rendered the burning of the Qur'an as a video projection of words, which slowly disappeared from the screen, the wisdom of ages disappearing in the face of Tamburlaine's self-assertion. In the wake of Zenocrate's death, the debate between the three sons became an important hook, with Wan presenting Calyphas's pacifism as deliberate and principled in contrast to the unthinking militarism of his younger brothers; his death was dignified, with Tamburlaine asking him to stand up straight before snapping his neck. But the image of the conscientious objector lingered in the mind during the closing speech, which began as a vaunting lecture on political conquest delivered by Tamburlaine, who was left alone on stage as the lights faded on Tamburlaine's offer to take on the heavens. The production's scepticism about toxic masculinity allowed it to seemingly reject its hero at the moment when his confidence seemed to soar, a powerful political gesture.

Finally, in the most recent and important production of the century to date, Michael Boyd turned Marlowe's continent-bestriding hero into an Atlantic-bestriding one, beginning at New York's Theatre for a New Audience in 2014, and then remounting the same production with a new cast for the RSC in 2018. In an interview before the RSC run, Boyd suggested that 'the world and our understanding of the nature of tyranny have changed so much since 2014 that we will have no choice but to reread the play anew for a contemporary audience'.[81] Certainly by the 2018 production, with both the US and Russia being headed by combative and performatively masculine figureheads, Boyd's *Tamburlaine* seemed to be less about the concerns of how a conqueror like Tamburlaine comes to power, and more about what that kind of power does to the soul. This Tamburlaine – John Douglas Thompson in New York, Jude Owusu in Stratford-upon-Avon – was quite literally haunted.

Boyd's innovative solution to the problem of coherence in a compressed production was to revive the elaborate thematic doubling that distinguished his 2006–8 productions of Shakespeare's history plays at the RSC. There, history was figured as a cyclical series of recurring events, in which the same actors – often in the same costumes – were forced to relive events in different guises. Here, as Tamburlaine's victims were killed, actors paused before getting up and walking off. When they returned in their next role, the actors' bodies continued to bear the scars of their previous life. Capolin had his neck snapped in 1.4 of *Part I*; in the actor's subsequent roles as Magnetes and Amyras, he wore a surgical neck brace. The treacherous Agydas had his throat cut; as Arabia and Orcanes, a red line remained visible on his neck. And Cosroe still had blood on his face when returning as the King of Fez, and screamed vengeance from the balcony as he watched Cosroe's Persian crown placed on Zenocrate's head.

Claire M. L. Bourne notes that the design 'made Tamburlaine's ever-growing empire feel like an abattoir', with 'tall, thick, plastic curtains' covering the industrial scaffolding that formed the production's backdrop.[82] The macabre associations of the plastic were further stressed in the choice to stylize onstage deaths through the use of a child actor playing Young Callapine 'to carefully paint the faces of the dead with stage blood he carried in a bucket ... that culminated, devastatingly, in his throwing bucketfuls of blood at his parents when they brained themselves against their cage'.[83] The blood that spattered across the walls and curtains of the stage was mirrored in the scars and matted blood that marred the bodies of the actors, and the presence of these scars even on the bodies of his sons allowed the dead to gradually close in around Tamburlaine. Dan Venning felt that the doubling was played too often for comedy, seeming 'to ridicule the repetitive nature of *Tamburlaine*, thus making the play seem ineptly crafted';[84] Bourne, however, singled out the doubling of Zenocrate with Callapine, noting that '[Merritt] Janson's Callapine routinely appeared on the upstage scaffolding – above and behind Tamburlaine. As Callapine pursued Tamburlaine, so did the ghostly Zenocrate. Elusive adversary and lost wife were one and the same: reminders that Tamburlaine's earthly powers had their bounds'.[85] To this end, Tamburlaine's treatment of Zenocrate was revisited upon himself. He raised her body – played by the actor – as the monument at the site of the destroyed Larissa, utilizing her corpse as an emblem of destruction. That this emblem then followed him about the stage suggested that even this megalomaniac could no longer escape the consequences of his own actions.

Pascale Aebischer notes the shifting emphasis from the New York reviews – which made little if any reference to the contemporary political climate, and especially to the significance of casting the African-American Thompson in the title role during the closing years of Barack Obama's presidency – to an emphasis on topicality in the RSC's programme, which explicitly identified Trump, Putin, Salvini, Orban, Farage and

Galloway in its 'exploration of political charisma and the ruthless pursuit of power by white, predominantly right-wing leaders of dubious moral credentials'.[86] Aebischer was struck by the potential confusion in (both times) casting a black actor in a role designed to critique a distinctively white manifestation of totalitarian leadership. McJannet, discussing the New York production as the culmination of her discussion of the racial politics of casting in *Tamburlaine*, felt that the integrated casting across the ensemble (including a black actor, Chuk Iwuji, as Bajazeth; the role was taken by the Indian actor Sagar I. M. Arya in Stratford) 'challenged simplistic assumptions about inheritance and physical versus temperamental leadership qualities', offering a more dialogic treatment of race than the Orientalizing tendencies of earlier productions.[87] Tom Piper's metal set and the mixed-period dress presented a world out of time that foregrounded the repetitive qualities of the action, climaxing in an extraordinary dance of death, during which Tamburlaine was pulled about the stage on his enormous chariot by the conquered kings accompanied by an entourage of corpses, including Zenocrate's in a chair, with all of the bodies convulsing every time Tamburlaine cracked his whip. Tamburlaine's power was undisputed, but his actions literally took him around in circles, a potent visualization of contemporary political impasse.

Conclusion

The stage history of *Tamburlaine* suggests that the play's significance is assumed – few plays have inaugurated so many theatres – but that the nature of that significance is more ambiguous. Tamburlaine himself is sometimes a righteous defender of wrongs, sometimes a tyrant, sometimes a cannibal. The need for the play to be heavily adapted to work as a single performance complicates its reception even further, as characters who become crucial to one production such as Olympia or Calyphas are reduced or cut in the next. The rare choice to stage *Part I* in isolation, as the American Shakespeare Center did in 2011, offers yet another set of possibilities. Eric Minton argued that, with the final scene playing out over the brained bodies of Bajazeth and Zabina, Tamburlaine's play became 'The Tragedy of Bajazeth'.[88]

Irving Wardle remarked of the 1992 RSC production that 'What remains constant is [Tamburlaine's] impious defiance of all forms of authority – hence his persisting glamour'.[89] Yet a glamorized or exoticized Tamburlaine has struggled to endure in an age so sceptical of this brand of machismo. The most exciting development in *Tamburlaine*'s afterlife is the growing confidence of small-scale and fringe organizations in exploring the play, offering an alternative to commercially appealing spectacle and diversifying the pool of political and aesthetic responses to the play. Far from Nightingale's fears of monotony, *Tamburlaine* is potentially beginning to speak to broader audiences than ever before.

3

The State of the Art: The Critical Landscape, 2000–Present

Sarah Wall-Randell

The first decades of the twenty-first century have seen a continued and accelerating interest in the *Tamburlaine* plays among scholars. A quantitative reckoning offers only a one-dimensional perspective, but it is nevertheless worth noting that the MLA International Bibliography catalogues about forty peer-reviewed journal articles and book chapters that deal centrally with *I* or *II Tamburlaine* published in English in each of the decades 1980–9 and 1990–9, but fifty-two for 2000–9 and over sixty so far since 2010. While *Doctor Faustus* remains, at present, the most-studied of Marlowe's works, *Tamburlaine* is clearly on the rise.

I. Anglo-Ottoman studies

One of the forces behind this flowering of *Tamburlaine* scholarship post-2000 has certainly been the larger growth of interest, within the field of early modern literary studies, in the relationship between England and the Islamic world in the sixteenth and seventeenth centuries. While, as Tom Rutter notes, the events of 11 September 2001 clearly sharpened scholarly focus on the history of Muslim–Christian interaction, the field was already active before the turn of the twenty-first century.[1] Following ground-breaking work by Nabil Matar, Jonathan Burton, and others, scholars have recognized the need to balance the enthusiasm with which early modernists of the 1980s and 1990s had taken up the idea of the New World and Atlantic exploration in the sixteenth- and seventeenth-century English imagination with a complementary investigation of English perceptions of the 'old' world, the multicultural Mediterranean: the Ottoman empire, the Arab world, northern Africa, and Central Europe.[2] Important critical work on early modern 'Turk plays' has informed our understanding of *Tamburlaine*'s depiction of the Ottoman and Islamic worlds.

A key part of recent critics' re-evaluation of previous generations' scholarship on England's relations with the early modern 'East' has been their warning against the application of Edward Said's influential analysis of 'Orientalism', the pervasive discourse of estrangement and subjugation through which European colonial powers justified and enforced their domination of other cultures. Orientalism does not 'work' as a paradigm to apply to sixteenth- and seventeenth-century English attitudes toward the Islamic world, critics such as Richmond Barbour advise, because, to put it simply, England did not yet have a position of strength from which to dictate its relations with the 'East'. 'To project [Said's] findings backward, to read precolonial ethnography as if its rhetoric bespoke European dominance of the world, or its defensive tropes necessarily foretold aggressive expansion, is anachronistic', asserts Barbour in *Before Orientalism: London's Theatre of the East, 1576–1626*.[3] New-World-minded critics of early modern drama had argued that Tamburlaine's lust for conquest was a stand-in for England's imperial ambitions; Burton contends instead 'that Marlowe's representation of Turkish strength is representative of actual Turkish strength, and that the two *Tamburlaine* plays interrogate European responses to that power'; responses that are more about anxiety than the presumption of mastery.[4]

Tamburlaine's sweep of geographic settings and references across the Near East and North Africa, its Persian, Turkish, and Moorish characters, and the spectacular blasphemy of Tamburlaine against Islam in *Part II*, when he burns a Qur'an onstage, make the plays a rich field for examining English perceptions of religious and racial difference that constituted the compelling and fearsome idea of the 'Mahometan'. The iconic acts of inhuman cruelty that Tamburlaine inflicts on enemies and intimates alike, using an emperor as his footstool, slaughtering civilians as they beg for mercy, murdering his own son for being insufficiently battle-hungry, and forcing kings to draw his chariot like beasts, darkly epitomize one early modern English stereotype of the 'barbarism' of the East.

As Burton says, however, English Islamophobia was not an immutable force; anti-Muslim or anti-Turkish sentiment was subject to strategic 'activation and suspension' depending on what financial or political interest England had in a given matter.[5] Elizabeth I sought common ground around religious iconoclasm in her diplomatic communications with Sultan Murad III. In a way that is typical of that complex and shifting English understanding of the allurements and depredations of Islam, and yet is also characteristically Marlovian, *Tamburlaine* refuses a simple confrontation between the familiar and the 'other'. Tamburlaine himself is a 'Scythian', a nomad from the steppes of modern-day northern Eurasia, not an Ottoman Turk or North African. While he relishes the trappings of wealth once he has clawed his way into them, his origins are not in the perfumed 'Eastern' luxury so resonant in the early modern English imagination, but in the humble life of a shepherd. Rather than attacking Christianity primarily, he rejects all religion in favour of the worship of individual power, all the while calling himself the 'scourge', or punishing tool, of God, carrying out the divine will against God's unfavoured of all persuasions. Far from reinforcing a rigid religious hierarchy by bowing to 'Mahomet' (early moderns erroneously believed that Muslims worshipped the Prophet), or blindly following superstition, as in Protestant England's idea of idolatrous Roman Catholicism, Tamburlaine overturns every available traditional order and smashes icons of religion and monarchy along the way.

Tamburlaine's oblique positioning vis-à-vis established categories of 'us' and 'them' thus means that the plays cannot simply be read as evidence of early modern English Islamophobia. Matthew Dimmock tracks the oppositions of Turk and Persian, Muslim and Christian, through the diptych, and finds that the demonization of Ottoman Turks set out in *Part I*, typical of earlier English writers such as Foxe, becomes more complex in *Part II*, which 'begins to offer a sense of the conceptual instability the east occupied in the English imagination'.[6] Linda McJannet makes a close study of the character of Bazajeth in *Tamburlaine, Parts I and II*. Based on a real historical model, Bayazid I (1389–1403), Marlowe's Bazajeth set the precedent for a type of stage Turk that held sway on the public stage into the seventeenth century in plays by Thomas Kyd, Robert Greene, Thomas Dekker, and others; yet Marlowe's sultan, as McJannet shows, is no two-dimensional 'raging Turk,' but a complex and even sympathetic character.[7]

Jonathan Gil Harris, meanwhile, reminds us that *Tamburlaine*'s geographical reach extends beyond the Mediterranean into the subcontinent, both in references to India in the play (historical and transhistorical, evoking the travels of the 'real' Timür – see Matthew Dimmock's chapter in the present volume – as well as the early modern Portuguese colonial presence in South Asia) and in the ways in which seventeenth-century English travellers to India, such as Sir Thomas Roe and Thomas Coryate, brought with them preconceptions and frames of reference based on Marlowe's play. Not only does Marlowe's version of Timür affect how Roe and Coryate see the Mughals of their own time, Harris argues, but Tamburlaine's 'ecstatic' self-transformations provide

Coryate with a model for his own reinvention as a trans-cultural 'shape-shifter'.[8]

A related avenue of inquiry, and one of the most vibrant areas of current scholarship on medieval and early modern culture, connecting directly to work on English views of the Islamic world and the East, is that informed by critical race studies (see Sydnee Wagner's chapter in the present volume). These theorists of 'race before race' challenge traditional scholarly assumptions that 'race' as we know it in the present day did not exist as a concept in premodern European societies, and that depictions of racial difference in the cultural productions of these societies, presumed to be made by white artists for a white audience, cannot be analysed meaningfully using contemporary race-studies' theoretical frameworks. Scholars of medieval and early modern race work to relocate the presence and experiences of actual people of colour in supposedly homogenous premodern European societies, to find the roots of present-day structures of racist hegemony in medieval and early modern literary and cultural discourses, and to contribute, through analysing those structures' expression in texts and artefacts, to dismantling their continuing effects.

II. Environmentalism

Another set of tools informed by urgent present-day issues that critics and scholars have used to engage with the *Tamburlaine* plays is that offered by ecocriticism. Through examining how humans understood the natural world in the premodern era, medieval and Renaissance ecocritics seek to historicize and de-essentialize the state of disconnection from and exploitation of the environment in which we live now. In an essay examining the history of the word 'environment' in the English language, and its earlier fraternal twin, 'environ', Vin Nardizzi finds that Marlowe and other writers of the 1580s and 1590s use the verb 'environ' in contexts very different from (and yet necessarily connected to) the modern sense of 'environment'. 'Environ' occurs in *Tamburlaine, Part I*, 'in interlinked discourses of physical protection, militarism, and ... peril',[9] always denoting a surrounding action by soldiers: palaces environed by troops (5.2.464); the sultan of Egypt environed with knights (4.3.2), which nevertheless fail to protect him from Tamburlaine's forces; Tamburlaine's five hundred thousand armed footmen guarding his flag, 'environing their standard round' (4.1.26). Nardizzi proposes that these uses can productively remind us that 'environment' denotes not only an ecosystem but also an experience of being environed, 'an ambience that can make us feel stifled and overwhelmed'.[10] Such an intellectual exercise, Nardizzi claims, helps humans escape from our own anthropocentric worldview, in which it is always we who do things, good or bad, to the environment; instead, we can imagine, in a play from a cultural moment just before the advent of European colonialism, industrialization, and the other human endeavours that have wreaked devastation on the globe, what it might be to be 'environed'.[11] Zümre Gizem Yilmaz takes up another ecocritical approach, finding an 'ecophobia' more broadly present in *Tamburlaine*: Tamburlaine conquers and subjugates not only peoples and nations but the natural world itself, and part of his exercise of his hard-won, nearly superhuman power involves rejecting what is earthy and 'natural' about the human body, as when he prevents the corpse of Zenocrate from decomposing and drags it around with him rather than allowing it to return to the earth.[12]

III. Religion

Recent readings of the diptych have engaged with the 'religious turn' that has become more prominent within literary studies in the last twenty years, finding the plays as much a mirror for debates within early modern Christianity as a perspective on the East. John Parker, for example, finds in Tamburlaine an evocation of the religious journey of St. Paul, comparing

'Tamburlaine's over-the-top grandeur' to 'Saul's pre-conversion cruelty [and] the later zeal for grace that his cruelty prefigured... [T]he villain here is both heaven's representative and its opponent; "the scourge of God" is both subjective and objective genitive'.[13] Joel Elliot Slotkin notes that the *Tamburlaine* plays 'do not seek to accurately reproduce the relationship between Islam and Christianity in the late sixteenth century but, rather, to use the interaction between religions to explore metaphysical questions of particular concern in the wake of the Protestant Reformation'.[14] Slotkin argues that Marlowe's subject is not Christianity or Islam per se, but religious belief itself, and that he ultimately valorizes a pragmatic open-mindedness: 'Marlowe insists that religious questions are worth asking, even if their answers prove impossible to determine with certainty'.[15] Leila Watkins, conversely, argues that the religious position the *Tamburlaine* plays most consistently take is not one of openness to different modes of the divine, but of radical scepticism; while resisting a too-easy association between the plays and the accusations of atheism levelled against Marlowe by Greene, Baines, and Kyd, Watkins maintains that the plays reject a religious viewpoint.[16]

IV. Book history/theatre history

As the only plays by Marlowe to appear in print during his lifetime, *Tamburlaine, Parts I and II*, printed in one volume in 1590, occupy a unique place in the textual and bibliographical history of his work, and in the history of his reception not just as a playwright but as an 'author' in the print marketplace. Accordingly, they have inspired work by scholars aligned with the enormous growth in the last twenty-five years in material book studies, the scholarship and analysis of print, manuscript, and reading cultures and technologies (see Claire M. L. Bourne's chapter in this volume). Some of this work in critical bibliography has aimed to strip away the accretions of convention and conjecture that have built up around early modern texts such as *Tamburlaine* through successive eras of 'best practices' in editing, while at the same time bringing back into view 'paratexts' previously thought incidental, like the size, formats, and typography of early printed texts, as well as prefaces, indexes, illustrations, and evidence of readerly use, to arrive at fresh revelations about their meaning.[17] Mathew R. Martin calls attention to how 'the modern tradition of editing the *Tamburlaine* plays suppresses the unruly materialisms of the two plays in order to discipline their unruly textual bodies';[18] he focuses on the relatively neglected 1597 edition, arguing that its verbal variants from more 'authoritative' printings, usually discounted by editors as printing-house misreadings, tend to draw the meanings of the lines in which they appear in a more concrete, corporeal, even sensual direction, and thus actually have their own, alternative value. Kirk Melnikoff sheds light on the edits to the play-text that the stationer Richard Jones claims in his preface to the 1590 first edition that he made, arguing that Jones was less concerned with shaping Marlowe's reputation, or with staking a claim for print drama as a 'literary' genre (motives that previous scholars have imputed to Jones), than he was with positioning himself and the products of his publishing operation in the print marketplace – with his 'brand', as we might say now.[19] Seeing the sales potential for 'improving' literature, Jones accordingly edits *Tamburlaine* and 'markets the text as providing a model for the behaviour of his ambitious "Gentlemen Readers"', while at the same time establishing his own name as an editor of 'agency and skill'.[20]

In 2018 Melnikoff and Roslyn L. Knutson produced the edited collection *Christopher Marlowe, Theatrical Commerce, and the Book Trade*, a major re-evaluation of 'Marlowe in repertory and Marlowe and the book' in which multiple essays – indeed, nearly a whole section of the volume – address the form and meanings of Jones's 1590 edition of *I* and *II Tamburlaine*.[21] Taken as a whole, these essays make a strong case for the idea that Jones's work with the *Tamburlaine* plays set important precedents for the printing of play-texts going forward. Adam G. Hooks reminds us that Jones's *Tamburlaine* does not bear Marlowe's name, and proceeds to demonstrate how surprisingly late in history – not until the nineteenth century, and even then not univocally – the play was clearly attributed to him.[22] Claire M. L. Bourne argues that Jones's formatting choices, including breaking the play up into discrete, numbered scenes, emphasize its origin in the theatre as well as the vivid theatricality of its style, and capture for the reader a bit of the experience of being a spectator to the play onstage.[23] Peter Kirwan's chapter extends Bourne's claims by analysing the ways in which the 1594 quarto of *The First Part of the Contention*, a version of which was later known as Shakespeare's *2 Henry VI*, shows the influence of the 1590 *Tamburlaine*'s 'theatrical' formatting and use of stage directions, and suggests that this *Tamburlaine*-ian page presence may have contributed to the theory that the play was co-authored by Marlowe.[24] Tara L. Lyons calls on scholars to recognize the pioneering quality of Jones's decision to print the two *Tamburlaine* plays together as one unit: 'when he gathered Marlowe's plays under the title *Tamburlaine the Great*, Jones was offering customers an unprecedented textual experience with professional plays: an opportunity to read a whole series from start to finish, in one sitting and setting'.[25] In the process of his sequential publication of editions of Tamburlaine, Lyons says, Jones invented the idea of a collection of plays, and showed that the relationship between the two parts of a diptych could be interpreted in multiple ways.

Like the history of books, print, and reading, theatre history is an ascendant field within early modern literary studies in the twenty-first century; indeed, as the focus of the Melnikoff and Knutson collection shows, these two critical conversations increasingly speak to and build upon each other. Tiffany Stern's edited collection *Rethinking Theatrical Documents* (2019) also brings theatre historians and scholars of early modern book culture together to consider the circulation of 'documents of performance' – playwrights' manuscripts, actors' 'parts', prompt-books, and printed plays, as well as the Qur'an that features centrally as a prop in *Tamburlaine, Part II* – in and out of the playhouse.[26]

One potential thread of textual scholarship on *Tamburlaine* is notable for its absence from the present-day critical conversation: any sense of an 'authorship controversy' (to borrow the disingenuous term from certain fringe Shakespeare studies). Once, Marlowe's authorship of the diptych had its doubters, including Milton's nephew Edward Phillips (1675), Edmond Malone (1811), and James Broughton (1818).[27] Hooks, in the Melnikoff and Knutson collection, follows the circuitous and belated process through which the play was assigned to Marlowe, emphasizing that it was often cautious readers who hesitated to call it Marlowe's, and sometimes unscrupulous ones, like John Payne Collier, who were the readiest to commit.[28] The attribution, possibly alluded to in Greene's preface to *Perimedes the Blacke-smith* (1588), and more substantially hinted at in Heywood's prologue to the 1633 printing of *The Jew of Malta*, was not firmly made until 1820, in an edition of Marlowe's collected plays assembled by William Oxberry.[29] Hooks's point is to unsettle certain circular assumptions that scholars have made about Marlowe's early reception, not seriously to challenge the attribution of *Tamburlaine*. But in light of our recently increased appreciation for the collaborative nature of early modern dramatic composition and theatrical production, which has inspired, among other innovations, some contentious claims for co-authorship of works in the Shakespeare canon by Middleton and others, and given the fact that we know from Jones's prefatory epistle that the play as we have it is not exactly the play as it was performed by the Admiral's Men, it is perhaps notable that there has been no recent attempt to challenge Marlowe's sole authorship of the plays.[30] It is possible that the 'high astounding terms' (*I Tam.*, Prologue, 5) of the play's language are now so closely associated with what we celebrate as Marlowe's style, and the audacious, violent hero with the poet-secret agent who died in a knife-fight, that it has become unthinkable that anyone else could have written *Tamburlaine*.[31]

V. The new philology

Scholars of the history of texts examine how we have arrived at our definition of Marlowe's 'authentic style'; others who work within more formalist methodologies examine the style itself. Formalism, the critical model that puts the close study of a text's uses of language at the forefront, long associated with the 'New' Criticism of the mid-twentieth century and criticized for its insularity, has been revived, with a difference, in the twenty-first century. This 'new philology' brings a more historically-, theoretically- or politically-informed perspective to bear on the analysis of the forms, textures, and patterns of language within early modern literature. Peter Gibbard takes the accepted view that the *Tamburlaine* plays employ a flowing, grammatically unbroken, end-stopped poetic line, and shows that this early version of the 'mighty line' is influenced by Ciceronian rhetoric and its characteristic 'periodic' structure, in which long, balanced clauses make up a regularly structured sentence.[32] Bryan Lowrance draws attention to *Tamburlaine*'s participation in the sixteenth-century rediscovery of 'wit', defined not simply as showy verbal quickness but as the actualization of the latent power in words, 'a leading out of inner capacity, of *in-genium*, into the actuality of *poesis*'.[33] Seen in this light, Tamburlaine's glittering oratory is part of early modern English poetry's 'attempts to come to grips with an emerging sense of the autonomy of literature itself'.[34] For Lowrance, Tamburlaine's advantage over his rivals and the reason for his success in love and war is his ability to replace the trivial 'mother-wits' of the prologue with his own 'new combination of wit and sovereignty, of poetry with power'.[35]

Catherine Nicholson also considers language and power in *Uncommon Tongues: Eloquence and Eccentricity in the English Renaissance*, in which she studies how three English Renaissance writers famous for their extravagant language, John Lyly, Edmund Spenser, and Marlowe, position 'eloquence' both as the pinnacle of English expression and as deeply foreign or 'outlandish'. The triumph of unrhymed iambic pentameter as the vehicle for Tamburlaine's military victory – the literal 'feet' that carry him forward – is far less inevitable than hindsight makes it appear, Nicholson says. In fact, the 'mighty line' was at first received with mixed feelings by theorists of English poetry such as George Puttenham and Samuel Daniel. Blank verse now may seem to contain language into a shapely form, but 'Marlowe identifies the open-ended capaciousness of blank verse with aggression' and with barbarism, not with Classicism and control: '[A]t the end of Elizabeth I's reign and the height of what we now call the Renaissance, English writers were far from agreed on the ideal trajectory of the English literary tradition – a tradition whose contours they refused to equate with those of England'.[36] For Nicholson, Tamburlaine's contentious foreignness becomes a matter of language and style as well as of race and geopolitics.

Using formalism in a slightly different way, Andrew Duxfield's *Christopher Marlowe and the Failure to Unify* looks at Marlowe's interest in the idea of unity as a theme that shapes the overall structure as well as the verbal patterns of the plays, reading this preoccupation with unification as a response to public anxieties about fractures and tensions within English society in the 1580s and 1590s. In the *Tamburlaine* plays, Duxfield notes the central image of a map, on which a vast, three-dimensional world is reduced and iconized into a graspable two-dimensional graphic, and argues that a major project for the titular character is not only to seize territories like squares in a board game, but to condense and rationalize himself, as well, body and mind, into a two-dimensional image. Yet this project must fail: 'Just as a map cannot represent its subject without simplification and distortion, Tamburlaine finds that complexity, both of the world and himself, stands in the way of the fashioning of a unified self'.[37] Ultimately, Duxfield says, '[t]he unitary identity of warrior-god that Tamburlaine attempts to construct cannot withstand the multiplicity of competing forces – moral, religious, physiological, erotic – which it attempts to contain'.[38] A useful complement to Duxfield's study of the map as object and hermeneutic for the play is the chapter by Jacques Lezra in Emily Bartels and Emma Smith's important collection *Christopher Marlowe in Context* (2013). Lezra's approach is not philological; indeed, he is intentionally not programmatic. 'We will not get very far with [Marlowe's] works if we hold fast to a distinction between interpretive approaches and archival or materialist ones, between mythopoesis and science, old and new ... in part because Marlowe consistently shifts the borders between types of geography and sorts of criticism in ways great as well as small', Lezra reminds us.[39] While the model of the map seems ordered and comprehensive, the verbal and conceptual multiplicity of the play both explodes its limits and denies the very premises of such a systematic way of imagining the world.

VI. Marlowe's debt to the literary past

Patrick Cheney warrants special mention for his singular contribution to Marlowe studies with a sustained investigation into Marlowe's sense of his own indebtedness to his literary forebears, ancient and modern. Cheney followed his 1997 account of the influence of Ovid on the shaping of Marlowe's literary career (see M. L. Stapleton's chapter in this volume) with another monograph, *Marlowe's Republican Authorship: Lucan, Liberty, and the Sublime* (2009), devoted to the poet and playwright's response to the anti-imperialism of Lucan. At some point, either early or late in his brief maturity, Marlowe translated the first book of Lucan's *De Bello Civili*; Cheney sees this anti-imperialist work as 'a keystone to Marlowe's canon of plays and poems', including the *Tamburlaine* plays.[40] Tamburlaine, for Cheney, is 'a republican freedom-fighter who wants to be a king'.[41] Cheney argues that the play explores 'the Tamburlainian sublime of ambition and beauty' not only through Tamburlaine's desire to be completely free in his exercise of power and his view that might (not anointed monarchy) makes right, but through the deployment of a language of republicanism – words like 'merit', 'equal', 'consent', 'right', 'liberty' – versus a language of injustice and constraint – 'slavery', 'birth', 'theft', 'tyranny'.[42] By tracking this use of language, Cheney says, we can chart the rise and fall of Tamburlaine through the plays, watching as *Part I*'s ideal of republican power atrophies into *Part II*'s imperial impotence. Cheney continued his study of Marlowe and the sublime still further in 2018's *English Authorship and the Early Modern Sublime*, in which he analyses Tamburlaine's characteristic verbal hyperbole as not merely gorgeous excess but a species of the Longinian sublime, carrying listeners beyond the boundaries of what had previously been possible in language. Cheney specifically locates the sublime in Tamburlaine's verbal construction of Zenocrate's surpassing beauty, which he enshrines through his elaborate praise of her into a poetic and literal monument, both during her life and after her death, when he drags her hearse everywhere with him. 'Tamburlaine's legacy to his sons', the veneration of Zenocrate, 'is Marlowe's sublime legacy to modernity'.[43] In the early modern period, Cheney says, 'the sublime becomes the concept that authors inscript to register their own literary greatness'.[44]

VII. *Tamburlaine* in Marlowe biography

In the historical cycle of critical approaches to early modern literature, while some interpretive methodologies once considered outmoded are now back at the centre of the conversation (religion-centred criticism, bibliography, formalism), others remain out of favour, such as the once-ubiquitous 'biographical criticism' (looking for traces of the author's persona embedded in the work, and for the roots of the work in the author's life). Nevertheless, the mysterious and persistently fascinating documentary shards of Marlowe's life have been assembled into full-length biographies more times in the twenty-first century than ever before, occasioning some important commentary on his poetry and plays, including *Tamburlaine*, as part of his life-story. A late-twentieth-century work of 'true-crime', Charles Nicholl's intentionally controversial *The Reckoning: The Murder of Christopher Marlowe* (1992), was criticized by scholars for its dependence on speculation, but its popular success presaged a millennial boom in more serious literary biographies of Marlowe, with four major lives of the playwright emerging at the turn of the century, by prominent Marlowe critics Lisa Hopkins (2000) and Constance Brown Kuriyama (2002), and by the lauded academic life-writers David Riggs (2004) and Park Honan (2005). These accounts of Marlowe's life contribute to our understanding of the *Tamburlaine* plays by presenting important evidence for their chronology within the Marlowe canon, and by considering Marlowe's influences and the *Tamburlaine* composition process, as well as through literary analysis of the plays themselves.

In *Christopher Marlowe: A Literary Life*, Hopkins builds on the work of those New Historicists who had found resonances between early modern English literature and the beginnings of European settler colonialism in the New World, proposing that Tamburlaine's relentless world conquest is partly informed by Marlowe's awareness of English adventurers like Ralegh and the Iberian *conquistadores*.[45] Following Matar and looking east as well as west, Hopkins also suggests a connection between Tamburlaine and another violent conqueror, a 'crucial figure in the westward translation of empire': Aeneas.[46] Founder of Rome in Virgil's epic and the grandfather of Brutus, the legendary first king of Britain, Aeneas is a touchstone of early modern England's cherished idea of its cultural inheritance from the Roman empire. By setting Tamburlaine in parallel both with European colonizers of the Americas and with Aeneas, Hopkins argues, Marlowe unsettles oppositions of heroism and villainy, and of England's status as the subject or object of the acquisitive imperial gaze.

Riggs, in *The World of Christopher Marlowe*, traces the influence of the university MA curriculum of the 1580s in

Tamburlaine's vision of world domination, particularly the discipline of cosmography, the study of the order of the universe from the largest to smallest scale.[47] Cosmography links divine and mythological accounts of how the world was first made with astronomy, physical geography, and the natural histories of the world's regions, to produce a total account of the structure and working of the cosmos and the earth. 'Advanced training in cosmography and astronomy ... produced subjects who were mentally positioned to grasp the entire field of spatial phenomena', writes Riggs, further noting that 'Marlowe's MA course, in Tamburlaine's words, produced "souls, whose faculties can comprehend / The wondrous architecture of the world"'.[48] Not only in Marlowe's formal university syllabus, but in his broader immersion in Classical and other literature, Riggs, like Cheney, sees him as deeply influenced by his reading. Riggs argues that Marlowe's Classical education planted in his imagination the idea of Orphic creation, of the godlike poet who sings the world into existence, and suggests this bardic figure as one of the inspirations behind Tamburlaine's ability to reshape the globe by speaking the rolling lines of Marlowe's poetry.[49] Marlowe's interest in the work of literary contemporaries such as Spenser is reflected in *Tamburlaine* too, Riggs shows, pointing to ironic echoes of *The Faerie Queene*'s Prince Arthur in *II Tamburlaine*'s spectacular barbarity.[50]

Finally, Honan's biography, *Christopher Marlowe: Poet and Spy* (2005), devotes a full chapter to 'The Tamburlaine phenomenon', characterizing the *Tamburlaine* plays as a major turning-point both in the life and career of Marlowe and in the theatrical world of late-sixteenth-century London. In *Tamburlaine*, Honan's Marlowe, with one foot still in his academic training but also natively endowed with a rich poetic voice, brought audiences a dramatic experience more intellectually and morally complex and also more sensuously overwhelming than any that had come before. Honan finds a compelling *ars dramatica* in *I Tamburlaine*'s Prologue, 'at once a sales pitch and an art manifesto ... the most influential lines ever written, in this age, about the theatre's purposes'.[51]

Marlowe issues a formal invitation to the audience to see for themselves, promising to 'lead you to the stately tent of War: / Where you shall hear the Scythian Tamburlaine / Threatening the world with high astounding terms' (*I Tam.*, Prologue, 3–5); in this opening offer, Honan says, 'Marlowe does not treat the stage as a place of moral example, proof, or beneficial demonstration, but as a place for story and experience'.[52] Essentially, according to Honan, Marlowe is announcing his intention to show, not to tell; to immerse playgoers in Tamburlaine's world and let them draw their own conclusions. Charles Whitney, in his study of audience and reader responses to early modern plays in their own time, concurs: 'Virtually from the beginning Tamburlaine came to symbolize the power of the popular theatre itself ... Marlowe and his audiences together challenged the didacticism of the popular theatre ... the Tamburlaine intervention was collaborative'.[53]

These characterizations of the *Tamburlaine* plays as not simply serving readers and audiences a passive, if exhilarating, spectacle of power, ambition, ruthlessness, and blood, but as challenging them to question, resist, and interpret for themselves the hero, the ethics of the tale, and the intoxicating rhythms of surge and yield inherent in the language, serve as a suitable, and invigorating, message to scholars present and future. Twenty-first-century *Tamburlaine* criticism is off to a vibrant start; and still, readers of the plays now are like the surviving sons of Tamburlaine in the final scene of *Part II*, surveying the map of their father's achievements, while he draws their eyes to the sweep of still-unconquered territories: 'see what a world of ground / Lies westward' (*II Tam.*, 5.3.145–6). There is still much for us to discover about the worlds – intellectual, social, material – in which these plays charting the rise and rise of the stalking Scythian were written, more work for us to do in reckoning with our own era's inheritance from those worlds, and much for us yet to uncover within the 'mighty lines' themselves.

4

New Directions: Mending *Tamburlaine*

Claire M. L. Bourne

In the introduction to *Book Destruction from the Medieval to the Contemporary* (2014), Adam Smyth and Gill Partington cite the post-9/11 burning of the Qur'an by a pastor in Florida and its desecration by guards at Guantanamo Bay as two of the most vivid examples of book destruction in the twenty-first-century Western imaginary.[1] Not only that: these acts of obliteration, they remind us, cost dozens of lives by sparking deadly protests in the Middle East. At the end of the second *Tamburlaine the Great* play, written more than four centuries earlier, Tamburlaine's command to burn the '*Alcaron*, / And all the heapes of supersticious bookes, / Found in the Temples of that *Mahomet*' has also been read as consequential – not for others, but for the perpetrator himself.[2] Tamburlaine's desecration of these books is often cited, by those who read the plays together as a *de casibus* tragedy, as the reason for the onset of an illness and, ultimately, for his death.[3]

These highly symbolic and spectacular acts reside at one end of the spectrum of human impact on books. The surviving physical books that transmit *Tamburlaine* exhibit many signs of less extreme damage: some of it purposeful, some of it inadvertent, and some of it due to normal wear and tear. These objects also preserve traces of reading that both affirm and dispute elements of the plays' fictional world, sometimes simultaneously. One such form of readerly engagement evident on the pages of extant copies is emendation – the act of removing literal and printing errors from a text. The practice of altering text to eradicate perceived mistakes has long been central to the editorial handling of early modern plays such as *Tamburlaine*. Even before editorial practices began to ossify in the eighteenth century, 'perfecting' playtexts for initial publication and, especially, for improved second-plus editions was not unusual, although it constituted labour that is now largely invisible because it went unattributed in print.[4] But readers also emended texts for their own private use. A copy of *II Tamburlaine* (1606) at the Beinecke Rare Book and Manuscript Library, for example, shows an early reader making a small but significant change to the speech Amyrus delivers upon inheriting his dying father's titles. The printed text reads: 'Heauens witnesse me with what a broken heart / and damned spirit I ascend this seate.' The reader suggested 'daunted' as a variant for 'damned', an adjustment that effectively absolves Amyrus of blame for his father's damning actions and mends any damage that those actions might have done to the son's reputation (see Figure 1).[5] The reader's emendation certainly draws attention to the question of genre. For Amyrus' spirit to be 'damned', Tamburlaine's must be, too. The burning of the Qur'an would be the most immediate explanation. Labelled 'commicall discourses' in the *Stationers' Register*, advertised as 'Tragicall Discourses' in their first two editions, and associated with 'Histories' by their first publisher Richard Jones, the plays have generated a great deal of generic confusion.[6] This reader's alteration of Amyrus' spirit from 'damned' to 'daunted' here suggests an understanding of the play's genre as something *other than* tragedy. Then again, the emendation is not decisive. The reader has underlined 'damned' instead of crossing it out, thus leaving it available as a viable reading. The reader has also crossed out the word 'daunted' in

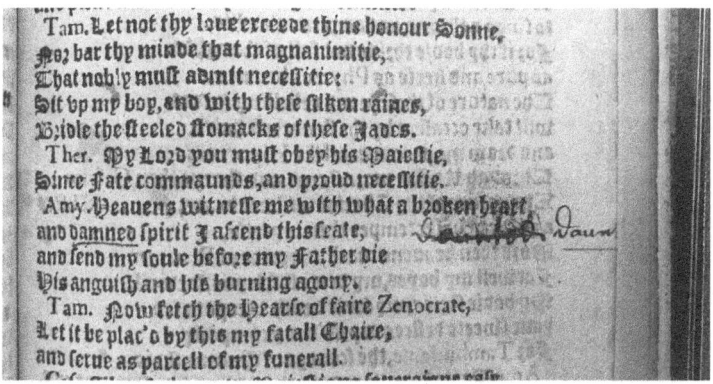

FIGURE 1 Tamburlaine the greate ... The second part *(London: Edward White, 1606)*, sig. L2r, 1977 2594, Beinecke Rare Book and Manuscript Library.

the margin and then rewritten and underlined it. It is almost as if they second-guessed the change before deciding to record both options.[7]

The Eberly Family Special Collections Library at the Pennsylvania State University stewards another copy of *II Tamburlaine* (1606) that presents models of emendation that are both more material and more figurative than the editorial mode exhibited in the Beinecke copy. Not only has the physical book been repaired, but several marginal marks and annotations suggest the reader's interest in the faults of the characters who populate the play's fictional world. In this chapter, I argue that reading *Tamburlaine* in the sixteenth and seventeenth centuries was characterized by efforts to mend Tamburlaine/*Tamburlaine*. I begin with an overview of *Tamburlaine*'s textual presence through 1700 to show not only that the plays were read heavily, especially early on, but also that they continued to be available as reading matter. Not only did all three of Jones's two-part octavo editions sell out between 1590 (the year they were first published) and 1605, but surviving copies of those editions along with the two single-play quartos from 1605 and 1606 exhibit signs of significant use and early readerly engagement. Even though it is more difficult to identify if and when *Tamburlaine* was read after the first decade of the seventeenth century, it is still possible to catch glimpses of copies in circulation.

Of course, we cannot ever know exactly what readers thought of the plays, or what they got out of reading them.[8] We do know that the practices that counted as 'play-reading' during the period were varied and sometimes left no marks. However, evidence suggests early modern readers could read with and against a text; they could read both holistically and selectively.[9] They assembled, gathered, and collected playtexts, but they also broke texts apart.[10] Because these practices required varying degrees of physical contact between reader and book, they wore away at the materials that constituted the object, causing damage that sometimes inspired small acts of care: of repair, or mending. Knowing how to understand and contextualize the evidence of reading is one of the greatest methodological challenges we face as historians of the book – *and* as literary critics. To what extent do non-textual reading practices (that is, the ones engaged with the book as a physical object) resonate with the content of the texts that those objects preserve?

Despite the infeasibility of reconstructing individual readers' full experiences of the plays they encountered in print, it is still possible to extrapolate something about early readings of *Tamburlaine* from marks, annotations, damage, and repair. In short, reading readers reading *Tamburlaine* is not so different from actually reading *Tamburlaine*: ambiguity, uncertainty, and paradox function as viable interpretive outcomes. Like all responsible histories of the book (and specifically of reading), the story I tell about how the vestiges of reading connect with the content of the plays is constructed out of plausible interpretations of the evidence, not provable facts. Sometimes it is necessary to – and sometimes the materials that endure require us to – hold more than one interpretation in play.

Tamburlaine in the early modern book trade: Allusions, availability, authorship

In the 1590s, Richard Jones published *I* and *II Tamburlaine* three times together in octavo (1590, 1593, and 1597). He made unprecedented efforts to tailor the plays for readers, heeding both book trade contexts and the plays' well-known theatrical effects.[11] Jones kept his finger on the pulse of readers' changing tastes and continued to adapt the way he marketed the plays as he brought out new editions.[12] When Jones sold his printing shop to Edward White in 1598, he also transferred the rights to print some of his titles, including *Tamburlaine*.[13] In 1605 and 1606, White published Parts I and II as bibliographically distinct quartos. It was the last time *Tamburlaine* would see print until 1820, when William Oxberry edited and published the two plays in his series of Marlowe editions.[14] The lack of subsequent early editions could have been because the 1605 and 1606 quartos took a while to sell out and that, when (or even if) they did, the plays were already too old-fashioned to justify another edition. But this gap in publication does not mean that the plays fell into complete obscurity, or even that copies of the early editions were completely unavailable to seventeenth-century play-readers.

The plays certainly persisted in memories of the early commercial theatre. *Tamburlaine* generated more contemporary commentary than any other play from the period.[15] And its reputation as a touchstone of the English stage was alive and well almost three decades after its last known edition was published. Thomas Heywood, if he was the person responsible for writing the prologue published with *The Jew of Malta* in 1633, praised both Marlowe and the actor Edward Alleyn, who premiered the role of Tamburlaine, in a tribute that famously equivocates on which of these men was famous for *Tamburlaine*:

> *In* Hero *and* Leander *one did gaine*
> *A Lasting memorie: in* Tamberlaine,
> *This* Jew, *with others many: th'other wan* [sic]
> *The Attribute of peerelesse, being a man*
> *Whom we may ranke with* (*doing no one wrong*)
> Proteus *for shapes, and* Roscius *for a tongue*[.][16]

The reference to Tamburlaine relies on spectators' familiarity with theatre history, especially their ability to name and pair playwright (and/or actor) with the play. Readers of the quarto get a little bit more assistance with a pair of marginal glosses specifying '*Marloe*' and '*Allin*' as the two famous men associated with *Tamburlaine* and this other old play, *The Jew of Malta*. If the prologue is, indeed, applauding Marlowe (instead of, or in addition to, Alleyn) for *Tamburlaine*, this would be the first time (we know of) that the plays were attributed to him. After all, none of the editions published by Jones and White named an author. Heywood's evocation of *Tamburlaine* situated the plays in a long, yet still relevant, theatrical tradition. So did William Prynne's censure of the their 'lewde' content in *Histrio-Mastix* that same year.[17] Revivals of *Tamburlaine* at the Red Bull in the 1630s seem likely, and allusions to the plays and their distinctive dramaturgy pop up in new plays written and performed for a new generation of Caroline play-goers.[18] By the time public performance was restored after the Interregnum, the *Tamburlaine* plays came to function 'as shorthand for an older dramatic tradition' which had endured despite changing tastes.[19]

But what about *reading* the *Tamburlaine* plays? Neither play is listed in Alan B. Farmer and Zachary Lesser's 'Caroline Canon of Classic Plays', which includes plays that went into third-plus editions between 1626 and 1642.[20] But several booksellers' catalogues that started to be compiled about fifteen years after public performance was banned offer glimpses of the plays' continued presence in the book trade, not as new books but as used ones. Although neither play had been published in a new edition for a half century, evidence suggests that copies of *I* and *II Tamburlaine* were possibly available for sale in the 1650s on the second-hand book market. There may not have been the same 'ongoing demand for these plays *as books*' as there was at the time for other by-then classics, like *Doctor Faustus*.[21] But London booksellers saddled with extra stock or sensing a demand among customers for reading and collecting the books of plays written for London's early commercial playhouses did what they could to generate and/or meet a demand for old plays.[22]

Those booksellers seem to have known *Tamburlaine* either as a book (i.e., they had seen it) or they knew *of* it (i.e., they had heard about it). Richard Rogers and William Lee listed 'Tamberlaine, both parts' in the 'exact and perfect Catalogue of all Playes that are Printed', which they assembled (rather hastily, it seems) to appear at the end of *The Careless Shepherdess* in 1656.[23] Aaron T. Pratt has argued that Rogers and Lee must have gathered the titles of the approximately 500 plays listed in the catalogue from their actual stock, 'or at least what they wanted to claim was their stock'.[24] In other words, they were advertising copies of playbooks in their inventory, and/or ones they had knowledge of from word-of-mouth and the broader London book trade. It is not clear whether their inventory actually included copies of *Tamburlaine*. At the very least, they knew that the play was a two-parter and that discrete editions of each part (and/or an edition of both parts) existed.

In the same year, Edward Archer published an expanded catalogue with a quarto of *The Old Law* (and possibly circulated it on its own).[25] The playbook title page promised that the appended catalogue was better than the Rogers and Lee version: it was 'more exactly Printed than ever before'.[26] Again, *Tamburlaine* was among the play-titles listed in the catalogue – 'Tamerlain. both parts.' But this entry included a little bit more information than Rogers and Lee had provided: here, the title was labelled with an 'H' for 'History'. If Archer had copies of *Tamburlaine* in stock or had seen a copy, then he might have gleaned this generic label from Jones's prefatory epistle to readers 'who take pleasure in reading Histories', which had prefaced all the early editions except for *II Tamburlaine* (1606).[27] It is also possible that Archer did not have access to actual copies but rather extrapolated the 'History' label from the title's reference to an historical figure.[28] If Archer did have or knew of copies for sale, then it would have been easy enough for prospective readers to find them. Unlike Rogers and Lee's catalogue, Archer's explicitly advertised where to buy books of the listed titles. Readers wanting to acquire a copy of *Tamburlaine* in 1656 might have been able to purchase one at Archer's own shop at the sign of Adam and Eve in Little Britain, or a bit further to the east behind the Royal Exchange at Robert Pollard's short-lived establishment at the sign of 'the Ben Johnson's Head'.

Five years later, the *Tamburlaine* plays showed up again in another, more robust catalogue of plays '*that were ever yet printed and published, till this present year*'.[29] It was compiled by Francis Kirkman, who may also have had a hand in assembling the earlier lists.[30] Kirkman styled himself as a voracious reader – and collector – of printed plays and romances. In language that echoed the title of the 1661 catalogue, he later claimed to have 'perfected' his own 'Collection of all the *English Stage Plays* that were ever yet Printed': 'I have them all, and have read them all.'[31] Indeed, if his own account of his obsessive, completist collecting project is to be trusted, Kirkman may just be the earliest reader of *Tamburlaine* we can name outside of the theatre besides Jones and White, the two publishers who had ushered the plays to market. Kirkman's 1661 catalogue was designed to achieve two complementary ends: to advertise playbooks for sale and to put feelers out for titles known to exist in print but not currently in the inventory held by Kirkman or his partners Nathanial Brook, Thomas Johnson, and Henry Marsh. The title of the catalogue encourages readers to 'either buy or sell' the listed books at one of these booksellers' shops. Each of the *Tamburlaine* plays gets its own separate entry in

Kirkman's catalogue, and both are labelled 'T' for 'Tragedy'. This means that Kirkman could have had access to a copy of the 1590 or 1593 octavos, both of which advertise their contents as 'Tragicall Discourses'. However, Kirkman's decision to revise the generic label from the 'H' used to describe the plays in the Archer catalogue to a 'T' could just as likely reflect Kirkman's judgement based on his own reading of the two plays.

The *Tamburlaine* plays continued to go unattributed in all three of these early catalogues. In the 1661 list, Kirkman positioned the plays' titles – 'Tamburlaine first part' and 'Tamburlaine 2d part' – directly underneath that of the Senecan tragedy 'Thebais', which he attributed to Thomas Newton. This probably led Edward Phillips to misread the layout and attribute the *Tamburlaine* plays to Newton in his *Theatrum Poetarum* (1675).[32] In the meantime, another attribution, already possibly made by Heywood in the 1633 *Jew of Malta* quarto, was gaining traction. When Kirkman published a slightly expanded and revised catalogue in 1671, he attributed 'Tamberlain, 1st part' and 'Tamberlain, 2d part' to '*Chr. Marloe*'.[33] Twenty years later, Gerard Langbaine picked up this attribution, along with Kirkman's labelling of the plays as tragedies, in his own catalogue of English plays.[34] Even though the plays were listed under Marlowe's name, Langbaine was not entirely sold on Marlowe as the playwright. In his *Account of the English Dramatick Poets* (1691), he cited Heywood's prologue to the *Jew of Malta* as the only reason why he listed the plays as Marlowe's: 'Had I not Mr. *Heywood*'s Word for it ... I should not believe this Play to be his [i.e., Marlowe's]'.[35]

A more immediate context for Langbaine's scepticism was the front matter published with Charles Saunders's *Tamerlane the Great* (1681), a play performed by the King's Company in Oxford on 19 March 1681 and at the Theatre Royal at Drury Lane either just before or just after.[36] In the preface to this edition, Saunders defended himself from accusations that his play 'was only an Old-Play Transcribed'.[37] He pleaded ignorance of any previous *Tamburlaine*, claiming to have 'never heard of any Play on the same Subject, until my own was Acted' and assured 'whoever was the Author' of this *other* version that he 'might e'en keep it to himself secure from invasion, or Plagiary'.[38] Saunders was no plagiarist. It was this second bit that Langbaine quoted to register his uncertainty about Kirkman's ascription of the plays to Marlowe. However, the attribution stuck. When revising Langbaine's *Account* for publication as *The Lives of the English Dramatick Poets* (1699), Charles Gildon stripped all doubt about Marlowe's authorship from the *Tamburlaine* entry.[39] And, about a century later, the actor and collector John Philip Kemble confidently wrote 'By Christopher Marloe' on the title page of his recently acquired copy of *II Tamburlaine* (1606).[40]

Authorship aside, Saunders's insistence on the originality of his *Tamerlane the Great* has usually been read as evidence that the earlier *Tamburlaine*, like all other Marlowe plays except *Doctor Faustus*, was unknown less than a century after first being performed.[41] Saunders mentions that others had told him of 'a Cock-Pit Play' called *Tamburlaine the Great*, which suggests that some of these informants had heard of (or maybe actually seen) the play. But Saunders did not appeal to the memory of *spectators* in attempting to differentiate his play from the older *Tamburlaine*. He appealed the memory of *readers*: 'Let those who have Read it Convince themselves ... that this [i.e., Saunders's *Tamburlaine*] is no second Edition, but an entirely new Play'. In order to make this comparison, sceptics about Saunders's version would have to have read the other version, too. As the presence of the *Tamburlaine* plays in bookseller catalogues from 1656 onwards suggests, doing so would not have been impossible. Saunders's claim that 'not a Bookseller in *London* ... could call [the older *Tamburlaine*] to Remembrance' was patently untrue. As we have seen, booksellers like Kirkman certainly knew about *Tamburlaine* and perhaps even had copies of the plays for sale in their second-hand stock.

Book in hand: Reading and repairing *Tamburlaine* (1606)

George Saunders might not have numbered himself among the sixteenth-century *Tamburlaine* editions' early readers, but the plays clearly made a good investment for their early publishers. Long before Kirkman, Richard Jones became *Tamburlaine*'s earliest known reader outside the theatre.[42] In reading and assessing the viability of the plays for publication, Jones determined that they needed to be fixed. And indeed from his engagement onward, the plays have been judged to be faulty: formally, textually, *and* morally. Jones famously admitted to having 'omitted' material from his version, characterizing the discarded episodes as 'vnmeet' (that is, unfit) to be 'mixtured in print with such matter of worth' (i.e., the course of Tamburlaine's rapid accumulation and consolidation of power). Jones vividly described the material he removed not only as 'fond and friuolous Iestures' when compared to the plays' other content but also as 'graced deformities' in performance. He thus presented his choice to remove them as an act of mending. It was an act that 'perfected' – re-formed – the plays both for a particular kind of reading public ('Gentlemen readers') as well as for the medium of print.[43] The temporal and geographic scope of the *Tamburlaine* plays meant that they (individually and together) violated the unities of time and place that critics like Philip Sidney insisted on.[44] But Jones transformed this fracturing from a liability into an asset. He addressed the plays' sweeping content by dividing them into discrete numbered scenes, highly unusual for the printed text of a commercial-theatre play at the time. These textual divisions simultaneously signalled and sutured fictional gaps in time and geography, while also smoothing over the breaches created by Jones's extraction of the comic bits. In the first part of the play, Jones's efforts to divide the play resulted in a clearer articulation of successive units of action that, in turn, rendered the relentless iteration of Tamburlaine's conquests legible to readers. There is even evidence that he may have tried reordering scenic units in the second part to produce a similar effect but, because of the second play's formal differences, was less than successful.[45]

According to its own prologue, *Tamburlaine . . . the seconde part* was written in response to the popularity of the first play on stage. It is generally agreed that there was not enough good source material left for a whole sequel. Because the second play drew on a wider range of sources, it has been described as more 'fragmentary' than the first.[46] If *I Tamburlaine* was relentlessly focused on Tamburlaine himself, the second play was cushioned by divergent episodes given over to his generals' exploits and his enemies' in-fighting.[47] The first play was implicitly viewed as the template for what a play about Tamburlaine *should* be. And because the second part broke this mould, it has always already been treated as full of fault lines. This assessment is based on – and conditioned by – access to texts that, as we have seen, were 'mended' by Jones when he brought the two plays to press as a single bibliographic entity in 1590. Until Edward White published *II Tamburlaine* as a stand-alone quarto, this play circulated as the sequel to the first play and has since been judged (in terms of form and quality) almost exclusively in relation to it.

Read together, the two *Tamburlaine* plays remain steadfastly agnostic about the direct consequences of intemperance, pride, and violence. Whether to read Tamburlaine's death at the end of the second play as divine punishment for burning the Qur'an (i.e., a tragedy), or whether to read it as the last episode in a storied life (i.e., a history) has lingered as interpretive crux since at least as early as Kirkman changed the plays' generic label from 'H' to 'T'. White's separate publication of *II Tamburlaine* allowed readers to encounter the second play without the protagonist's relentlessly iterative – and successful – rise to power in the first as necessary preamble. What readers got instead was a main character who does not exhibit his military prowess until more than halfway through the play.

This meant that the prelude to Tamburlaine's final 'conquests' consisted instead of loss (Zenocrate's death, his eldest son's failure to inherit the mantle of war) and delay (the slow, meandering build-up to war with the Turkish kings promised at the outset). In collection, Tamburlaine had already proved himself. In this stand-alone quarto, he had not. He was eminently fallible.

Sometime in the seventeenth century, a reader of Penn State's *II Tamburlaine* scored passages that draw attention to moral faults. In some cases, the reader even seems to call for reformed behaviour. Both kinds of interventions gesture towards a reading of *II Tamburlaine* as a tragedy, but like the 'damned'/'daunted' variant in the Beinecke copy of the same edition, the intentions behind the reader's interventions in Penn State's *Tamburlaine* are difficult to pin down. The reader has marked the speeches in which Tamburlaine's three sons answer their father's call for them to succeed him as 'scourge and terrour of the world'.[48] Amyrus and Celebinus embrace the charge, while Calyphas rejects it. Later, Calyphas explains that killing 'workes remorse in a man' and reasserts his decision not to war like his brothers – this speech is also marked.[49] One X marks the speech of a messenger who comes to tell Orcanes that Sigismond has violated their agreement to join forces against Tamburlaine.[50] An X marks Olympia's husband's dying words, while another (on the facing page) marks her son's plea for her to stab him and let him 'meet' his father.[51] Three Xs appear at the beginning of the last act: one marks the Babylonian governor's request for information about Tamburlaine's advance, one marks his demand that the white flags of truce be hung outside the city, and a third marks a plea from one of his citizens that he not 'yeeld vp the towne' to Tamburlaine.[52] All these marked passages highlight morally questionable behaviour – the breaking of a truce, the blind faith in (or, perhaps, the filial rejection of) a father, and the cowardice of suicide and surrender over resistance (or is it the behaviour of others that drives people to suicide and surrender that is being questioned?).

The final X in the quarto is the only one that marks a speech belonging to Tamburlaine. It appears next to the speech where he wonders that he has been so far 'vntoucht by Mahomet' for his audacious behaviour just before upping the ante by throwing the Qur'an onto the fire and declaring once more that he is the 'scourge' of a God.[53] Next to this X is inscribed the word 'Last', perhaps (quite simply) because this is the last passage the reader has marked or because it is the last, most extreme of Tamburlaine's actions (see Figure 2). The annotation also might indicate the reader's assessment that Tamburlaine is sorely wrong about his absence of punishment, as if the reader is saying: cf. the last page. If this is the case, then the reader was surely reading the play as tragedy – Tamburlaine's overweening pride and overreaching ambition are to blame for the sudden end of his 'progres'.[54] He will face consequences at 'Last'.

The reader has also written in the margins. Early readers used the margins of their books for all manner of inscriptions unrelated to the printed text, but the notes in Penn State's copy of *II Tamburlaine*, where they are legible, seem to relate to dramatic moment and circumstance. In the margin next to the speech where Theridamas describes Tamburlaine's magnificence in an effort to compel Olympia to come with him, the reader has inscribed a version of Ecclesiastes 8.1: 'Strive not with a mighty man lest thou fall into his hands.' Here: 'Quarrell not with a meitey man'.[55] What remains of the cropped note – 'nor rouse Comunecaytion with men of men of [. . .]' – is probably a version of Ecclesiastes 8.3: 'Strive not with a man that is full of tongue, and heap not wood upon his fire' (see Figure 3). Applied to the situation in which Olympia finds herself (that is, grieving for her husband's death and son's suicide and now captive to Tamburlaine's generals), the reader's inscription reads as a caution to Olympia *either* (1) to listen to (that is, quarrel not with) Theridamas (the 'meitey man') and go with him to Tamburlaine; or (2) to continue in her resistance by not going and thus not quarrelling with Tamburlaine (the 'meitey man'). She pleads for permission to 'caste her body in the burning flame' that 'feedes vpon' her 'Sonnes and Husbandes

> the Scythian Shepheard.
>
> Caf. Here they are my Lord.
> Tam. Well said, let there be a fire presently.
> In vaine I see men worship Mahomet:
> My sword hath sent millions of Turks to hell,
> Slew all his priestes, his kinsmen and his friendes,
> And yet I liue vntoucht by Mahomet: ╳ _last_
> There is a God full of reuenging wrath,
> From whome the thunder and the lightning breakes,
> Whose scourge I am, and him I will obey.
> So Casane, fling them in the fire.
> Now Mahomet if thou haue any power,
> Come downe thy selfe and worke a miracle,
> Thou art not worthy to be worshipped,
> That suffers flames of fire to burne the writ,
> Wherein the summe of thy Religion rests:
> Why sends thou not a furious whirlewinde downe,
> To blow thy Alcaron vp to thy throane,
> Where men report thou sits by God himselfe.
> Or vengeance on the blood of Tamburlaine,
> That shakes his sword against thy Maiestie:
> And spurns the Abstracts of thy foolish lawes.
> Well Souldiours, Mahomet remaines in hell,
> He cannot heare the voice of Tamburlaine:
> Seeke out another God-head to adore,
> The God that sits in heauen, if any God,
> For he is God alone, and none but he.

FIGURE 2 Tamburlaine the Great ... The second part *(1606), sig. H4r, PR2669.A1 1606, Rare Books and Manuscripts, Eberly Family Special Collections Library, Penn State University Libraries.*

flesh' – her body as wood upon a fire. Theridamas refuses: '[S]ooner shall fire consume vs both, / then scorch a face as beautiful as this.' In the left-hand margin, the reader writes: 'not with this m[an].' Quarrel not with this man. Olympia has quarrelled – she is now in Theridamas's hands. At the same time, though, death would prevent her from falling into the hands of the mightier Tamburlaine. Does that make her, in the annotating reader's eyes, a cautionary tale or an exemplary figure?

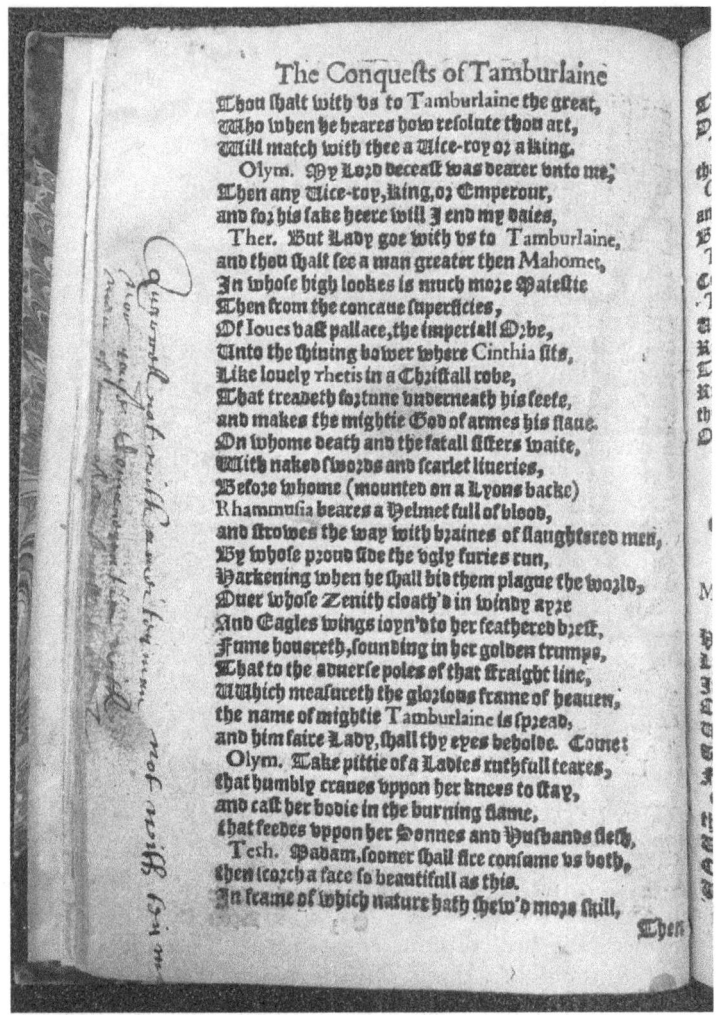

FIGURE 3 Tamburlaine the Great ... The second part *(1606), sig. E3v, PR2669.A1 1606, Rare Books and Manuscripts, Eberly Family Special Collections Library, Penn State University Libraries.*

Elsewhere, the reader notices Callapine's bid to defeat Tamburlaine. In a margin otherwise full of pen trials, the reader writes: 'God saue t[he] [...] / Church [...] / King, and / ggod send hi[m] [...] / in Christ [...].'[56] Callapine, the son of the much abused Zabina and Bajazeth, is right to revenge his parents. God be with him? A few pages later, the reader writes something similar underneath Tamburlaine's demand that his 'Charyot' be ready so that, after the battle against the Turkish kings, he can 'ride in tryumph through the Campe': 'ggod sende you life and breth / [...] / god send him long life.'[57] You, the reader? Tamburlaine? The enemies he will eventually bridle to pull the chariot? These inscriptions suggest an abiding concern with questions of divine ordination and divine justice in relation to human actions. They are therefore consistent with the passages marked by the marginal Xs and the citation of Ecclesiastes. So, here is a reader who seems to connect with the play's wide-ranging exploration of how people behave when something significant – life, chastity, pride – is at stake. Here is a reader who expressed interest in a series of speeches that could possibly be used to stake a claim for the play, if not as a tragedy writ large, then at least as a series of tragic episodes.

The printed text is the product of Jones mending the play's form, while the annotations and marks left in the blank spaces of this copy evince a reader noting the moral choices and faults of the play's characters. A reader of the Penn State copy of *II Tamburlaine*, perhaps the same one, also attended to faults with the physical book. The word 'mend' appears on three pages. In the first instance, it is written on a small slip of paper that pasted over cuts in the page (see Figure 4).[58] But this is also the page where Tamburlaine turns sharply away from eulogizing Zenocrate and towards steeling his sons for war. Was it too sharp a turn for this reader? What is so suggestive about the page that was razed and repaired in this way is that it faces the page where Tamburlaine 'cuts his arme' so that his sons can prove their loyalty by touching his wound. The reader seems to have taken notice of this stage direction, as it is scored on both sides (see Figure 5).[59] 'Mend' is also inscribed in the

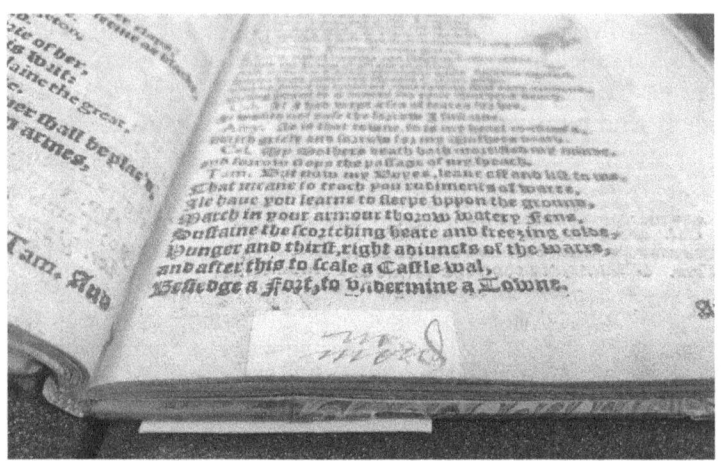

FIGURE 4 Tamburlaine the Great ... The second part *(1606), sig. D4r*, PR2669.A1 1606, *Rare Books and Manuscripts, Eberly Family Special Collections Library, Penn State University Libraries.*

same hand at the top of the page where Olympia stabs her son and the bottom of the page (three times) where Tamburlaine tells the Turkish kings they are to be bridled.[60] Physical violations of the body all, where the mending of behaviour could mean the difference between life and death. It is as if these annotations speak from the page to the play's fictional world in the imperative mode: 'Mend!'

Mending also made the difference in the survival of this book, as it has in the survival of most extant copies of *Tamburlaine*. In Penn State's copy of the 1606 quarto, another slip of paper reinforces the top corner of a page towards the end – a corner that has started to wear away from heavy use. This repair, and the other patch discussed above, must have been applied before the book was rebound (likely in the late eighteenth or early nineteenth century) because they are cropped and probably a good deal earlier based on the letter forms of the 'mend' written on the repair slip and elsewhere.

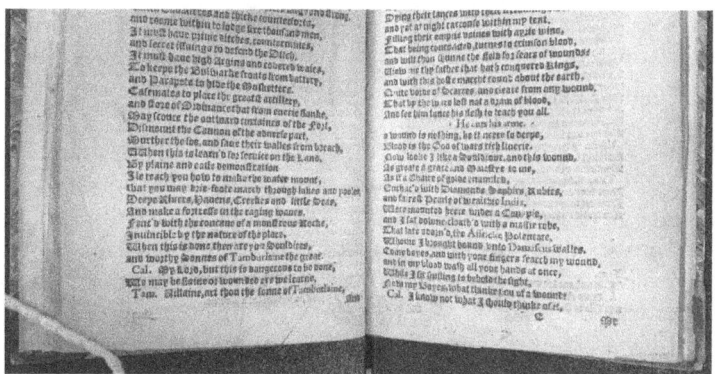

FIGURE 5 Tamburlaine the Great ... The second part *(1606)*, sigs. D4v-E1r, PR2669.A1 1606, Rare Books and Manuscripts, Eberly Family Special Collections Library, Penn State University Libraries.

The title page, which was heavily damaged, has been patched back together and backed with early manuscript waste paper. Indeed, the title pages of at least eleven extant copies of *Tamburlaine* are missing, inlaid, or damaged badly enough to have been backed, inlaid, or re-margined.[61] In contrast to so many Shakespeare quartos that have been made to look pristine through later techniques of restoration and repair, copies of *Tamburlaine*, especially ones that have been mended with paper patches, new margins, and lost pages supplied in facsimile, do not belie their histories of use.

The history of reading is full of cautionary tales about extrapolating too much – and too creatively – from readers' marks, inscriptions, and other physical interactions with the material text. We are eager to know what early readers thought of the plays they bought, bound, collected, and read. We hope that the 'discovery' of historically embedded interpretations might confirm our own readings of the play – for example, *did*

early readers read *Tamburlaine* as a tragedy? – or even bring new ones to light. But often, even the most suggestive marginalia and proofs of book-use usually end up raising more questions than they answer.

My story that the early history of reading *II Tamburlaine* – and Tamburlaine – is a history of readerly attention to and engagement with mending is conditioned by what I think of as the most fascinating material features of the Penn State copy as it survives to us: the two paper patches that repair physical faults on the book's pages along with the repetition of the word 'mend'. The Xs and the marginal notes therefore function as corroborating evidence that this reader was interested in the play's explorations of faulty behaviour – and even that these interventions (read in this way) show an early reader interested in the play as tragedy. As a literary scholar, I have been trained to examine words from every angle – to excavate all of their operative, historical meanings. To mend: to fix, to repair, to improve, to rectify moral faults. I am practised in thinking capaciously – to imagine readers as clever as this one might have been (a reader who might be as clever as I think I am in suggesting that 'mend' is operating here on registers both material and figurative). I *want* this story to be true because it is a perfect example of how literary criticism and a concern for books as material objects can be mutually informing.

The more I consider this book (that is, the more I look *at* it rather than *through* it), the more I am persuaded that the condition of working with objects such as this one mimics the condition of reading *Tamburlaine* itself. As historians of reading, we have to be okay with not knowing for sure. Like the scene of book destruction at the end of *II Tamburlaine* that may or may not have led to Tamburlaine's death and, therefore, unlike the modern scenes of book destruction that Smyth and Partington point out had delayed but very real consequences, the slow wearing away of books due to readerly attention and the small acts of interpretation and preservation that have kept them in play are never not going to be shrouded in ambiguity. This does not mean we should back away from these objects and the traces of human behaviour they transmit. In the place of arguing *this is what was*, it is our place to argue (as I have done here) *this is what might have been*.

Acknowledgements

Special thanks to Mark Bainbridge, Becky Fall, Tara Lyons, and Dyani Taff for their help describing and photographing copies of *Tamburlaine* that I was not able to see in person.

5

New Directions: Tamburlaine the Weather Man

Tom Rutter

In the opening scene of *Tamburlaine, Part I*, Cosroe, brother of the hapless Mycetes, King of Persia, recalls that in the past their country was led by 'mighty conquerors',

> That in their prowess and their policies
> Have triumphed over Afric and the bounds
> Of Europe, where the sun dares scarce appear
> For freezing meteors and congealèd cold.
>
> (1.1.7–11)[1]

By 'bounds' he means the furthest northern region of Europe, a place he imagines as being so cold that it discourages the sun from appearing. Even in a place of such extremes, to the modern eye or ear 'freezing meteors' seems a bit picturesque, implying cold space-matter hurtling across the sky. To Marlowe and his audience, however, 'meteor' did not have the specific modern meaning of 'a small mass or particle of rock or metal, usually originating from a decaying comet, which enters the earth's atmosphere from space' (*OED* 'meteor', *n.*¹, 3.a). Certainly, 'meteor' could be used to mean much the same as 'comet', as when in William Shakespeare's *Richard II* the Welsh Captain recounts a series of alarming occurrences:

> The bay trees in our country are all withered,
> And meteors fright the fixed stars of heaven;
> The pale-faced moon looks bloody on the earth,
> And lean-looked prophets whisper fearful change.
>
> (2.4.8–11)[2]

At the same time, though, 'meteors' could refer to a whole range of phenomena occurring within the earth's atmosphere, including mundane weather events (as in our modern use of the term 'meteorology'), but also optical effects such as rainbows, and even earthquakes. In Cosroe's speech, the words 'freezing meteors' therefore have quite a complex effect. On the one hand they seem impressive, out of the ordinary, even portentous, in a manner in keeping with *Tamburlaine*'s often elevated poetic register. On the other, they are technically accurate: northern Europe can indeed be a place of ice and snow. Cosroe's use of the word 'meteors' is an appropriate beginning to a pair of plays where hyperbolic language and the claim that things that happen are signs from God often turn out to disguise more worldly realities.

The current chapter is about Marlowe's use of meteorological imagery across the two *Tamburlaine* plays. It reflects an interest among recent critics in what Howard Marchitello and Evelyn Tribble describe as 'the ways in which both science and literature are mutually informing and mutually sustaining' – that is, a reciprocal interest not only in the inherently literary nature of a great deal of early modern scientific writing, but also in the uses to which literary writers put scientific knowledge.[3] Juliet Cummins and David Burchell emphasize the interdisciplinary nature of much modern scholarly work in this area, being 'not primarily concerned with either literature or science understood as discrete enterprises, but rather with the way that each participates in general developments in early modern thought and culture.' Poetry and drama should thus be understood not simply as reacting to new theories or discoveries, but as part of the way in which scientific knowledge, at a communal level, was made: 'Poets and dramatists of the late sixteenth to early eighteenth centuries, usually at a remove from the main hub of scientific thinking, provided critiques of the practices and methodologies of natural philosophers [see endnote], while paradoxically appropriating many of their key assumptions.'[4]

An important recent text in this field, discussed later on in this chapter, is Mary Thomas Crane's *Losing Touch with Nature: Literature and the New Science in Sixteenth-Century England*, which looks at the way challenges to 'settled [...] accounts of how the universe worked' influenced the work of poets and dramatists.[5] In her section on *Tamburlaine*, Crane shows how new theories in astronomy and meteorology gave Marlowe language and imagery with which to convey Tamburlaine's immense ambition. Where I depart from Crane, however, is in stressing the way Marlowe uses meteorological images and ideas as a way of mounting a radically heterodox religious critique: I argue that in his treatment of the causes of meteorological phenomena, Marlowe is as much concerned with theological questions as with the physical nature of the universe. This emphasis on Marlowe's subversive treatment of religion aligns me with critics such as Chloe Preedy, who in *Marlowe's Literary Scepticism* emphasizes the 'sustained uncertainty in Marlowe's writings about divine providence, the immortality of the soul and life after death'.[6] It also sets me apart from another significant critical approach to early modern weather, namely that of ecologically focused critics such as Todd Borlik, Gabriel Egan and Steve Mentz who discuss the literature of the period, and its treatment of relationships between the human and the nonhuman, in light of the environmental catastrophe that threatens the modern world.

Conceptions of the weather clearly form a part of this: Mentz, for example, finds in the storm scenes in Shakespeare's *King Lear* a vision of nature as both hostile and resistant to 'human attempts to construct survivable narratives'.[7] The current chapter acknowledges both the productiveness and the urgency of analyses like these while aiming at something different: an account of the sceptical, subversive uses to which Marlowe put his depictions of meteorology. In her recent book *Shakespeare's Representation of Weather, Climate and Environment*, which appeared as this chapter was being completed, Sophie Chiari argues that early modern playwrights 'used weather and climate imagery in their works in order to represent and question men's behaviour in connection not just with the natural world but also with religion, power and politics'.[8] Chiari's focus is on Shakespeare, but, as the following paragraphs will demonstrate, her words are equally applicable to Marlowe, whose treatment of weather engages with questions of divine Providence, the political uses of religion, and the nature of God. I begin by setting out, briefly, some of the core meteorological assumptions that underlie the two *Tamburlaine* plays, before going on to discuss the dramas themselves.

The dominant set of theories informing the science of meteorology in Marlowe's time was ultimately derived from the Greek philosopher Aristotle, whose writings on a vast array of topics had occupied a central place in university curricula since the Middle Ages. Although the authority of Aristotle had received significant challenges in a number of fields by the early modern period, his views on meteorology retained a wide currency. In his 2011 account of Renaissance meteorology, Craig Martin suggests that this was partly because they seemed in accordance with everyday experience of how clouds, mists and the like are formed, and partly because, being conjectures based on empirical observation, they could accommodate new ideas based on new observations without their core theory being fatally undermined.[9] As with Aristotle's other works of natural philosophy such as his *Physics*, *On the Heavens*, and *On Generation and Corruption*, his *Meteorology* was increasingly taught at Bachelor's as well as Master's level in sixteenth-century universities.[10] Since Marlowe's Cambridge education extended to MA level, it is a certainty that he would have come into contact with this text and the extensive Latin commentary upon it, as well as with other important meteorological texts such as Pliny's *Historia naturalis* – although as S. K. Heninger shows, Aristotelian ideas about the weather were also widely disseminated in English in texts such as William Fulke's *A Goodly Gallery . . . to Beholde the Naturall Causes of All Kind of Meteors* (1563).[11]

Aristotle's meteorology is informed by his understanding of the cosmos as a series of concentric spheres with the earth at its centre and the Moon, Mercury, Venus, the Sun, and the other planets turning in successive spheres around it, with the fixed stars (as opposed to the wandering planets) in the outermost sphere or *primum mobile*.[12] The heavenly bodies above the moon are understood to move in regular courses through the celestial fifth element or *aether*.[13] However, in the sublunary realm, objects are made of the four elements of fire, air, water and earth; are subject to change and decay; and move erratically, although the elements of earth and water naturally tend downward and fire and air, upward. The specific concern of meteorology is 'the conditions which affect them' in the region 'continuous with the motions of the heavens': in effect, with the material action of the heavens upon objects on earth.[14]

According to Aristotle, meteorological events are caused by the sun drawing up two kinds of 'exhalations' from the earth: 'one is more vaporous in character, the other more windy, the vapour arising from the water within and upon the earth, while the exhalations from the earth itself, which is dry, are more like smoke'.[15] (For convenience, this chapter follows S. K. Heninger's *Handbook of Renaissance Meteorology* in referring to the wetter kind as 'vapours' and the drier kind as 'exhalations'.)[16] As these undergo changes in temperature in what Tamburlaine in *Part I*, 4.2.30 calls 'the triple region of the air' (consisting of a cold middle region between upper and lower regions, which are warmer), they produce phenomena such as clouds and rain (which occur when moist vapours condense in the middle region), thunder and lightning (the result of hot exhalations getting trapped in clouds), and comets (hot exhalations that reach the uppermost regions of the air and are ignited by the friction of the turning spheres). Comets were therefore considered meteorological phenomena rather than astronomical ones (the same was true of the Milky Way); earthquakes, too, were meteorological, being caused by vapours and exhalations trapped within the Earth.

Although Aristotle is concerned primarily with the natural causes of meteors, religious traditions have often sought to identify the hand of God in unexpected or extreme weather events. A significant influence on sixteenth-century beliefs about weather was the emphasis placed by Reformation theologians on divine Providence, the processes by which God orders and guides the workings of the Universe. Martin Luther's insistence on the notion that all things 'take place through the working of the Word' makes it harder to see meteorological occurrences as accidental, and as Craig Martin argues, Lutheran writers on meteorology (such as Johannes Garcaeus and Wolfgang Meurer) 'considered the purpose of rare or violent weather events to be found in their prophetic nature; they were signs of God's will, which could be at times providential and at times wrathful'.[17] This way of thinking is evident in many responses to one of the most alarming meteorological events (in the Aristotelian sense of the term) of Marlowe's lifetime, the earthquake that took place on 6 April 1580 and was felt throughout England. (It was followed on 1 May by a more localized earthquake in Marlowe's home county of Kent.)[18] In his *Discourse vpon the Earthquake*, for example, Arthur Golding treated it as an instance of God calling people 'to the amendemente of their Religion and conuersation' before laying 'his heauy hande in wrathfull dyspleasure vpon them'. Golding describes a sequence of recent meteorological occurrences:

> the strange appeerings of Comets, the often Eclipses of Sunne and Moone, the great and strange fashioned lights seene in the firmament in the night times, the suddaine falling, and vnwonted abiding of vnmeasurable abundance of Snow, the excessiue and vntimely raynes and ouerflowing of waters, the greatnesse and sharpe continuance of sore frostes, and many other such wonderfull things.

After these 'signes and tokens' of coming punishment, the earthquake proves both God's mercy (in giving people another warning) and 'the certaintie of Gods irreuocable iudgements'.[19]

Although he himself interprets the earthquake in religious terms, Golding complains that there are some who 'wil not sticke to deface the apparant working of God, by ascribing this miracle to some ordinarie causes in nature', and indeed, there were some in Marlowe's England who preferred to see unusual meteorological events as part of the natural course of things. In his 'short, but sharpe, and learned Iudgement of Earthquakes' within a letter to the poet Edmund Spenser published in *Three Proper, and Wittie, Familiar Letters* (1580), the Cambridge scholar Gabriel Harvey offers the conventional Aristotelian view of earthquakes as caused by windes 'emprysoned in the Caues, and Dungeons of the Earth [. . .] seeking to be set at libertie', while accepting that, through the action of the sun and other celestial bodies, it is ultimately 'God himselfe, the Creatour, and Continuer, and Corrector of Nature' who brings this about. Like Golding, he states that the purpose of earthquakes may be 'to testifie and denounce the secrete wrathe, and indignation of God', but unlike Golding, he disclaims any ability to tell when this is the case:

> But yet, notwithstanding, dare not I aforehand presume thus farre, or arrogate so much vnto my selfe, as to determine precisely and peremptorily of this, or euery the like singular

Earthquake, to be necessarily, and vndoubtedly a supernaturall, and immediate fatall Action of God, for this, or that singular intent, when as I am sure, there may be a sufficient Naturall, eyther necessarie or contingent Cause in the very Earth it selfe.[20]

It is noticeable that in Harvey's account of the earthquake, it is the gentlewomen with whom he is dining who, after the earthquake has taken place, begin 'very demurely, and deuoutely to pray vnto God', and one of the gentlemen who entreats the Cambridge scholar Harvey to discourse on the cause, observing that 'woomen are euery way vehement, and affectionate'.[21] A pious response is associated with women (who do not have the benefit of a formal education) and implicitly disparaged, while the proper role of gentlemen is not to repent but to intellectualize.

Marlowe's period of study at Cambridge began a few months after Harvey wrote his letter, and while the mercurial poet and the pedantic scholar seem utterly unlike in most respects, the *Tamburlaine* plays are informed by a similar learned scepticism about the possibility of identifying the hand of God in earthly affairs. Perhaps the most sustained discussion of this topic, albeit in a non-meteorological context, comes in *Part II*: Sigismund, King of Hungary opportunistically breaks his truce with the Turks, only for his forces to be unexpectedly routed. The dying Sigismund (who swore by 'Sweet Jesus Christ' to observe the truce, 1.2.58) attributes his defeat to 'vengeance from on high / For my accursed and hateful perjury' (2.3.2–3), and the victorious Orcanes (who, notwithstanding his Muslim faith, called upon Christ to avenge the wrong done him) points out that in the battle's outcome the power of Christ 'appears as full / As rays of Cynthia to the clearest sight' (2.3.29–30). Both characters see divine intervention at work, but the Turkish viceroy Gazellus demurs: ''Tis but the fortune of the wars, my lord, / Whose power is often proved a miracle' (2.3.31–2). This dialogue encapsulates a question repeatedly asked throughout both plays: namely, whether earthly events, in particular Tamburlaine's own unexpected rise to power, reflect divine will, as is implied by the epithet attached to Tamburlaine, 'the scourge and wrath of God' (*I Tam.*, 3.3.44). The inherently debatable nature of meteorological events, which authorities variously ascribed to natural causes and to divine Providence, offers Marlowe an appropriate and fruitful source of imagery with which to explore this theme.

From his first appearance in *Part I*, Tamburlaine expresses confidence that his rise to power has been divinely ordained. The 'possession of the Persian crown', he tells Zenocrate, is something that 'gracious stars have promised at my birth' (1.2.91–2); if Theridamas draws his sword against him, 'Jove himself will stretch his hand from heaven / To ward the blow and shield me safe from harm' (1.2.180–1). Against the armies of the Turks, 'Legions of spirits fleeting in the air / Direct our bullets and our weapons' points' (3.3.156–7). By contrast, other characters' hopes and pleas for divine aid prove utterly ineffectual, from the moment when the captured Zenocrate states her belief that 'The gods, defenders of the innocent, / Will never prosper your intended drifts' (1.2.68–9) to the Turkish empress Zabina's plea that Mahomet 'solicit God himself / And make him rain down murdering shot from heaven / To dash the Scythians' brains' (3.3.195–7). It is unclear whether by 'murdering shot' Zabina means the artillery that human soldiers might use, or the bolts of thunder more appropriate to a deity. However, her husband's words are clearer in the invocation he delivers after his defeat:

> Ye holy priests of heavenly Mahomet,
> That, sacrificing, slice and cut your flesh,
> Staining his altars with your purple blood,
> Make heaven to frown and every fixèd star
> To suck up poison from the moorish fens,
> And pour it in this glorious tyrant's throat!
>
> (4.2.2–7)

This account of the weather is accurate in early modern terms. As S. K. Heninger notes, 'Many authorities ascribed the power of exhaling evaporations not only to the Sun, but also to the other planets and stars'; furthermore, 'Evaporations from fens were thought to incorporate the infectious qualities inherent in such places'.[22] What Bajazeth is asking for, then, is not an unmistakeable moment of divine intervention like that in Thomas Lodge and Robert Greene's play *A Looking-Glass for London and England* (printed 1594), where 'A hand from out a cloud, threatneth a burning sword'; instead, he is asking for God to work through natural meteorological processes to bring about Tamburlaine's downfall.[23] This view of God operating through nature resembles Harvey's observation that 'God hath all these secondarie inferiour thinges, the foure Elementes, all sensible, and vnsensible, reasonable, and vnreasonable Creatures, the whole worlde, and what soeuer is contayned in the Compas of the worlde' to achieve 'such Effectes, either ordinarie or extraordinarie, as shall seeme most requisite to his eternall Prouidence'.[24] However, it also envisions a universe that is, in religious terms, difficult to read, because it is impossible to distinguish the working of God through nature from mere accidental natural occurrences.

This understanding of God's relationship with the universe creates obvious questions when it comes to the interpretation of Tamburlaine's string of victories across the two plays, as well as that of the apparent failure of God to defend the innocent Zenocrate, to prevent the deposition of kings and emperors, or to avert atrocities such as the slaughter of the virgins of Damascus. Just as a storm or earthquake could be either a divine warning or punishment, or part of the ordinary course of nature, so Tamburlaine's conquests could be either God's means of punishing tyrannical rulers such as Bajazeth, or the entirely natural successes of a supremely able warrior. Indeed, the analogy between Tamburlaine and a meteorological event is one that the plays themselves encourage. After Tamburlaine's famous speech over the dying Cosroe in which he speaks of the human soul 'Still climbing after knowledge infinite' until it reaches 'The sweet fruition of an earthly crown' (*I Tam.*, 2.7.24–9), Theridamas concurs that 'he is gross and like the massy earth / That moves not upwards' (2.7.31–2): by implication, Tamburlaine does move upwards because he is not earthy but fiery, like an exhalation ascending from the earth's surface (Cosroe earlier called him a 'fiery thirster after sovereignty', 2.6.31).[25] Tamburlaine makes this metaphor more explicit later on when, stepping onto his 'royal throne' using Bajazeth as a footstool (*I Tam.*, 4.2.15), he states:

> My sword struck fire from his coat of steel,
> Even in Bithynia, when I took this Turk,
> As when a fiery exhalation,
> Wrapped in the bowels of a freezing cloud,
> Fighting for passage, makes the welkin crack,
> And casts a flash of lightning to the earth.
>
> (4.2.41–6)

The action of Tamburlaine's sword against Bajazeth's armour is compared to that of a hot exhalation against the sides of a cloud, and the sparks that are produced by metal on metal are like the lightning that appears as a result. A lengthier comparison of Tamburlaine to the weather appears a few scenes earlier, when he overhears Agydas disparaging him to Zenocrate. Agydas describes his silent, wrathful glare in meteorological terms: Tamburlaine's eyes

> shine as comets, menacing revenge,
> And casts a pale complexion on his cheeks.
> As when the seaman sees the Hyades
> Gather an army of Cimmerian clouds,
> (Auster and Aquilon with wingèd steeds
> All sweating tilt about the watery heavens
> With shivering spears enforcing thunderclaps,
> And from their shields strike flames of lightning),

> All fearful folds his sails and sounds the main,
> Lifting his prayers to the heavens for aid
> Against the terror of the winds and waves:
> So fares Agydas for the late-felt frowns
> That sent a tempest to my daunted thoughts,
> And makes my soul divine her overthrow.
>
> (3.2.74–87)

Just as comets portend divine punishment, so Tamburlaine's eyes threaten the revenge he will take against Agydas; his frowns are described in a lengthy epic simile that imagines a mariner watching storm clouds gather. Although the two images have somewhat different connotations, implying a sign from God in the first instance and the workings of nature in the second, they both imagine Tamburlaine's look as a meteorological phenomenon that demands interpretation. Agydas is able to interpret it all too well as a sign that storms are on the way.

Tamburlaine himself, of course, insists both that his victories are meaningful and that he knows what they mean. As he tells the captured kings in *Part II*, he is 'made arch-monarch of the world, / Crowned and invested by the hand of Jove' (4.1.149–50), and 'these tyrannies ... I execute, enjoined me from above, / To scourge the pride of such as heaven abhors' (4.1.145, 147–8). Tamburlaine thus interprets his conquests as facilitated by Providence in order to punish God's enemies. As early as his first appearance in *Part I*, he claims to be able to read the signs of God's favour, telling Theridamas:

> See how he rains down heaps of gold in showers
> As if he meant to give my soldiers pay,
> And as a sure and grounded argument
> That I shall be the monarch of the East,
> He sends this Soldan's daughter rich and brave
> To be my queen and portly emperess.
>
> (1.2.182–7)

Tamburlaine is being disingenuous here. Not only have both Zenocrate and her treasure been 'ta'en' (1.2.2) by Tamburlaine, rather than sent from God; having instructed his soldiers to 'Lay out our golden wedges to the view / That their reflections may amaze the Persians' (1.2.139–40), he uses her as he uses the treasure: as a means of persuading Theridamas to defect. Although the meteorological metaphor of 'rains' suggests God working through natural processes (not to mention, perhaps, the myth of Jupiter and Danaë), the artificial processes by which Tamburlaine has produced a spectacular image to imply divine favour are readily apparent.[26]

This opportunistic use of convenient events as proof that God is on one's side is something that appears elsewhere in Marlowe, for example in *The Jew of Malta* when the Christian Governor of Malta, Ferneze, who benefits from the Jewish Barabas's double-crossing of the Turks only to double-cross Barabas in turn, insists that 'due praise be given / Neither to fate nor fortune, but to heaven' for his victory.[27] As a cynical view of how leaders use religion, it recalls the Italian writer Niccolò Machiavelli, who in his *Discourses on Livy* praises the politic use made of religion by Numa Pompilius, one of the earliest founders of Rome: 'As he found a very ferocious people and wished to reduce it to civil obedience with the arts of peace, he turned to religion as a thing altogether necessary if he wished to maintain a civilization'; in order to bolster his authority when devising new laws, he 'pretended to be intimate with a nymph who counselled him on what he had to counsel the people'.[28] Machiavelli was certainly being read while Marlowe was at Cambridge: in a letter dating from around 1579 that describes scholarly life at the university, Harvey mentions that 'sum good fellowes amongst us begin nowe to be prettely well acquayntid with a certayne parlous booke' called *Il principe* (Machiavelli's *The Prince*), as well as the *Discorsi* and other texts.[29] Marlowe's depiction of the way Tamburlaine interprets events in self-servingly religious terms may owe something to this school of thought; it also anticipates the view attributed to Marlowe (by Thomas Kyd) that 'things esteemed to be donn by devine power might haue a aswell [*sic*] been don by observation of men'.³⁰

Like the meteorological occurrences to which they are sometimes compared, Tamburlaine's victories are phenomena that can be interpreted either as natural or as divinely ordained – not least by Tamburlaine himself, who has obvious reasons for asserting the latter.³¹ Marlowe's depiction of this process implies a critique of the way religious explanations can be used to bolster political power. Tamburlaine does not stop at interpretation, however: he imposes himself on the world in ways that produce the appearance of meteorological events – or, indeed, the real thing. As he exclaims in *Part I*, after comparing his clash with Bajazeth to a 'fiery exhalation':

> As was the fame of Clymen's brain-sick son
> That almost brent the axle-tree of heaven,
> So shall our swords, our lances and our shot
> Fill all the air with fiery meteors.
> Then, when the sky shall wax as red as blood,
> It shall be said I made it red myself,
> To make me think of naught but blood and war.
>
> (4.2.49–55)

Tamburlaine here doesn't merely compare his men's artillery to 'fiery meteors', as when at 2.3.19 he refers to 'bullets like Jove's dreadful thunderbolts'; he says it will actually *produce* fiery meteors that will make the sky 'as red as blood', blurring the boundary between metaphor and fact. He anticipates creating an aerial spectacle that will correctly be read by others not only as Tamburlaine's own handiwork ('I made it red myself') but as a spectacle for him to interpret ('To make me think of naught but blood and war'). He makes a similar assertion following his victory over the King of Arabia at the end of *Part I*:

> And here in Afric, where it seldom rains,
> Since I arrived with my triumphant host,
> Have swelling clouds drawn from wide gasping wounds
> Been oft resolved in bloody purple showers,
> A meteor that might terrify the earth
> And make it quake at every drop it drinks.
>
> (5.2.395–400)

This sounds like hyperbole, but it describes a phenomenon that was recognized in the Renaissance: in his chapter 'Of monstruous or prodigious rayne', the meteorological writer William Fulke explains that 'the sunne from places where bloud hath ben spilt, draweth vp great quantitie of bloud, & so it rayneth bloud'.[32] The sheer quantity of blood spilt by Tamburlaine produces a weather event that is simultaneously natural and portentous, 'A meteor that might terrify the earth'.

A final instance of Tamburlaine literally making the weather appears after the death of Zenocrate in *Part II*, when he decides to burn the surrounding town 'Because this place bereft me of my love' (2.4.138):

> So, burn the turrets of this cursèd town,
> Flame to the highest region of the air
> And kindle heaps of exhalations
> That, being fiery meteors, may presage
> Death and destruction to th'inhabitants.
> Over my zenith hang a blazing star,
> That may endure till heaven be dissolved,
> Fed with the fresh supply of earthly dregs,
> Threat'ning a death and famine to this land.
> Flying dragons, lightning, fearful thunderclaps,
> Singe these fair plains and make them seem as black
> As is the island where the Furies mask,
> Compassed with Lethe, Styx, and Phlegethon,
> Because my dear Zenocrate is dead.
>
> (3.2.1–14)

Once again, extreme levels of destructiveness are imagined as actually changing the weather: the flaming town will generate exhalations that will turn to meteors when they rise to the heights of the atmosphere. (These include 'flying dragons', which here refer to a type of fiery meteor, not an animal.) Tamburlaine even envisages creating a permanent spectacle (unlike the inherently temporary nature of normal weather events) in the form of a blazing star 'Fed with the fresh supply of earthly dregs, / Threat'ning a death and famine to this land'.

These notions are, in the strict sense of the word, preposterous, in that they place events in the wrong order. As Mary Thomas Crane notes, the 'destruction of the town is imagined as the direct cause of meteors, which thus stand as signs of the destruction that caused them'.[33] The havoc that Tamburlaine says the meteors portend actually came before, and indeed produced, the meteors, and the 'death and famine' foretold by the blazing star have, surely, already happened. This demystification of apparently prophetic meteorological events as effects of the things they seem to anticipate resembles Fulke's argument in *A Goodly Gallery*: comets 'ar sayd to betoken drought', but this really occurs because 'a *Comet* can not be generated without great heat, & muche moisture is consumed in the burning of it'.[34] The actual cause of the drought is the same heat that generates the comet. Tamburlaine, however, wants to have it both ways: he exploits the science, but he also insists on the prophetic nature of the spectacles that he plans to create. As with his capture of Zenocrate and his appropriation of her treasure, the events he claims to interpret are ones that he has produced himself.

In her discussion of this passage, Crane focuses in particular on the blazing star 'That may endure till heaven be dissolved'. As has already been noted, a star that endures until the end of time is not, strictly speaking, a meteorological phenomenon, since such phenomena arise out of the imperfect mixtures that characterize the sublunary world and are temporary in nature. An everlasting star belongs, instead, in the changeless spheres above the moon; but, given that such regions are supposed to be unchanging, a new star ought not to appear there in the first place. Crane discusses this paradox with reference to the new star (really a supernova) that appeared in the constellation of Cassiopeia in November 1572 and remained visible for several months. Using their understanding of parallax, early modern astronomers such as Thomas Digges 'were able for the first time to determine that the new star was located in the realm of the fixed stars, where no change was supposed to be possible', rather than beneath the moon.[35] This observation contradicted established assumptions about the nature of the universe and therefore posed a problem for contemporary commentators; however, instead of encouraging a wholesale abandonment of those assumptions, it tended to be read as exceptional and therefore portentous. Eight years later, following the appearance of another 'blazyng starre', Francis Shakelton would say of the star of 1572

> it semed so straunge: as from the beginnyng of the worlde, the like was neuer sene: for in the iudgement of the moste experte Astronomers, (and suche as are moste skilfull in the Mathematiques in this our tyme and age) that starre which did then appeare vnto our sighte, was no Comete, but mere supernaturall.

Shakelton went on to cite Digges's '*Alae, seu Scalae Mathematicae*, where the miracle is by demonstrations Mathematicall, plainly and most manifestly proued'. Rather than prompting a paradigm shift, the fact that the new star had appeared above the moon was understood by Shakelton as miraculous, a sign from God 'to be mindfull of the Iudgement daie'.[36] Only a few months after its disappearance, incidentally, the aurora borealis was visible in Canterbury, in November 1574, a spectacular and unusual event that may have added to the young Marlowe's interest in celestial phenomena.[37]

For the adult Marlowe, however, the challenge to astronomical orthodoxy posed by the star of 1572 had, as Crane argues, a different effect: by hinting at the possibility of 'a universe newly secularized and open to change', it provided the playwright with 'a language adequate to convey Tamburlaine's immense ambition and will to conquest'.[38] Tamburlaine's vision of creating a new, permanent feature in the sky is just one of several 'imagined transgressions of the heavens' in *Part II*, including his command that his followers 'Raise cavalieros higher than the clouds / And with the cannon break the frame of heaven' (2.4.103–4) and his promise to the captured kings that after sacking their cities he will 'with the flames that beat against the clouds / Incense the heavens and make the stars to melt' (4.1.193–4).[39] Crane might have added the dying Tamburlaine's injunction, 'Come let us march against the powers of heaven / And set black streamers in the firmament / To signify the slaughter of the gods' (5.3.48–50). In effect, Tamburlaine's images of entering, changing or damaging the heavens do literally break their frame: in refusing to accept that the heavens are immutable and invulnerable, Tamburlaine shatters the boundary between them and the world he lives in, between astronomy and meteorology.

It is worth noting, however, that all of the lines cited in the above paragraph are uttered at moments of crisis for Tamburlaine, when the limits of his power become all too apparent: after the death of Zenocrate, whom Tamburlaine is unable to keep alive; after his killing of his son Calyphas, in whom Tamburlaine is unable to achieve a satisfactory reproduction of his own martial ethos; and when Tamburlaine has become conscious of his own approaching death. That gives them an ironic potential that is not fully accounted for in Crane's view of Marlowe as using astronomical imagery to convey Tamburlaine's power and ambition, and which might be more akin to the spectacle of the grief-deranged protagonist of George Peele and Shakespeare's *Titus Andronicus* asking his family and friends to shoot letters up to heaven with their bows and arrows (4.3).[40] It also raises the wider question of how, ultimately, to interpret Tamburlaine's use of meteorological imagery across the two plays: as splendid assertions of world-shaking achievement and intent, or as bombastic verbiage that bears little relation to what is actually going on. When he talks of filling 'all the air with fiery meteors', for example, or states that he has spilt so much blood as to produce 'purple showers' from the clouds, it is impossible to know whether the audience is expected to understand such things as having happened, or being able to happen, or whether they are mere hyperbole. One feature of the plays that makes this question even harder to resolve is their lack of detail regarding any visual effects that may (or may not) have been used to accompany Tamburlaine's speeches. In *Shakespeare's Storms*, Gwilym Jones discusses the spectacular use of fireworks to accompany another, later play concerned, like *Tamburlaine*, both with the nature of political power and with 'the human interpretation of the weather': Shakespeare's *Julius Caesar*, where Casca's account of 'a tempest dropping fire' (1.3.10) is preceded by '*Thunder and lightning*' (1.3.0 SD), with similar stage directions recurring over the scenes that follow (1.3.100 SD, 2.2.0 SD).[41] Such effects were evidently available when Marlowe was writing *Tamburlaine*: in George Peele's *The Battle of Alcazar* (1588–9), for example, the Presenter's description at the start of Act 5 of 'lightning', 'fiery stars and streaming comets' is accompanied by stage directions calling for 'Lightning and thunder', 'the blazing star', and 'Fireworks'.[42] The text of *Tamburlaine*, by contrast, gives no indication of what effects were used at moments such as the burning of the town after Zenocrate's death (although the New Mermaids editor suggests fireworks, smoke effects and/or a scenic backdrop).[43] The lack of any such information in print means that Tamburlaine's words have to carry the whole weight of the episode's significance.

The difficulty of identifying how far Tamburlaine's meteorological imagery matches up to the actual phenomena only serves to amplify Marlowe's religious critique in the play. As this chapter has attempted to argue, one reason why this imagery proved so useful to Marlowe was because of its inherently debatable nature: weather events could variously be interpreted as messages from God, or as part of the natural course of things. This made such imagery very appropriate to a play that raises the question of whether the astounding victories and conquests of a figure like Tamburlaine are to be understood as part of God's plans for the world, or as mere accidents. At a further level of complexity, the play depicts the ways in which a personality like Tamburlaine can exploit the debatable nature of the weather to assert his God-given right to the power he enjoys – with an implied critique of the tendency of other rulers to do the same. If the reality of the events being described is itself open to question, however, then that adds yet another twist: other characters' acquiescence in Tamburlaine's interpretations of meteorological events can be understood as the effect, not of his convincing rhetoric, but of the power of his violence to compel assent. This modifies the notion ascribed to Marlowe by the informer Richard Baines, that 'the beginning of religion was only to keep men in awe'.[44] Instead, the beginning and maintenance of a specific religious interpretation depends on men being kept in awe through astonishing acts of violence and sadism such as those employed by Tamburlaine.

Marlowe's religious scepticism may go further than this, however. In depicting a character who describes, creates, or invents meteorological signs that demand interpretation, Marlowe not only subverts the claims of religious commentators to make sense of the universe; he can also be seen as parodying the very understanding of God that such writers assume. In his account of blazing stars and similar phenomena, Francis Shakelton writes that God uses comets 'to threaten, and prognosticate condigne punishemente, to light vpon all persones generally, who daiely and howerly doe (of set purpose and malice, wilfully offende, Gods diuine Maiestie) and doe continually wallow and perseuer in their wicked and abhominable synne and transgression'.[45] Arthur Golding makes the similar point that God uses signs such as earthquakes to call men 'to the knowledge of themselues, and to the amendemente of their Religion and conuersation, before he haue layd his heauy hande in wrathfull dyspleasure vpon them'.[46] This understanding of meteorological events as warnings of divine punishment is theologically conventional; but it also brings to mind ways in which Tamburlaine himself exercises power and domination. After '*looking wrathfully on* AGYDAS' with eyes that shine like comets and brows that threaten storms (*I Tam.*, 3.2.65 SD), Tamburlaine has Techelles present him with a '*naked dagger*' (3.2.87 SD) and the words, 'See you, Agydas, how the king salutes you. / He bids you prophesy what it imports' (3.2.88–9). Agydas correctly interprets the dagger as implying the alternatives of suicide and agonizing punishment, of which he chooses the former. Tamburlaine's use here of a non-verbal threat to which Agydas must respond with a gesture of submission so as to avoid future punishment seems a lot like Protestant commentators' vision of a wrathful God who sends earthquakes and blazing stars as warnings to sinners to repent. So does his use of white, red and black tents before besieged cities to signify progressive offers of mercy, death to soldiers, and wholesale slaughter. His implacable response to the virgins of Damascus when, too late, they plead for their city – 'They have refused the offer of their lives / And know my customs are as peremptory / As wrathful planets, death, or destiny' (5.2.63–5) – makes him sound like the God described by Golding:

> Terrible and moste true is this saying of his by the mouth of Salomon: *For as much as I haue called, and you haue refuzed: and I haue stretched oute my handes, and you haue not regarded it: but haue despized al my counsel, and set my correction at nought: therefore wil I also laugh at your destruction* [. . .]. Soothly it is a dreadful thing to fall into the handes of the Lorde. For as he is merciful, so is he also iust, and in all his determinations he is vtterly vnchangeable.[47]

In depicting a protagonist who interprets weather events, some of them created by himself, in manifestly self-serving ways,

Marlowe can be seen as questioning similar interpretations from the commentators of his own day. But in having that protagonist offer spectacular warnings of mass punishment that are enacted with unswerving severity, Marlowe goes further, questioning the notion of a God who not only allows Tamburlaine to flourish, but who seems terrifyingly similar to Tamburlaine himself.

6

New Directions: Towards a Racialized *Tamburlaine*

Sydnee Wagner

During Othello's speech to the Duke of Venice, he apologizes for his words, declaring, 'Rude am I in my speech' (1.3.82), before notably winning the Duke over with his masterful rhetoric.[1] Othello's downplaying of his intellect speaks to attitudes about race and the unintelligibility of language in the early modern period. Even Desdemona tells Othello that his speech has become unintelligible to her due to his affect when she exclaims 'Upon my knees, what doth your speech import? / I understand a fury in your words / But not the words' (4.2.31–3). Despite deeming his speech 'rude', in his final moments before death Othello recognizes the importance of rhetoric when he reflects on how his story will be told after he is gone, evoking the use of affect in rhetoric by imploring others to 'Speak of me as I am' (5.2.340). He continues by asking those who will write about him to not revert to preconceived notions of racialized passions, but to 'speak / Of one that loved not wisely, but too well; / Of one not easily jealous, but, being wrought, /

Perplexed in the extreme' (5.2.341–4). Gratiano, having witnessed this speech, responds in turn: 'All that's spoke is marred' (5.2.355), a phrase that seemingly subverts the notion of Othello's 'rude speech' introduced at the beginning of the play.

Although a growing number of scholars are now attending to race in Shakespeare's plays (including *Othello*), few, if any, have begun to explore the possibilities of racialization in Marlowe's *Tamburlaine The Great*. In *Tamburlaine*, the titular character is remarkably European in physical description (despite being from Kesh in Central Asia), yet through the efforts of rhetoric and affect he becomes racially 'othered' to the audience. These works may seem like different plays in their theatrical reproduction of racial difference (*Othello* historically employs the use of blackface cosmetics and textiles) and both have vastly different scholarly traditions in early modern studies (*Othello* is the most notable 'race play' from the period, whereas *Tamburlaine* is rarely discussed through technologies of race-making), and yet the rhetoric around race within these texts is strikingly similar. By highlighting the rhetorical devices that racialize beyond the physiological difference at play in *Othello*, I wish to bridge these plays and the parallel treatments of the titular characters. Despite *Tamburlaine* rarely being attended to through theoretical frameworks that employ critical race theory or postcolonial theory, this essay makes a case that race is a central anxiety of the play through the titular character of the play. Rather than making the case for one mode of race-making in the early modern period, I will gesture towards a variety of technologies of race-making that are at work, both in *Tamburlaine* and in early modern English society, in hopes that future *Tamburlaine* scholarship takes up this call towards a racialized *Tamburlaine*.

Despite the play being located outside of Europe and centring around non-European characters, the critical tradition surrounding Marlowe's *Tamburlaine* is surprisingly devoid of attention to race. While scholars have made tangential gestures to race in *Tamburlaine* in the form of geography, foreignness, or vagabonds, they have done so without explicitly naming these formations as 'race'.[2]

In an essay on *Tamburlaine* and Anglo-Ottoman relations, Jonathan Burton calls for the use of postcolonial theory in case-specific historical studies. In his attention to the Turk in Marlowe's dramatic work, Burton argues that 'Marlowe's plays are crucially marked by England's reciprocative commerce with the Ottoman Empire.'[3] Likewise, Emily Bartels, in her scholarship on imperialism and Marlowe's dramatic work, argues that early modern English representations of 'The East' were generative for imperialist self-construction because this space could be represented through extremes, allowing for 'England's supremacy' to be 'triumphantly mapped out'.[4]

Mark Thornton Burnett calls attention to the similarities between vagrancy and Tamburlaine's rebelliousness and his occupation as a shepherd, yet does not attend thoroughly to the strong ties between vagrancy, itineracy, and race within the period. Instead, Burnett argues that anxieties about Tamburlaine within the play mirror Elizabethan concerns about rogues and other 'masterless men'.[5] Garrett Sullivan makes a connection between geography and character in Marlowe's work, contending that early modern concepts of 'new' and 'old' geography shape identity formation in *Tamburlaine*, *Doctor Faustus*, and *The Jew of Malta*.[6] Mary Floyd-Wilson's *Race and Ethnicity in Renaissance Drama* has the most sustained work on race and *Tamburlaine*, attending to the use of early modern geo-humoral theory to describe Tamburlaine's Scythian nature. In her chapter on Tamburlaine's ethnicity, Floyd-Wilson claims Tamburlaine's violent character is rooted in English identity, 'white barbarity,' and a 'fraught affiliation with the Scythians'.[7]

While some scholars, such as Judith Haber, have paid particular attention to Tamburlaine's rhetoric and affect, they do not do so through thinking about the intersections between feelings and race.[8] When discussing possible influences on Shakespeare, Stephen Greenblatt cites *Tamburlaine* as one of the first plays Shakespeare likely saw in London, later influencing his plays *Titus Andronicus* (which features another prominently racialized character, Aaron the Moor) and the second tetralogy.[9] Despite the lack of scholarship on race within *Tamburlaine*, Marlowe's collected works are no stranger to race criticism, usually through another of Marlowe's plays, *The Jew of Malta* (1589).[10] This dramatic work relies heavily on early modern racialized stereotypes about Jewish people, particularly Jewish men, and the character Barabas is often regarded as a precursor to Shakespeare's Shylock from *Merchant of Venice* (1596).[11]

Although all of the scholarship above intersects with early modern race studies, the question of race rarely crops up in the writing. Compared to Marlowe's other plays, Tamburlaine is the only character consistently 'blackened' by both language and clothing, textual and material cues that stand paradoxically with Tamburlaine's pale complexion. By exploring the implications of Tamburlaine's blackness that reside outside an elementary understanding of physiological difference, I aim to show how race manifests in complex and complicated ways in early modern English ideologies and on the early modern stage.

Early modern race

Before discussing Tamburlaine's racialization, it's important to define what 'race' really means, in the early modern period and our own contemporary moment. In the early modern period, skin colour was but one means of racially identifying or othering people. Clothing, language, religion, geography and place of origin, sexuality, and humoral theory (among many other markers) were all technologies of race-making in the period. As Ian Smith notes:

> A new orthodoxy has emerged as a corrective to the predominant but unsustainable – for the period – sole

emphasis on skin color. Researchers now typically posit that race in the early modern period is the product of several, often interrelated, categories of identification, a complex amalgam of codes that can be mobilized to ratify group exclusion and marginalization.[12]

Geraldine Heng likewise uses critical race theory to attend to Medieval formations of racial ideologies, arguing that:

'Race' is one of the primary names we have ... that is attached to a repeating tendency, of the gravest import, to demarcate human beings through differences among humans that are selectively essentialized as absolute and fundamental, in order to distribute positions and powers differently to human groups. Race-making thus operates as specific historical occasions in which strategic essentialisms are posited and assigned through a variety of practices and pressures, so as to construct a hierarchy of peoples for different treatment ... race is a structural relationship for the articulation and management of human differences, rather than a substantive content.[13]

Like Heng, in this essay I will engage with race as not a 'substantive content'; that is, I will not use early modern theories of race to try to rationalize racial ideologies (which are, by nature, inherently irrational) nor will I try to reaffirm racist narratives through popular pseudo-sciences of the period. Instead, I will engage with the technologies of race-making in the period to demonstrate the reproductions (and new formations) of racial ideologies at work in Marlowe's play, which are used to encourage audiences into viewing Tamburlaine as fundamentally 'Other'.

In his book, *Habeas Viscus: Racializing Assemblages, Biopolitics, and Black Feminist Theories of the Human*, Alexander Weheliye coins the phrase 'racializing assemblages', which he describes as 'constru[ing] race not as a biological or cultural classification but as a set of sociopolitical processes that discipline humanity into full humans, not-quite-humans, and nonhumans.'[14] In my readings of race in *Tamburlaine* I will also use Weheliye's notion of 'racializing assemblages' as a basis for thinking through Tamburlaine, the character, and how he is racially othered on the early modern stage. In order to take this approach, I will be looking at rhetoric, affect, and the materialization of these technologies of race through the evocation of clothing and objects and how they, like Tamburlaine, are coded racially throughout the play.

How can scholars locate racialized affect, or better yet, differentiate racialized affect from affect that is seemingly non-racial, if such a thing were possible? Sianne Ngai's scholarship on affect, conceptualized in her book *Ugly Feelings*, focuses predominantly on negative affect modes, which she quite vividly explains: 'if *Ugly Feelings* is a bestiary of affects, in other words, it is one filled with rats and possums rather than lions, its categories of feeling generally being, well, weaker and nastier.'[15] Within her project on ugly feelings, Ngai locates individual modes of 'ugly' affect as, 'envy, anxiety, paranoia, irritation, a racialized affect I call "animatedness," and a strange amalgamation of shock and boredom I call "stuplimity"'.[16] These 'ugly feelings,' likewise, were simultaneously prescribed to racialized subjects in early modern writing as well as employed in white European discourse on race. It is important to note that, while affect in the early modern period is discussed through the Galenic tradition, relying on notions about the humours to talk about passions and melancholy, this scientific tradition does not negate the conscious race-making produced, in part, out of this science.[17] That is, while some of the scholars I engage with in this essay, like Mary Floyd-Wilson and Surekha Davies, posit that early modern ideas of race and ethnicity are formed out of humoralism as a reaction to encountering non-European people, this tradition of scholarship overlooks the fact that humoral theory was only one mode of understanding race in the early modern period, and certainly not the dominant mode.[18] By focusing solely on this form of race-making, scholars risk reasserting an ahistorical, and often dangerous, notion that race in the early modern period was far different from contemporary understandings of race. As Robert Young reminds us, 'a racist society will have a racist science'.[19] Thus, by situating geo-humoral theory as a mode of understanding racial difference, scholars risk the possibility of neglecting analysis of these scientific tools as conscious acts of race-making for the purposes of white supremacy, just as they risk forgetting that racism is the very locus in which these modes of science are conceived.

While the majority of *Tamburlaine*'s characters are coded, geographically, as non-European, Tamburlaine, as the titular character of the play, is prominently hyper-visible, addressable not only by the other characters in the play but also by the audience. So how would an early modern audience read Tamburlaine? With his recognizably European physical characteristics and his paradoxically barbarous behaviour, Tamburlaine displays a particular type of racial ambiguity. It is important to stress, however, that even racial ambiguity is a point of racial otherness. Race as a product of racism seeks to compound and collapse people into categories for the purposes of nation building and citizen forming.[20] That is, by placing people into categories that structurally deem them 'not-quite-human' or 'non-human', racial ideologies justify the brutality of Western colonial projects. 'Human', then, became a project shrouded in whiteness.[21] Thus, those who may be 'ambiguously raced' and not easily categorized or racially marked, to us as readers or to an early modern audience, also posed a threat to a white national project. Tamburlaine's racial ambiguity, then, is less of an invitation for an early modern audience to identify with him as a possibly white-washed character, and more of a site of possible threat for both the more identifiably racialized characters and for a predominantly white audience.

While some may locate this play before any semblance of English ethnonationalism, as England was a small country yet to fully realize imperial power, it is important to understand that the Elizabethan era was fraught with burgeoning nationalist rhetoric, even while larger empires, like the Ottomans, posed a significant threat.[22] By the late sixteenth century, England had already mandated laws that excluded non-white ethnic groups from civic participation, starting with expulsions of the Jewish population in the middle ages and continuing with the Egyptians Act of 1530 and Elizabeth I's public concern for 'blackamoors'.[23] English explorers, likewise, were already setting out with charters to establish colonies in the Americas, a strategic act to strengthen England's colonial project. So, while phrases like 'white national project' or 'ethnonationalism' may seem rooted in a present American context, England was surely participating in their own nation-building that was formed, in no small part, by emerging ideas of racial difference.

Geo-humoral theory, affect and Scythians

Tamburlaine's pale skin, while read by some scholars as proof that Tamburlaine was not racialized, is conceptualized in tandem with his 'barbarous' affect. When Cosroe, the Persian emperor and Tamburlaine's enemy, requests a description of Tamburlaine, Menaphon states that he is 'Pale of complexion, wrought in him with passion' (*Part I*, 2.1.19).[24] In this description, the proximity of Tamburlaine's '[p]ale ... complexion' to the mention of 'passion' evokes early modern geo-humoral theory. Concerning the relationship to humours and geography in the early modern period, Mary Floyd-Wilson asserts, 'climatic explanations of color and disposition were grounded in humoralism ... humoral theory is also the foundational knowledge for making ethnological distinctions'.[25] While I do not necessarily agree with Floyd-Wilson's claim that 'regionally inflected humoralism, reductively construed as "climate theory" by modern scholars, proves to be the dominant mode of ethnic distinction in the late sixteenth and early seventeenth centuries', as it ignores the heavily prevalent, and I would argue *dominant*, material ways in which race-making manifests outside of humoral theory, I find this particular model for thinking of skin colour and racial difference useful when discussing Tamburlaine's paleness. Just as being too hot (or from a geographic location south of Europe) can cause dark skin in early modern humoral discourse, being too cold, or from a far north region, can also cause an individual to be too *pale*. Tamburlaine's complexion, thus, may not entirely evoke a Eurocentric physicality as much as it may suggest he has a kind of humoral imbalance that could be the cause of both his pallor and excessive passions.

But humoral theory is only one reading of the textual proximity between Tamburlaine's pallid appearance and notable passions. If we are to read Tamburlaine's pale complexion as a marker of Eurocentric similarity through physicality, his 'passion' that is 'wrought in him' is decidedly not a Eurocentric ideal in early modern England. While Tamburlaine's exterior may be recognized by an early modern English audience as 'civilized' or even English itself, his affect proves to be as 'barbarous' as his actions are perceived. This juxtaposition then lends itself to imagining paleness as a type of barbarousness, suggesting unsettled racial similarities between white English and non-white barbarians.

Tamburlaine's pale complexion is perceived as 'wrought', or formed, by his racialized passions. Outside of a humoral reading of the correlation between humours and skin colour, the use of 'wrought' specifically connotes a materiality behind Tamburlaine's affect. That is, 'wrought' does not merely mean 'created' or 'formed', but was intrinsically linked to labour-related skills like metal-working and fabric-making in the early modern period. Tamburlaine's passions, thus, are imagined as materializing Tamburlaine's skin colour, as a blacksmith wrought metal.

Menaphon's description of Tamburlaine is not the only place in which Tamburlaine's paleness is contextualized through affective language. After Zenocrates expresses love and devotion to Tamburlaine and leaves with him, Agydas continues to express his qualms:

Betrayed by fortune and suspicious love,
Threatened with frowning wrath and jealousy,
Surprised with fear of hideous revenge,
I stand aghast; but most astonièd
To see his choler shut in secret thoughts
And wrapped in silence of his angry soul.
Upon his brows was portrayed ugly death,
And in his eyes the fury of his heart,
That shine as comets, menacing revenge,
And casts a pale complexion on his cheeks.

(*Part I*, 3.2.66–75)

Agydas begins his concerns by mapping out Tamburlaine's unruly passions, which are intrinsically linked to his 'choler shut in secret thoughts', a reference to early modern humoral theory in which 'choler' or bile, is directly related to temper. 'Choler' itself is often imagined as black or dark in colour, a direct opposition to Tamburlaine's references to 'pale complexion'. This contradictory relationship between Tamburlaine's pale skin being a product of his passion is further complicated by the hot and dry nature of 'choler'. In geo-humoral theory, a body too heated was more likely to be dark in complexion. Agydas's twin description of Tamburlaine's affect and physicality mirrors Menaphon's blazon-like portrait of Tamburlaine, breaking down his features until they are disembodied 'brows', 'eyes', 'amber hair', and 'cheeks'. Agydas's conceptualization of Tamburlaine's paleness, similarly, parallels Menaphon's notion that his pallid complexion is materialized through his ill temperament.

Tamburlaine's own humanity is called into question by Cosroe and Meander during their conversation. Answering Cosroe's frustration about Tamburlaine, whom he calls a 'devilish shepherd' and 'monstrous slave' (*Part I*, 2.6.1, 7), Meander muses on Tamburlaine's conception, concluding that '[s]ome powers divine, or else infernal, mixed / Their angry seeds at his conception: / For he was never spring of human race' (*Part I*, 2.6.9–11). This rhetoric parallels early modern notions of people of colour and their conception, which was perceived as unnatural compared to Europeans. Like *The Tempest*'s Caliban who is called a 'mooncalf' (a reference to an animal-like abortive foetus), Tamburlaine is perceived as having unnatural origins, which accounts for his 'monstrous' personhood. In addition to claiming that Tamburlaine is conceived out of unnatural conditions, Meander also suggests that, instead, Tamburlaine was again 'wrought' by negative affect such as 'their angry seeds'.

While Tamburlaine is described as pale in complexion, he's associated with blackness through rhetoric and prosthetics like clothing and military tools. When the Soldan of Egypt exclaims that Tamburlaine '[h]ath spread his colours to our high disgrace' (*Part I*, 4.1.7), the Messenger remarks:

> The first day when he pitcheth down his tents,
> White is their hue, and on his silver crest
> A snowy feather spangled white he bears,
> To signify the mildness of his mind
> That satiate with spoil refuseth blood;
> But when Aurora mounts the second time,
> As red as scarlet is his furniture –
> Then must his kindled wrath be quenched with blood,
> Not sparing any that can manage arms;
> But if these threats move not submission,
> Black are his colours, black pavilion,
> His spear, his shield, his horse, his armour, plumes,
> And jetty feathers menace death and hell;
> Without respect of sex, degree, or age,
> He razeth all his foes with fire and sword.
>
> (*Part I*, 4.1.49–63)

Here, the Messenger imagines that Tamburlaine's colours change with his military affect. First, his colours are 'white' the 'first day when he pitcheth down his tents'. This trend of white is also signified by the 'silver crest' and 'snowy feather spangled white' that Tamburlaine reportedly adopts. Notably, the way in which Tamburlaine's white military colours are described by the Messenger resonate with an earlier speech of Tamburlaine's, in which he describes Zenocrate's beauty like a blazon:

> Brighter than is the silver Rhodope,
> Fairer than whitest snow on Scythian hills,
> . . .
> More rich and valurous than Zenocrate's;
> With milk-white harts upon an ivory sled
> Thou shalt be drawn amidst the frozen pools
> And scale the icy mountains' lofty tops . . .
>
> (*Part I*, 1.2.88–100)

Zenocrate's complexion is described through white imagery, yet unlike Tamburlaine this fairness is compared to nature, emphasizing that Zenocrate's paleness is naturalized and desired. Tamburlaine first describes Zenocrate as 'brighter' than the 'silver Rhodope', a mountain range in southern Europe. He continues his snow-white metaphors in the next line when he exclaims that Zenocrate is 'fairer than whitest snow on Scythian hills', referring to the geographic location in Eurasia from which the Scythians, a nomadic ethnic group, originated. Relying on ancient Greek notions of the group, early modern English references to Scythians depicted them as barbarians and cannibals. Tamburlaine himself is called a 'Scythian' multiple times throughout the play, a rhetorical move by his enemies to paint him through barbaric lenses. Thus, Zenocrate being 'fairer than whitest snow on Scythian hills' not only implies that she is whiter than the geographical location, but also whiter than the inhabitants of that region, including Tamburlaine.

Since their first mentions in classical European writing, Scythians have been racially coded as 'Other'. From the Latin *Scythia*, which derived from the Greek *Skythia*, 'Scythian' was a name given to the region near the north coast of the Black Sea, and is thought to be from an Indo-European root meaning 'shepherd', the occupation that was popularly attributed to

Scythians. While Scythia is an ill-defined region, popularly attributed to parts of Russia, Scythians, as nomads, were also thought to live all over Eurasia, the Middle East, and parts of South East Europe.[26]

Hippocrates mentions a 'race' of Scythian Amazons in *On Airs, Waters, Places* (400 BCE) that are notably 'different from all other races'.[27] Classical writers like Claudius Ptolemaeus claimed that although 'white in complexion', their geographic location caused Scythians to be savage.[28] This precursor to early modern rhetorics of geo-humoral theory led sixteenth-century French philosopher Jean Bodin to describe Scythians as violent and volatile, comparing them to 'southerners':

> The cruelty of the southerners and of the Scythians is...very different, because the latter are driven to wrath by impulse alone and to revenge by a certain magnanimous valor of the soul; after they have been irritated, they can easily be mollified. The southerners are not easily angered, but when once angry they can with difficulty be softened: they attack the enemy with a foxlike cunning, not with open violence, and they inflict horribly painful torture upon the conquered. This savagery comes partly from the despotism which a vicious system of training and undisciplined appetites have created in a man...[29]

Scythians were often used as a measurement of racializing other groups, like Ethiopians and the Irish. In a similar comparison, in *A new description of Ireland* (1610), Barnabe Rich claims that 'the wild uncivil Scythians, do forbear to be cruel the one against the other. The cannibals, devourers of men's flesh, do leave to be fierce amongst themselves.'[30] Fynes Moryson, likewise, thought the 'wild Irish' were so brutal that 'a man would think these men to be Scythians, who let their horses' blood under the ears, and for nourishment drink their blood, and indeed (as I have formerly said), some of the Irish are of the race of Scythians, coming into Spain, and from thence into Ireland'.[31] Edmund Spenser, in his infamously anti-Irish treatise *A Veue of the present state of Irelande* (1633), connected Scythian-Irish relations not by violent acts like cannibalism, but through discourse on affect and mourning rituals: 'There be other sorts of cries also used amongst the Irish which savour greatly of the Scythian barbarism; as their lamentations at their burials with despairful outcries and immoderate wailings, the which Mr. Stanihurst might also have used for an argument to prove them Egyptians.'[32]

Tamburlaine's material blackness

Tamburlaine's racialization also takes the form of rhetorical and material blackening. In the Messenger's description of Tamburlaine's military colours, he says that Tamburlaine goes from 'spangled white' to 'red as scarlet' in attempt to dissuade his opponent into 'submission'. While these colours are described through affective language, as white represents the 'mildness' of his mind and red his 'kindled wrath', they also mimic Petrarchan beauty standards for women, in which the Petrarchan beloved is described as having fair skin with red cheeks.[33] These colours are quickly succeeded by Tamburlaine's black, imagined as a type of contagion on the previous white and red colours. This invasion of blackness mirrors a type of humoral infection as well, with black symbolizing bile caused by melancholia, which can change supposedly healthy white and red complexions.[34]

In reply to Tamburlaine's transformative blackness, the Soldan describes Capolin as the 'fair Arabian king' (*Part I*, 4.1.68), setting up a rhetorical juxtaposition between the two sovereigns based on European racial hierarchies that privilege 'fairness'. This metaphorical blackness is seen as an invasive element, mimicking not only Tamburlaine's conquest trajectory, but also early modern anxieties of 'swarming' non-white groups, who were discussed through plague-like imageries. The sentiment that Tamburlaine's blackness has an infectious quality is again repeated by the Governor of Damascus later in the play, in which he states, 'His coal-black colours everywhere advanced' (*Part I*, 5.1.9). This notion of invasive blackness was not limited to threats of military conquest, but also anxieties of miscegenation, particularly of black men with white women.[35] If Zenocrate represents the pinnacle of white womanhood in the play (despite actually being non-European), Tamburlaine's blackness, even if a rhetorical or material construction, implies a potential for audiences to read him as racially hypermasculine. Likewise, while the white, and even the red, that preceded Tamburlaine's black were seen as dormant colours, black is the colour of Tamburlaine's mobilized empire. It is imagined as 'advancing' on the geopolitical boundaries that Tamburlaine's military invades. Similarly, this anxiety of invasive blackness mirrors early modern English qualms revolving around both the threat of non-white groups entering England's borders (like the 'Blackamoors' or 'Gypsies') and the looming presence of the Ottoman empire.

Tamburlaine explicitly associates himself with black materials, adopting his enemy's rhetoric about his colour-coded campaign:

But if he stay until the bloody flag
Be once advanced on my vermilion tent,
He dies, and those that kept us out so long.
And when they see me march in black array,
With mournful streamers hanging down their heads,
Were in that city all the world contained,
Not one should 'scape, but perish by our swords.

(*Part I*, 4.2.116–22)

Here, Tamburlaine echoes the ominous words of the Messenger, using this association of military affect and colours to threaten his enemies. Tamburlaine's blackness is not just in direct relation to his military colours, but also a part of his mourning garb. Near the end of *Part I*, Tamburlaine enters '*all in black, and very melancholy*' (5.2.0), a disposition similar to Hamlet's correlation between clothing and affect. While an early modern audience would associate black clothing with the traditional garb of mourning (as in the case of *Hamlet*), black cloth was also used in place of (or with) cosmetics to transform white actors into black characters. In his ground-breaking article, 'Othello's Black Handkerchief', Ian Smith argues that though some early modern scholars have asserted the power of cultural materials to affirm and constitute subjects,

> in the theatre of racial cross-dressing, claiming that the materials of staging confer meaning takes on a radically perverse sense ... The prosthetic black cloth covers and masks the body beneath; its primary function is to materialize the imagined and absent real black subject and to give it meaning. Black cloth's primary meaning does not reside in its constitutive relation to the actor's body as clothing, but in the representational and semantic space of the theatre, it is a body – a material or textile body.[36]

That is, black cloth not only signified racial difference in the early modern imagination, but was used, in addition or instead of the technologies of cosmetics, to transform a white actor into a black character. Despite Tamburlaine's complexion being 'pale', the use of black clothing and other material has the possibility to transform him, for the characters interacting with Tamburlaine and for the audience, into a racially black character. Tamburlaine's black clothing, then, functions as what Alexander Weheliye would call a 'racializing assemblage'. That is, the black cloth, specifically in *Tamburlaine* and largely on the early modern stage, is a material marker, like flesh, of racialization.

Of course, a racialized Tamburlaine is not limited to the early modern stage. A 2014–15 production of *Tamburlaine The Great* at Theatre for a New Audience, directed by Michael Boyd, featured a cast predominantly of colour, starring black American actor John Douglas Thompson as Tamburlaine. While this production clearly uses a black man to play the titular role, negating the textual evidence for a pale, Scythian Tamburlaine, Zenocrate was kept 'fair' through the performance of white actress Merritt Janson. In 2018, Michael Boyd brought his production of *Tamburlaine The Great* to the Royal Shakespeare Company, this time casting black British actor Jude Owusu as Tamburlaine.

The Royal Shakespeare Company has produced other performances of *Tamburlaine The Great*. In 1992, popular Shakespearean actor Antony Sher played the title role.[37] Although Sher is not a person of colour, the production played up his Jewish ethnic heritage and further exoticized his stage presence through the use of vaguely eastern costume. Notably, in stills of the production, Sher is often photographed wearing black cosmetic paint rubbed across his cheeks, forehead, nose, and neck. While ambiguous whether this choice was informed by practices of theatrical blackface, the stills conjure the text's use of black materialities to further racialize Sher's performance.[38] Like the Tamburlaine of Marlowe's text using black banners and clothing to signify his racialized conquest, the use of black cosmetics to mark Tamburlaine's face in this production reflects on the complexity of racialization, and how paint and inkiness can be signals for an audience to read Tamburlaine's body as 'Other'.[39]

Analysing early modern texts like *Tamburlaine* becomes particularly important to the growing field of early modern race studies when we consider that race, as a product of racism, does not begin or end with physiological differences. This sentiment does not diminish the fact that notions about racial difference often centre on the marked body, the visibly brown and black body, but this articulation does account for the fact that even language around physiological difference contains notions of difference that go beyond the body, and seep into ideologies about language, occupation, place of origin, culture, and clothing. *Tamburlaine*, with the emphasis on these non-physiological differences and how they may materially manifest, conveys a type of early modern race-making that cannot be chalked up to ignorant reactions to encountering people of colour, or the pre-existing humoral model. These representations reveal a more conscious formation of racial difference used to construct notions of civility and nationalism during the inception of England's colonial projects.

7

New Directions: Retooling Timür

Matthew Dimmock

It is surprising how little interest scholars of Christopher Marlowe's remarkable *Tamburlaine* plays (1587–8) seem to take in the plays' historical model, Amir Timür Gurgan (1336–1405). Potential sources have been exhaustively identified, of course, and Marlowe's transformation of them scrutinized, but these approaches tend toward the assumptions embedded in Frederick Boas's characterization of Timür (in 1940) as 'so exotic a subject'.[1] Two years earlier, John Bakeless had benignly encouraged his readers in the same direction with the affirmation that 'one may have a very interesting time tracing down all the strange avenues along which news of the far-off Asiatic warrior reached the young English university scholar in Cambridge or London'.[2] Timür is distanced and made strange, blurred into the 'first heir' of Marlowe's invention, and thereby becomes a creature of the London playhouses rather than a historical actor and vital cultural presence in his own right.[3]

In a move familiar from reams of Marlovian criticism Timür, in becoming Tamburlaine, somehow becomes Marlowe in an apotheosistic coupling that enables the initial flourishing of the playwright's genius. For Una Ellis-Fermor, Marlowe found 'in the half-obliterated records' of Timür's aspiration 'an echo of his own, as yet untried and untested. Mind rushes to mind and the inevitable union is achieved across the barrier of years and race'.[4] The notion that a generative cultural charge might be sparked through a 'strange' identification is a valuable one for thinking about Tamburlaine's particular affect and his profound impact on late sixteenth-century English audiences, something extensively charted in recent scholarship.[5] However the nature of Marlowe's own identification with his protagonist is, in the terms used by Ellis-Fermor and others, more destructive, for it always seems to entail the total absorption (if not erasure) of Timür.

Boas, Bakeless, and Ellis-Fermor all approached the *Tamburlaine* plays from an early twentieth-century, late British-imperial context that in a Saidian sense required earlier histories of non-European conquest to be ruined, half-obliterated, largely marooned in an Asian barbarism populated by 'half-tame Tartars'.[6] Yet for them, Marlowe's originality could only go so far: in seeking heroism beyond the limits of Christendom and classical civilization, he apparently sought out a known, established type – specifically a kind of Alexander, Caesar or Cyrus.[7] In these terms, Marlowe's working method becomes a type of proto-imperial archaeology, digging through obscure tracts, seeking out historical *übermenschen* and refiguring them in established forms for the use and glory of the nascent empire.[8] Any innovation was necessarily sparked by a 'remote character', someone 'looming up vaguely in the mist of Eastern history', necessarily distant, exotic, and unfamiliar, ready to be resuscitated by Marlowe's genius.[9]

Although there have been notable attempts to challenge this paradigm, either by reframing the two plays as 'one of the boldest experiments in world literature' or by reconsidering the implications of their cultural, religious, and geographical coordinates, elements of it continue to linger in the assumptions of some contemporary scholarship.[10] What inspired Marlowe to choose Timür, and the reasoning behind his transformation of the narrative of Timür in his sources, remains a matter that requires scholarly attention. Twentieth-century tendencies to either sidestep the question entirely or erroneously argue that the appeal lay in Timür's 'lostness' and obscurity now seem unsatisfactory. Through turning some of these underlying assumptions inside out, recognizing Timür's prominence in a wider late sixteenth-century world, and rethinking the established dynamics of Marlowe's relationship with his sources, new possibilities emerge. In this chapter I ask: what do these plays look like if, rather than us imagining a Tamburlaine lifted out of obscurity by Marlowe to become a short-lived English phenomenon, we instead consider Marlowe being lifted out of obscurity by the long-established Eurasian phenomenon that was Timür?[11]

Timürid legacies

Timür was certainly a phenomenon. Born into a minor Barlas Turkic family in Samarkand in 1336 and a milieu that remained dominated by the legacy of the Mongol warlord Chinggis Khan (who had died in 1227), Timür rose to power in Transoxiana before leading long campaigns to conquer Persia (1383–93) involving the brutal destruction of Herat; and against the Golden Horde (1385–95).[12] Later he would move eastward to devastate the Tughlaq Delhi Sultanate (1398), in a campaign that resulted in the sacking of Delhi, 'at that time one of the richest and most powerful cities in the world'; and then westward, conquering Armenia, Georgia and Syria (in 1400), razing Aleppo and Damascus in the process.[13] He then turned to besiege and ultimately destroy Baghdad (1401), before sweeping across Anatolia after the defeat of the Ottoman army under Bayezid I (Marlowe's Bajazeth) at the Battle of Ankara in 1402 (this is the point where Marlowe's first part ends). Following a peripatetic life of military campaigning that is notable for a sequence of ostentatious massacres – a warning to all those who would rebel against or defy him – Timür died at the start of a campaign to conquer Ming China, in 1405.

Unlike his Marlovian manifestation, who relentlessly craves 'the ripest fruit of all, / That perfect bliss and sole felicity, / The sweet fruition of an earthly crown' (*Part I*, 2.7.27–9) and is finally crowned 'Emperor of the earth' (*Part I*, 5.2.11), Timür never took a crown and retained the title Amir (general) throughout his life.[14] Although he married into the illustrious line, Timür was not of the blood of Chinggis and therefore chose to govern through a sequence of Chinggisid puppet kings in accordance with the dominant Chinggisid *yasa* code. Nevertheless, Timür's expanding realm came at a time of change for the Mongol state, as Asfar Moin has insightfully demonstrated. The nomadic existence that had defined Mongol culture for generations was being gradually supplanted by 'a pattern of seminomadic, Persian, and Muslim life'.[15] A tension between the two existed throughout – and to some extent defined – Timür's rise and supremacy (it is there in Marlowe's appropriation of the narrative too). This tension generated a peculiarly messianic, millenarian role for Timür: that of *Sahib Quiran*, or Lord of Conjunction. A sacred category of sovereignty that crucially resonated with 'Muslims and non-Muslims alike', the notion of *Sahib Quiran* emerged from a rich astrological culture, but was inflected with elements of Sufi sainthood to present a transcendent, universalist model – a new type of preordained, divinely sanctioned 'world conqueror'. The dominance and potency of Chinggisid precedent meant that Timür was unable to openly acknowledge this status in his lifetime (despite his repeated association with the role by others), but it was much elaborated by his successors in a hagiographical refiguring of the conqueror that rapidly erased the memory of the Chinggisid puppet monarchs in whose name he had ruled, and enhanced his Islamic associations. In this way a distinctly Timürid model of authority displaced the earlier Mongol models. This process began almost immediately on Timür's death: his son Shahrukh publicly signalled the shift by declaring 'the supremacy of the Islamic *shari'a* over the Mongol *yasa*'. He then proceeded to abandon 'the practice of taking Chinggisid brides for his sons, and together with his sons patronized the production of official histories that elided many references to Mongol practices in Timur's time'.[16]

It is this new Timürid idea of sovereignty that had such a profound effect on the subsequent political history of 'west Asia, the Ottoman Empire, Iran, North India, and Central Asia' as well as (in part at least) China.[17] As an idea it certainly intoxicated Marlowe, and these epoch-defining transformations and their import leap from the pages of his potential sources, whether in George Whetstone's *The English Mirror* (1586, taken from Pedro Mexia's *Sila de Varia Lección* of 1542) or Petrus Perondinus's *Magni Tamerlanis Scytharum Imperatoris Vita* (1553). In each of these books Timür's acts and paradigm-shifting legacy are transmuted into the mould of a medieval *vita*, as they report, awestruck, the scale of armies assembled, territories conquered, and the unnerving, acetic quality of Tamerlane's commitment to violence and disdain for mercy or worldly goods.[18] As in the near-ubiquitous early modern English narratives of the life of the Prophet Muhammad, 'strange' agents of political, cultural or theological change seem to appear as if from nowhere: from poverty and illiteracy in the case of 'Mahomet', from landless criminality in the case of Tamerlane.[19] It is from this lowly position that they rise to challenge and overturn moribund and immoral dynastic regimes (reflecting perhaps the Christological origins of the biographical model). For Marlowe's sources this is a means of identifying either the arbitrary mechanisms of Fate or of fashioning Tamerlane as a brutally effective instrument of a Christian god; in the plays this becomes a means for Tamburlaine to discover 'his unique role in history'.[20]

Of greater importance for an understanding of the relevance of Timür's life for the sixteenth-century contexts in which Marlowe lived and wrote is its vivid afterlife. Any informed early modern English sense of Islam and those Islamic states ranging from the Ottoman Empire through Safavid Persia eastward to the Mughal Empire in India – each prominently represented in the *Tamburlaine* plays – was necessarily shaped by Timūr's legacy. Both the Safavid and Mughal dynasties were founded by monarchs who lived and flourished 'under the shadow of Timur': Shah Isma'il I (1487–1524) and Mirza Babur (1483–1530).[21] In response to complex circumstances, new religious movements, and a Timūrid synthesis of kingship and saintliness, these two ostensibly different figures found unlikely common sovereign ground: as Moin notes, 'Babur, the heir of Timur, became a devotee of Ali. Shah Isma'il, a son of Ali, became another Timur'.[22] In the sixteenth century their successors continued to elaborate the Timūrid inheritance, as the Ottoman Sultan Süleyman I (1494–1566) simultaneously began to characterize himself as world conqueror and Lord of Conjunction in a paradoxical assumption of the title of a man who had routed the Ottoman forces at the Battle of Ankara (1402) and humiliated his ancestor Bayezid I (1389–1403).[23] That Timurid inheritance later found very different expressions in the postures adopted by Mughal Emperor Jalal al-Din Muhammad Akbar (1542–1605) – who modelled his own chronicle, the *Akbarnama*, after Timūr's *Zafarnama* (Book of Victory) – and the Safavid Shah 'Abbas I (1571–1629), although both incorporated the universalist, messianic millenarian strain bequeathed by the original Lord of Conjunction, an element that only gained in prominence with the fervent anticipation of the millennial Islamic year 1000 AH (1591/2 CE).[24]

For Marlowe and his contemporaries, then, Timūr's was a living legacy, active in the world he sought to represent. It is through a rich and innovative anachronism that this legacy feeds into the drama: cannons can roar across pre-artillery battlefields; mid-fifteenth-century Persian dynastic struggles and late sixteenth-century Ottoman–Persian conflicts can be layered onto late fourteenth-/early fifteenth-century Timūrid campaigns; Achaemenid Persia can intrude on Safavid; and Tamburlaine can erroneously claim a sixteenth-century Portuguese dominion, from 'the Indian continent / Even from Persepolis to Mexico' (*Part I*, 3.3.254–5).[25] Marlowe clearly indicates an awareness of

Timür's direct inheritance by moving beyond his sources to incorporate the figure of Usumcasane (sometimes just Casane) into the action. Mexia (in Fortescue's translation) identifies this 'Usancasan' as a direct descendant of Tamburlaine and an opponent of the Ottomans, asserting that 'the Heirs of this Usancasam ... advanced themselves to the honour and name of the first Sophy [Shah], whence now is derived the empire of Sophy [Persia], which liveth this day as sworn enemy of the Turk'.[26]

In Whetstone's version of the same narrative, 'Usuncasan' and his successors carry on Tamburlaine's 'mortall wars against the great Turk' to the 'great benefit of all christendom'.[27] Abid Masood has identified at least seven instances of Usuncasan in English texts that repeat the same spelling (or close versions of it) as that used by Fortescue or Whetstone, but only one that accords with Marlowe's Usumcasane: another potential source, John Foxe's *Acts and Monuments* (1583 edition).[28] For Foxe this 'Vsumcassanes' was an implacable enemy of Ottoman Sultan Mehmed II (the famed conqueror of Constantinople), whom he twice defeated in battle. Once again this historical successor to Timür is defined by his Persian identity, and through that as a foil to the Ottomans: an ideal, time-travelling companion for Tamburlaine, the reliever of Constantinople, who initially asserts that his destiny is 'the possession of the Persian crown' (*Part I*, 1.2.91), and once that has been achieved he repeatedly identifies himself as 'the King of Persia' (*Part I*, 3.3.132) and his followers as 'Persians' (*Part I*, 3.3.165).[29]

If nothing else, Marlowe's interpolation of Usumcasane into both parts of *Tamburlaine* indicates that he was fully aware of the dynastic connections that linked his protagonist to the contemporary ruler of Persia, Shah 'Abbas, and therefore understood, at least in part, the efficacy of Timür in his present. It might suggest something more. A devotee from the very start, Usumcasane plays a role in all of Tamburlaine's campaigns, and his occasional speeches are notable for their concern with the future, with fame, and with legacy. First, he has a vision of things to come in which:

> . . . kings shall crouch unto our conquering swords
> And hosts of soldiers stand amazed at us,
> When with their fearful tongues they shall confess
> These are the men that all the world admires
>
> (*Part I*, 1.2.220–3)

Later he imagines that to become a king will be 'half to be a god' (*Part I*, 2.5.56), and at the plays' conclusion he reflects that if Tamburlaine were to die, the glory of heaven 'is disgraced, / Earth droops and says that hell in heaven is placed' (*Part II*, 5.3.40–1). He also plays a small but conspicuous part in the brutal sacking and slaughter that takes places as Tamburlaine destroys the apocalyptically resonant city of Babylon, when this implacable opponent of the Ottomans hands over the 'Turkish Alcoran' (*Part II*, 5.1.171) and accompanying superstitious books for the fire in Tamburlaine's final hubristic set-piece.[30] Enlisting Usumcasane in this fashion offers Marlowe a measure of Persian authenticity, but it also enables him to lay conflict over conflict and individual onto individual, drawing out a defining, multi-generational anti-Ottomanism, hinting at the continuous resurfacing of the past in the present, reminding his audience of Tamburlaine's contemporaneity.

The plays achieve the same kind of effect more bluntly through the invocation of place. Marlowe's potential sources broadly concur on the nature and extent of Timür's conquests: for Mexia and his derivatives these begin with Persia and extend through Syria, Armenia, Babylon, Mesopotamia, Scythia, Asiatica, Albania, Media, and Egypt.[31] For Perondinus, Persia is followed by the defeat of 'the Hyrcans, the Margians, the Amazons, the Bactrians, the Sogdians, the Sacae' and the Tartars, with Timür ultimately subduing 'all the peoples between the Pamir Mountains, the Red Sea, the Caspian and the [Indian] Ocean'.[32] For both writers Persia is the first, scene-setting move in a long and wide-ranging campaign, invoked primarily in order to explain the conquest and slaughter that followed. Only the brief account in Baptista Fulgosius's *De dictis factisque memorabilis collectanea* (1509) identifies Tamerlane as 'King of the Persians' (Perondinus characterizes him and his army as Tartars), as Marlowe consistently does, suggesting that for Marlowe the Persian context was crucially important.

Even more curious is the anachronistic prominence that Marlowe accords India, a location that does not feature at all in Mexia or Perondinus. It is initially, in Jonathan Gil Harris's words, 'a metonymy for untold wealth' but it becomes something more, a means for Tamburlaine to articulate the scale of his ambition and the provocative combination of desire and disdain he feels for the world. The 'Indian continent' (*Part I*, 3.3.254) is where his newly imperial reach will stretch from; his meanest soldier is, however, worth more than 'all the gold in India's wealthy arms' (*Part I*, 1.2.85); and he plans to gouge a channel between Alexandria and the Red Sea to short-circuit the established late sixteenth-century trade routes eastward, and enable men to 'quickly sail to India' (*Part II*, 5.3.135). Tamburlaine is forging a new world in which the complex, partly mythic and above all crowded political landscape of medieval Eurasia is erased, wiped clean in favour of a different, early modern dispensation. Marlowe's audience watched as a world they recognized, dominated by considerable universalist Muslim empires – the Ottomans, the Safavids, the Mughals – all vying for Timür's legacy, came into being.

Worldly riches

Folding Timür's political, military, cultural and sovereign legacies back into a version of his life offered an innovative way to capture the scale of the transformations he wrought and their strongly millenarian flavour. Thus the cult of personality that had already flourished around Timür in Asian contexts was reborn, even reinvented, in sixteenth-century England as a relevant and potent force.[33] Another element that these Timurid campaigns accelerated and expanded was trade, and Marlowe seizes upon the few and often contradictory references to the exchange of goods and amassing of booty in his sources to create a version of Timür much more attuned to the 'acquisitive energies' of late sixteenth-century London, a city that was rapidly becoming, in Joan Thirsk's words, 'a glittering center for consumer goods'.[34] In this he departs from precedent to offer a markedly different Timür, adapting and refashioning his protagonist in order that he can master a different kind of world.

Others have noted the material preoccupations of these plays and their protagonist. Thomas Healy has written of Marlowe's 'inflationary vision, building in its accumulating images, its lists of exotic places or gems, a picture of excess which combines space and wealth', a perspective at odds with Stephen Greenblatt's famous celebration of Tamburlaine's vacant stage and its insistence on 'the essential meaninglessness of theatrical space'.[35] 'To rule', in Healy's take on Tamburlaine, 'is to possess abundance'; Marlowe's plays are, in this reading, an exploration of 'the possibilities generated by abundance', a 'vision of plenitude in commodity and space' that the dramatist shares with the commercially oriented catalogue of English travels compiled by Richard Hakluyt in his near contemporary *Principal Navigations* (1589).[36] Earlier, Malcolm Kelsall had identified 'the substratum of mercantilistic opportunism' in these plays but he argued that it is Bajazeth, not Tamburlaine, who functions as the emblem of all worldly power and wealth, to be scourged in defeat at the Battle of Ankara. He also saw a profound difference between the presentation of material wealth in the *Tamburlaine* plays and *The Jew of Malta*; a difference that lay chiefly in the way Barabas's wealth was intended to be antagonistic and satirical.[37] Michel Poirier recognized the 'amazing exuberance' of the two parts of *Tamburlaine*: 'gold, silver and precious stones are lavished everywhere' he wrote, 'in the descriptions and the imagery'. Poirier intriguingly suggested that it was this new focus on materiality that pushed Marlowe to 'utter strains hitherto unheard on the English stage'. Indeed, for Poirier it was the very presence of such worldly abundance that enabled Marlowe 'to conjure up the barbaric East in all its splendour'.[38]

Poirier's sense of the 'East' as barbarous because of its material excesses, or that an 'Eastern' barbarism is somehow typified by material excess, is again characteristic of a later 'high' Orientalist mode, one that seems misplaced when applied to Marlowe's depiction of Timurid, Ottoman and pre-Safavid Persian empires in the two parts of *Tamburlaine*. There is of course excess – as Healy notes – but rather than signalling barbarism it perhaps indicates its opposite, particularly when considering the carefully delineated nature of these goods and Tamburlaine's own deliberate assumption of them. These are not random catalogues of 'eastern riches' but are designed to resonate in particular ways. Marlowe's probable sources for the two parts of *Tamburlaine* are very different in this regard: most emphasize Tamburlaine's meagre beginnings and a consequent lifelong frugality and humility. This is a man whose fame and command result from a commitment to dispense all spoils amongst his soldiers. What goods and treasures he does accumulate are presented as an unsought and natural consequence of conquest, so Mexia's account (in Fortescue's translation) records that 'having conquered so many countries, subdued and done to death sundry kings and princes', Tamburlaine

> returned home again into his country, charged with *infinite* heaps of gold and treasure, accompanied also with the most honourable estates of all the countries subdued by him, which brought with them in like manner the greatest part also of their wealth and substance, where he did to be built a most famous and goodly city and to be inhabited of those, as we foresaid, that he brought with him, which all together no less honourable than rich, in very short time with the help of Tamburlaine, framed the most beautiful and most sumptuous city in the world ... [my emphasis].[39]

Perondinus (echoing almost exactly Paulo Giovio writing a few years before) also focused on the founding of Samarkand, Timür's capital, recording 'the trophies, the plunder and the immense booty taken from his enemies with which he endowed it', treasure won especially in his conquest of Persia, a land 'packed thick with the flourishingly wealthy treasuries of kings'.[40] Again and again Tamburlaine is depicted 'loaded down' with largely unwanted 'plunder and glory'.[41] Only Cambinus, in the 1562 Shute translation, offers a different narrative: his Tamburlaine is driven by worldly desires, severely punishing theft 'to the end that he alone might rob and spoil according to his own desire the whole world'.[42] Notice the characteristic lack of detail in these accounts concerning the nature of the treasure: Tamburlaine's spoils are 'immense', his treasure 'infinite', which is perhaps not surprising in such accounts, but does reaffirm the effort Marlowe went to in order to flesh out the material dimensions of his two-part epic.

To do so Marlowe drew on a relatively restrained palette of materials that he could dependably associate with India, the Ottoman Empire, or the domains of the 'great Cham' further east (whose gifts Zenocrate carries when she is captured by Tamburlaine). He also chooses goods whose value he can realistically assert as universal, at least across the 'Old Worlds' of Afro-Eurasia. So gold – which for Marlowe was *the* global currency, sought after from London to Aleppo to Baghdad to Samarkand – features heavily, particularly in his imagining of Persia, whose soldiers are memorably described as wearing 'pluméd helms ... wrought with beaten gold, / Their swords enameled, and about their necks / Hangs massy chains of gold down to the waist' (1.2.124–6). And gold was a key element of the actual exchanges between England and North Africa, as well as the Ottoman court: there is perhaps an echo of these 'massy chains' in the gift of a 'chain of gold' weighing fourteen and a quarter ounces the English Queen Elizabeth I sent to Mulay Ahmad Al-Mansur, the King of Morocco in 1589.[43] The prominence of gold in the *Tamburlaine* plays and the vision they engendered is later ironized in imaginings of distant worlds such as Seagull's depiction of Virginia in Act 3, Scene 3 of *Eastward Ho!*:

Why man, all their dripping pans and their chamber pots are pure gold; and all the chains with which they chain up their streets are massy gold; all the prisoners they take are fettered in gold; and for rubies and diamonds, they go forth on holidays and gather 'em by the seashore to hang on their children's coats, and stick in their caps.

(3.3.25–31)[44]

In this play, and in the two parts of *Tamburlaine*, such hyperbolic references contain an implicit acknowledgement of the fundamental shifts underway in the global market in commodity metals. Marlowe's repeated references to 'Indian gold' and the 'Indian mines' as well as to the 'gold of rich America' and 'armadoes from Spain' reflect not an actual glut of gold but instead the 'massive influx of silver' that transformed the global economy from the 1540s onwards, beginning first in Germany, then Japan, and then the New World, the engine throughout being the huge demand for silver in Ming China. This was the celebrated 'silver cycle' that came to generate and underpin all international early modern wealth and commodity exchanges.[45] From this perspective much of the material world of the *Tamburlaine* plays is the product of a slowly clarifying awareness of such developments in late sixteenth-century England, an awareness and an accompanying set of anxieties that are here displaced onto a nostalgic preoccupation with gold.

After gold, the next most frequently mentioned material commodity is precious stones; both wrought jewellery and unwrought raw materials. They are often undifferentiated, but diamonds, sapphires and rubies – all associated in Richard Eden's translation and augmentation of Pietro Martire d'Anghiera's *Decades of the new worlde* (1555) with the oriental 'Indias' – are specified.[46] Then there are fabrics: silks of crimson, silks of Media, silken reins; costly cloths, cloths of gold, cloths of Damascus; and pearls (a category all by themselves): orient pearl, crowns of pearl, rocks of pearl. Less frequently appearing, but nevertheless valued trading goods associated with non-Christian locales, are items like ivory, camels, or pure-bred Barbarian and Scythian steeds. Sometimes Marlowe combines different elements of this list in sumptuous imaginary assemblages specifically designed to celebrate worldly power. They feature repeatedly in *Part II*: for instance, Callapine's dream of a 'golden canopy enchased with precious stones' (*Part II*, 1.2.48–9), or Tamburlaine's detailed appraisal of an imaginary enamelled chair of gold 'enchased with diamonds, sapphires, rubies, / And fairest pearl of worthy India' (*Part II*, 3.2.119–21), or the 'triple plume' he imagines wearing on his helm, 'spangled with diamonds, dancing in the air, / To note me Emperor of the threefold world' (*Part II*, 4.3.116–19) – are all attempts on Marlowe's part to realize a material iconography of universal power within the material constraints of the early modern stage.

Clothes are also an important visual element: the scarlet robes put on by the Soldan of Egypt in Part I (5.1.524), for instance, as well as the crimson robes worn by Tamburlaine before the siege of Damascus (*Part I*, 4.4) or the references to bassoes clad in 'crimson silk' (*Part II*, 1.2.46) are all examples of the most difficult colour to vividly achieve in the period, a colour which also features prominently in courtly gifts to Elizabeth I.[47] Crimson was made, as Jane Schneider has detailed, from a dye that was produced by grinding, fermenting and boiling 'wood that was Asian in origin ... imported into Europe by Venetian merchants from the old ports of Gujarat, Ceylon and the East Indies [and later from Brazil]'.[48] So even the 'breeches of crimson velvet' recorded in the diary of the theatrical impresario and cloth dyer Philip Henslowe signalled distant worlds and international trading networks.[49] The prominence of crimson is just one example, but this element can only have been magnified in performance, for Marlowe's crowded stage must have been, in Jean MacIntyre's words, a riot of 'rich and colourful garb'.[50]

Some of the material goods incorporated by Marlowe into the *Tamburlaine* plays, whilst invariably co-opted into this accumulative iconography of imperial power, might well have had a more immediate resonance for his first audiences. In the documents that accompanied the establishment of amity between Elizabethan England and the Ottoman Empire in 1580 are a number – including memoranda written by Francis Walsingham and William Cecil, Lord Burghley – that reflect upon the material advantages for England of such an association. Amongst other items, the import of fabrics is identified as highly desirable with silk, both 'unwrought and wrought' and Ottoman carpets prominent, alongside 'all spyces' and 'all sortes of Drugges'.[51] Similarly prominent in the English analysis of the material elements of the Levant trade, and again much desired, are 'all sortes of Iuells [jewels]' and 'Corrall' which is described as 'estemed above Gold'.[52] Silks and jewels, as mentioned above, appear prominently in the *Tamburlaine* plays, and their presence in 1580s England as a product of the 'Turkey trade' makes them yet more concrete and immediate, not imaginary trifles indiscriminately littering a 'barbaric East' as Poirier and others have implied. Marlowe also makes reference to drugs and antidotes, to 'Turkey carpets', and coral is one of the ingredients that Tamburlaine imagines his soldiers drinking, mixed with 'liquid gold' and 'orient pearl' after their conquests are done (*Part II*, 1.6.96–7). Coral is a particularly noteworthy inclusion, because it features as one of the defining elements of the 'Turkey trade' when it begins to be critiqued by writers and dramatists within two years of its establishment.[53] In a way that suggests that the riotous colours and fashions of the Tamburlainean stage were not quite as 'other' as is sometimes imagined, the immediate impact of the Ottoman relationship was the wholesale bewitching of Londoners, who were apparently already susceptible to such goods.[54] This was the world into which Marlowe's *Tamburlaine* plays emerged, and their protagonist is accordingly programmed to seize and accumulate across regions already defined for English audiences by material desires.

Conclusion: Revisiting Thomas Roe's Mughal confusion

When, on his first embassy to the Indian Mughal court in the city of Ajmer in 1616, Sir Thomas Roe was presented with a robe of honour by Emperor Jahangir's son Prince Khurram (the future Shah Jahan), he interpreted this celebrated episode in terms of his memory of Marlowe's Tamburlaine. Late in the evening he had been visited by a party sent from the prince that consisted of 'an Eunuch and diuers of his Captaynes' who bustled him out of his lodgings with the promise of 'a great Present... and made such a busines as if I should haue receiued his best Chayne of Pearle'.[55] His high expectations of favour were not met in the way he had anticipated, however. On arriving at the court,

> By and by came out a Cloth of gould Cloake of his owne, once or twice worne, which hee Caused to bee putt on my back, and I made reuerence, very vnwillingly. When his Ancestor Tamerlane was represented at the Theatre the Garment would well haue become the Actor: but it is here reputed the highest fauour to giue a garment warne by the Prince, or, beeing New, once layd on his shoulder.[56]

When confronted by this curious ritual, and its central material element, Roe turns to *Tamburlaine*, and to his knowledge of Timürid legacies. Jahangir had crafted an elaborate imperial image as a Timürid millennial being and upon his own accession, his son would style himself 'as the Second Lord of Conjunction, openly embracing his millennial legacy and asserting his oneness with Timur'.[57] This ongoing, mutating cult of personality was profoundly important for the Mughal court, and Roe's uneasy acknowledgement of its presence in distant and peripheral England is a further indication of its potency and the connections it enables. Of course Roe is not all admiration: he is deeply suspicious of this *khil'at* ritual and the general theatricality of Mughal elite culture, suspicions he voices at various points elsewhere in his journal.[58] Such theatricality easily shades into conspicuous artifice, even idolatry, and inevitably undermines – for the Anglican Roe at least – the nature of imperial power.

Between the great chain of pearls that Roe anticipated and the second-hand cloak that he received is a gulf which may reveal something of his experience of *Tamburlaine*. Roe probably saw and may have read *Part I* at least, and it seems to have had quite an impact on him, for he quotes from it elsewhere in his correspondence.[59] Both plays feature pearls in abundance, as already noted, and they are invariably more than just emblems of wealth and power that were easily translatable across cultures. The pearl was, in Marcia Pointon's words, a 'synecdoche for the whole of the East'.[60] Marlowe depicts the crowns Tamburlaine disburses to his followers 'enchased with pearl and gold' (*Part I*, 2.5.60), victorious soldiers 'sweat / With carrying pearl and treasure on their backs' (*Part II*, 3.5.166–7), and he is compared to a great pearl (*Part I*, 2.1.12). This was a 'common language' that Roe readily understood.[61]

In contrast, the *khil'at* exchange, in which ceremonial robes were given by potentates as marks of special favour, was more culturally specific and thus more opaque to Roe's English eye. Nevertheless it does appear obliquely in *Tamburlaine*, and in materially similar forms. It is invariably associated with types of conquest: Tamburlaine imagines himself 'clothed with the massy robe / That late adorned the Afric potentate' (*Part II*, 3.2.123–4), whilst Theridamas promises Olympia that he will clothe her 'in costly cloth of massy gold' (*Part II*, 4.2.40). Given these contexts, perhaps Roe's uneasiness is less surprising. He certainly seems to have been typical of Marlowe's early audiences in his fixation on the material foundations of power – the pearls – and this was something that he could easily assimilate in terms of his own experience and desires, with its emphasis on ownership over transaction and on the physical over the metaphorical. Although he routinely brandished his ambassadorial credentials, Roe's mission consisted primarily of securing privileged status for the East India Company factory at Surat: his desire for pearls was in keeping with that commercial role, but his expectation of pearls from an Indian prince had been primed by his experience of Marlowe's *Tamburlaine*.

Thomas Roe's uncertainty at the Mughal court in Ajmer when confronted with a gift from the illustrious Timür's ancestor usefully connects up the different strands of this chapter. Marlowe chose Timür as a subject not because he wanted to play 'a great game of chess with kings and conquerors for pieces' as Ethel Seaton memorably imagined in 1924, but because that particular biographical narrative enabled Marlowe to respond to, and engage with, a fundamentally changed world.[62] In Marlowe, the cult of personality that surrounded Timür found new purpose and resonance in a late sixteenth-century English context that fervently sought access to the stories, material goods, and culture of a newly accessible Asia. For all their brutality, the *Tamburlaine* plays suggest that when the late sixteenth-century English looked out at the non-Christian world they were not confronted by incommensurability, by an absolute failure of comprehension and communication.[63] Instead the 'amazing exuberance' of those plays can be seen to contribute to the ways the English actually and imaginatively integrated themselves into established narratives and iconography that made that wider world more knowable.

All this was of limited use to Roe, however. His knowledge of Tamburlaine and his legacies only gives him a partial understanding of what was expected of him in the Mughal court: he found the cloak of cloth of gold he was offered to be suspiciously theatrical in nature even as he recognized it as a key token of courtly exchange, but what unnerved Roe was less the object itself than the obligations and potential compromises its acceptance might entail. Marlowe may have brought Timür to the London stage and adorned him with the material elements of a wider world into which the English were actively emerging, but he could not physically take the English to Timür.

Whereas the silks, jewels, porcelains and carpets of India, China, and North Africa that arrived in the English capital in this period might be imagined shorn of all but the basic associations of wealth and power, when presented in person and in non-Christian courts they were inevitably imbued with a range of subtle transactions of which the English could only be dimly aware. Roe may have ruefully reflected that Marlowe's Tamburlaine had no need of such subtlety in his material dealings.

8

Three Tents for *Tamburlaine*: Resources and Approaches for Teaching the Play

Liam E. Semler

Teaching *Tamburlaine* is fun. What's not to like about a play that mischievously courts 'trigger warnings' in the twenty-first-century classroom? Marlowe is anything but safe. He is shocking and intelligent. His plays are poetically and theatrically innovative as well as conceptually brave and probing. He is an artist fully aware of his audience's hunger for spectacle and insight – and he delivers both by the chariot-load. A key element of the spectacle in *Tamburlaine, Part I* is Tamburlaine's military deployment of coloured tents, flags and clothes as part of his imperial style. Should a governor find his town besieged, Tamburlaine's 'tents of white now pitched before the gates' will signal the opportunity for amity and life for all therein through surrender (4.2.111–15).[1] 'But if he stay until the bloody flag / Be once advanced on my vermilion tent', says Tamburlaine ominously, '[h]e dies, and those that kept us out so long' (4.2.116–18). Yet even this is mercy, for 'when they see me march in black array', he intones apocalyptically, '[w]ere in that city all the world contained, / Not one should 'scape, but perish by our swords' (4.2.119–22). Such bravado would have little meaning if Tamburlaine did not always follow through on his words with machine-like execution. And so, he does. In the *Tamburlaine* plays his word is his bond and that bond is, incredibly, as steadfast as destiny.

Tamburlaine's tents are an ingenious expansion of his self because they broadcast his will – its absoluteness and power – on a grand scale. In what we might think of as a Marlovian reinterpretation of sumptuary law, Tamburlaine's will clothes earth and sky, dresses human allies and lieutenants as extensions of his psyche and thereby radically curtails his enemy's options. His enemies look out from their battlements and where once they saw their dominions spread before them, now all they see is the vivid will of Tamburlaine. White. Red. Black. Reality has been 'countermanded by a greater man' (1.2.22) and there is, in fact, no way out of the tunnel of his will. It is already too late.

The outlook may be grim for the besieged governor, but it's not all bad news for us. If the daunting task of teaching *Tamburlaine* to your students gives you chills, perhaps it is time to learn a few tricks of tent warfare from the Scythian master. First, let's remove to the White Tent for basic equipping with biographies, editions and sources. Then on to the Red Tent to hear tales of campaigners who have gone before you into the bloody classroom. After that, you must visit the Black Tent of execution to taste the keen edge of scholarly contention around the play. Finally, audacious and loquacious, you will take the field and conquer. Or die trying.

The White Tent: Equipping for the campaign

1. Biographies

We are spoilt for choice when it comes to modern, scholarly biographies of Marlowe. If you are seeking a concise and easily digestible biography accompanied by chapter-length analyses of all the plays including *Tamburlaine*, Tom Rutter's *Cambridge Introduction to Christopher Marlowe* (2012) is ideal. If you are settling in for a longer campaign, book-length biographies by Hopkins (2000), Kuriyama (2002), Riggs (2004) and Honan (2005) offer reliable and detailed accounts, each with different emphases. If a teacher of Marlowe were to read one or two of these works they would be well equipped with an overall understanding of Marlowe's life and numerous insights into how his writings engage with intellectual and cultural issues of his day.

If you desire more detail, it is easy to find because Marlowe's biography continues to fascinate scholars. One could read, for example, Hopkins's book-length *Chronology* (2005) of Marlowe and his works, which also includes annotated dates relating to his sources and the historical inspirations for his protagonists, including Timur the Lame. Hopkins's *Chronology* could be read in tandem with Knutson's more recent chapter, 'Marlowe in Repertory 1587–1593', in Melnikoff and Knutson's critical collection (noted in the Black Tent, below). The intrigues around Marlowe's spy work and death are tackled in Nicholl's *The Reckoning* (2002) and Kendall's *Christopher Marlowe and Richard Baines* (2003). An array of other approaches may be found in: Kozuka and Mulryne's collection of essays on biography, which includes a piece by Riggs linking *Tamburlaine* to Marlowe's life; Gurr's book on the Admiral's playing company, which references *Tamburlaine* frequently; and Wraight and Stern's old, yet well illustrated *Pictorial Biography*. It is safe to say that most modern collections of critical work on Marlowe include at least some essays investigating aspects of his biography (visit the Black Tent for a selection of critical collections). It is also safe to say, just in case you have heard to the contrary, that Marlowe died in 1593 and was an individual quite distinct from William Shakespeare who had a not undistinguished writing career of his own.

Gurr, Andrew, *Shakespeare's Opposites: The Admiral's Company 1594–1625* (Cambridge: Cambridge University Press, 2009).
Honan, Park, *Christopher Marlowe: Poet and Spy* (Oxford: Oxford University Press, 2005).
Hopkins, Lisa, *Christopher Marlowe: A Literary Life* (Houndmills: Palgrave Macmillan, 2000).
Hopkins, Lisa, *A Christopher Marlowe Chronology* (Houndmills: Palgrave Macmillan, 2005).
Kendall, Roy, *Christopher Marlowe and Richard Baines: Journeys through the Elizabethan Underground* (Madison, NJ: Fairleigh Dickinson University Press, 2003).
Kozuka, Takashi, and J. R. Mulryne (eds), *Shakespeare, Marlowe, Jonson: New Directions in Biography* (2006; rpt. New York: Routledge, 2016).
Kuriyama, Constance Brown, *Christopher Marlowe: A Renaissance Life* (Ithaca: Cornell University Press, 2002).
Nicholl, Charles, *The Reckoning: The Murder of Christopher Marlowe* (1992; rev. London: Vintage, 2002).
Riggs, David, *The World of Christopher Marlowe* (New York: Henry Holt and Company, 2004).
Rutter, Tom, *The Cambridge Introduction to Christopher Marlowe* (Cambridge: Cambridge University Press, 2012).
Wraight, A. D., and Virginia F. Stern, *In Search of Christopher Marlowe: A Pictorial Biography* (1965; rpt. Chichester: Adam Hart, 1993).

2. Editions

The enduring popularity of *Tamburlaine* has ensured that it is available in various inexpensive, modern editions. If you want to use a single-volume scholarly edition of both Parts of *Tamburlaine*, you could ask your students to obtain the New Mermaids edition by Dawson, the Broadview edition by Mathew R. Martin, or the Revels edition by Cunningham and Henson. While they are all user-friendly and prefaced by introductions, some teachers may find Martin's edition especially useful because, unlike the others, it has four appendices (totalling about sixty pages) containing early modern paratexts. These appendices include extracts from

Renaissance accounts of Tamburlaine's life, Tudor representations of Islam, literary intertexts such as Marlowe's 'Passionate Shepherd to his Love' and Thomas Nashe's *Christ's Tears over Jerusalem*, and texts relating to Marlowe's death and reputation including Thomas Kyd's 'Letters to Sir John Puckering' and Richard Baines's notorious Note. If you are keen for students to have a single-volume collection of Marlowe's plays so they can readily see comparison passages in context or simply read other brilliant examples from the canon such as *Doctor Faustus, The Jew of Malta* or *Edward II*, then Romany and Lindsey's *Complete Plays* (which I regularly teach from) or Bevington and Rasmussen's *Doctor Faustus and Other Plays* are worthwhile. Both contain *Tamburlaine, Parts I* and *II*.

Tamburlaine's demesne, as one might expect, reaches beyond the limits of hardcopy editions and into digital territory. The Folger Shakespeare Library's open-access Digital Anthology of Early Modern Drama provides an authoritative, searchable, original-spelling text of *Tamburlaine, Parts I* and *II* (1590) and all of the other plays by Marlowe. ProQuest's Early English Books Online (EEBO) holds digital facsimiles of many early copies of Marlowe's published plays and, thanks to the Text Creation Partnership, fully searchable, open-access transcriptions of Marlowe's plays including the 1590 publication of *Tamburlaine the Great* (which includes *Parts I* and *II*). The Boston Public Library's 1605 edition of *Tamburlaine, Part I* is freely available as a digital facsimile on Internet Archive.

Drama Online is a subscriber-only collection developed by Bloomsbury Publishing and Faber and Faber that includes *Tamburlaine* (in Dawson's edition of both Parts). It has a 'Play Tools' feature called 'Character Grid' which enables you to see all the scenes in which a character speaks and to produce printable texts of any specific character parts for teaching or performance purposes. So, for example, if I want to foreground female speech in the play, I could print out all Zenocrate's or Zabina's lines for students to explore in class; or I could ask students to select any character they like and do their own analysis of the way Marlowe has written the part. Students could conduct comparative analyses of different characters' parts, or of Tamburlaine's words in *Part I* versus his words in *Part II*, or use parts for blocking or acting out scenes.

Tamburlaine features in various open-access collections such as Renascence Editions, Project Gutenberg, Perseus Digital Library, Online Library of Liberty, Peter Lukacs's Elizabethan Drama, Anniina Jokinen's Luminarium and Peter Farey's Marlowe Page. These are useful editions, but most are based on much older, out-of-copyright, print editions and despite some being helpfully re-edited, annotated and introduced, should not be seen as replacements for the single-volume, hardcopy editions noted above. For some students, by choice or necessity, an audio experience of the texts is what they need to engage best with the play. Moreover, everybody can benefit from hearing at least some passages of the play read aloud because it brings out aural qualities that can easily remain hidden in silent reading. LibriVox has made freely available online readings of *Tamburlaine, Parts I* and *II*.

Bevington, David, and Eric Rasmussen (eds), *Doctor Faustus and Other Plays* (1995; rpt. Oxford: Oxford University Press, 2008).

Crane, Gregory R. (ed), Perseus Digital Library, Tufts University. http://www.perseus.tufts.edu/hopper/

Cunningham, J. S. and Eithne Henson (eds), *Tamburlaine the Great* (1981; rev. Manchester: Manchester University Press, 1999).

Dawson, Anthony B. (ed), *Tamburlaine, Parts One and Two* (1997; rpt. London: Bloomsbury, 2018).

Drama Online, Bloomsbury Publishing Plc and Faber and Faber Ltd, 2020. https://www.dramaonlinelibrary.com/

EEBO (Early English Books Online), Chadwyck-Healey and ProQuest LLC, 2020. https://search.proquest.com/eebo

EMED: A Digital Anthology of Early Modern English Drama, Folger Shakespeare Library, 2020. https://emed.folger.edu/

Farey, Peter (ed), Marlowe Page. http://www.rey.prestel.co.uk/

Internet Archive, *Tamburlaine the Greate*, 1605 (Boston Public Library). https://archive.org/details/tamburlainegreat1605marl

Jokinen, Anniina (ed), Luminarium. http://www.luminarium.org/
LibriVox: Free Public Domain Audiobooks. https://librivox.org/
Lukacs, Peter (ed), Elizabethan Drama. http://elizabethandrama.org/
Martin, Mathew R. (ed), *Tamburlaine the Great, Part One and Part Two* (Toronto: Broadview, 2014).
Online Library of Liberty. https://oll.libertyfund.org/
Project Gutenberg. http://www.gutenberg.org/
Renascence Editions. http://www.luminarium.org/renascence-editions/
Romany, Frank, and Robert Lindsey (eds), *The Complete Plays* (London: Penguin, 2003).

3. Sources

In addition to biographies and editions, the final piece of basic kit one needs is a choice of sources and related texts. I noted above that Martin's edition provides an array of intertexts relating specifically to *Tamburlaine*. More general documentary sources on Marlowe's life and death are reproduced in the biographical works by Honan, Kendall, Kuriyama and Wraight and Stern. The Baines Note and other related manuscripts are presented in facsimile, with transcription and explanation, on the British Library's 'Discovering Literature' webpages. The only comprehensive sourcebook on all Marlowe's plays is Thomas and Tydeman's excellent collection, which contains forty-two extracts from source texts with introductions and annotations. The sources are reproduced in modern spelling and foreign-language texts are translated into English. The section on *Tamburlaine the Great* includes 100 pages of extracts from sixteenth-century texts.

The 'milk-white tent' (*Part I*, 3.3.161) has served you royally, but to dwell here any longer in preparatory diversions might suggest you have a touch of the cowardly Calyphas about you. 'Fie, for shame, come forth!' (*Part II*, 4.1.31) and march with me to the tent of 'bloody colours' (*Part I*, 4.4.1) to search the wounds of those who've tasted battle.

Discovering Literature: Shakespeare and Renaissance Collection Items, The British Library. https://www.bl.uk/shakespeare/collection-items

Thomas, Vivien, and William Tydeman (eds), *Christopher Marlowe: The Plays and Their Sources* (1994; rpt. London: Routledge, 2011).

The Red Tent: Learning from those who went before

Let us ease into the Red Tent by acknowledging that there are innumerable books and articles addressing the teaching of early modern drama in general and Shakespeare in particular. Many of the insights and strategies they offer are transferrable to the teaching of Marlowe's plays. This is true, for example, of Gibson's *Teaching Shakespeare*, Stredder's *The North Face of Shakespeare*, Shand's *Teaching Shakespeare*, Banks' *Creative Shakespeare* and Thompson and Turchi's *Teaching Shakespeare with Purpose*, bearing in mind the dual caveat that not everything that works for Shakespeare works for Marlowe and that some of this material is targeted to secondary students and some to tertiary. But let's not over-invoke the 'S' word – it makes even seasoned Marlowe teachers jittery and we need all our nerve for the task in hand. If you have found this mention of Shakespeare upsetting, please consult the 'Resources' chapters of the Arden Early Modern Drama Guides to Marlowe's *Doctor Faustus*, *The Jew of Malta* and *Edward II* to get yourself back in a happy place.

Essay collections with broad or survey-style scope such as Conroy and Clarke's *Teaching the Early Modern Period*, Bamford and Leggatt's *Approaches to Teaching English Renaissance Drama* and Hackel and Moulton's *Teaching Early Modern English Literature from the Archives* have much to offer in terms of historical and literary context and awareness of current trends in teaching. The open-access journal *This Rough Magic* is a venue for scholarship and reviews relating to the teaching of medieval and early modern literature. It is peer-reviewed and searchable, but returns only a few hits on *Tamburlaine* including Pecan's article addressing genre and part of another discussing the use of *EEBO* in class.

Engle and Rasmussen's *Studying Shakespeare's Contemporaries,* and Hiscock and Hopkins's *Teaching Shakespeare and Early Modern Dramatists* are both highly readable and give attention to Marlowe. The latter book includes a chapter on Marlowe by Hopkins (pp. 42–53) in which she describes how various pairings of Marlovian and Shakespearean plays can be 'very productive' (p. 46) in class. Her suggestion of matching *Tamburlaine* with *Henry V* is fascinating (p. 47) and she also explains in detail how she teaches *Tamburlaine* in relation to both the life of Timur the Lame and the Elizabethan presence in Ireland (p. 48). In laying this out, Hopkins lists the contextual material she uses (via hardcopy handouts and e-copies on Blackboard LMS) and presents some generative discussion questions. Logan also has an evocative chapter on *Tamburlaine* and *Henry V* in *Shakespeare's Marlowe* that addresses influence, language and genre.

As with Hopkins, I've found students respond well to some account of Timur the Lame because his empire evokes such a different world from today's and also points us to the trade and tensions between East and West being played out in the Mediterranean in Tudor times. *The Jew of Malta* is a superb additional text via which students can develop a fuller sense of Marlowe's interest in the geopolitical clash of empires and religions. While students' imaginations are captured by the historical record of Timur, they are even more enthralled when directed to online material describing his extant fifteenth-century mausoleum, Gur-i-Amir in Uzbekistan, and his exhumation and reburial in 1941–2. This archaeological inquiry into his remains shed light on his physical appearance and also triggered tales of his posthumous impact on the course of the Second World War.

Setting aside the historical figure, I ask my students to consider the varied portraits of Tamburlaine in *Part I* as 'Scythian thief' (1.1.35–55), 'princely lion' (1.2.1–67), transcendent hero (2.1.1–30), devil (4.1.1–72), lover (1.2.82–108; 5.2.72–127) and rhetorician (1.2.165–211). These passages may be examined in relation to some interesting images: Robert Vaughan's engraving of 'Tamerlane' as a magisterial historical 'worthy' (reproduced by Bowers); the more mundane bust of 'Tamburlaine, the great' set between *Parts I* and *II* in the 1590 publication visible on *EEBO*; and Lawrence Johnson's image (1603) of a rather dapper Tamburlaine coiffured to impress (compare the 'wanton majesty' of Tamburlaine's hair in 2.1.23–6). These textual and visual angles on Tamburlaine (not to mention the other evocative images reproduced in Astington's article) can drive discussion around the complexity of Marlowe's protagonist and how he functions in the play. Two of the best passages in *Part I* to discuss in depth for their poetry, imagery and complexity are Tamburlaine's 'Ah, fair Zenocrate' speech on love and virtù (5.2.72–127) and Menaphon's portrait of the man as a type of beautifully incarnate destiny (2.1.7–30).

Another approach I take to the play is to emphasize a number of scenes or sequences that illustrate Marlowe's extraordinary blend of intellectual provocation and innovative stagecraft – this is the combination of spectacle and insight I noted above. In *Part I*, think of the ingeniously flamboyant translation of Tamburlaine from shepherd to warrior in 1.2, the bizarre – or do I mean metatheatrical or ridiculous or horrendous? – scene of Zenocrate and Zabina flyting while Tamburlaine and Bajazeth are fighting (3.3), and the rolling juggernaut of tension and atrocity that careens through Act 5 and ends with a blissfully blood-soaked betrothal. In addressing these scenes it is crucial to keep students focused on how the stage is used (and when it is fully cleared or not) because the orchestration of live, dead and dying bodies with their props, words and movements is at the core of Marlowe's achievement. If you can keep this theatrical side of Marlowe's mighty lines in the front of students' minds, they will be astonished by what (and how much) he is doing in front of (and to) his audience.

In considering some of these scenes, one could include discussion of the printer Richard Jones's preface to the 1590 edition, 'To the Gentleman Readers', which simultaneously raises three binaries relating to medium (readers versus audiences), status (gentlemen versus 'fondlings') and genre (serious content versus light). An excellent scholarly text to refer to along the way is Lunney's *Marlowe and the Popular Tradition* because her opening chapters explain so well, and via specific reference to *Tamburlaine*, how Marlowe moves theatre away from the conventional didacticism that late-Tudor audiences expected to newly complex and disturbing forms of story-telling that resist inherited certitudes. Also valuable in this context is Cartelli's account of *Tamburlaine* as a complex, staged event in Tudor England.

Before departing the Red Tent we need to acknowledge that Marlowe pedagogy is not just about historical context and literary analysis. This experimental playwright has a tendency to provoke experimental pedagogies requiring active, exploratory and student-directed learning. Here are a few examples. Bowman explains how she uses Augusto Boal's Brechtian 'Joker System' in undergraduate performance courses 'to explore a variety of "classic" texts by such authors as Euripides, Shakespeare, Marlowe and Chekhov' (p. 139). Her article is well worth reading because although she does not use Marlowe as her specific example in it, she explains lucidly how the system works to enable students to enter, dismantle and reconstruct the classic text in sophisticated, creative and authentic ways. By 'joking around with a text and its possibilities' (p. 147) in structured, yet improvisational ways the students learn about the play, about play itself, and about the discipline within which they are consuming and producing both.

This is not that far from my use of complexity theory and metalearning in teaching Marlowe in the literature classroom. I share Bowman's sentiment that '[i]n a pedagogical context. . .I am more than willing to live with a little chaos' (p. 147) because complexity theory argues that the zone of greatest energy and fertility in any system (and courses, classrooms and disciplines are all systems) lies at the 'edge of chaos' where inherited structures are most troubled by unpredicted forces. In *Teaching Shakespeare and Marlowe* and 'Prosperous Teaching and the Thing of Darkness' I describe experimental learning tasks and assessment exercises that put complexity theory into pedagogical action when teaching Marlowe. In the spirit of complexity theory, I have my students push the boundaries of what might be considered relevant to the study of Marlowe by injecting their radically unexpected and disjunctive ideas into the class discussion in order to provoke collaboratively the emergence of new approaches to the plays. This is in the context of teaching my Marlowe students about how the disciplinary frameworks in which they learn can become inhibitors of thought and insight if they are performed as mere reiteration of truisms rather than consciously critiqued by intellectually effortful strategies.

Coincidentally, and with no connection to Boal, one of the assessment levers in my Marlowe course I call the 'Joker Card' because it allows students to intervene at a point of their choosing in the regular assessment structure and play with their assessable response to Marlowe by producing anything other than a regular essay (see 'Prosperous Teaching'). In so doing they play with the educational system enveloping them. This is not a creative free-for-all; rather, a student's Joker Card assessment response must demonstrate considered analytical insight into Marlowe's texts delivered via personal creativity, which is harder than it sounds, but generates extraordinary creative-critical engagements with texts such as *Tamburlaine*. I won't forget the student who submitted an illustrated, verse-form, children's book (for primary school readers) that translated *Tamburlaine* into a parable of schoolyard bullying. As simple as this retelling sounds, it was an inspired move that actually got to grips with some fundamentals of human power relations at the same time as dealing with the affordances of translating stories between literary genres and audiences. This response gains extra resonance when one considers that many senior-level literature students are doing teaching degrees and will be in the primary or secondary classroom in just a few years.

Pendergraft describes a carefully structured 'Marlowe Project' that involved students in close reading and script analysis, dramaturgical charting of historical and literary parameters for the play, and participation as actors and directors in 'Composition' groups rehearsing sections of Marlovian plays. 'Composition' is a tightly structured set of techniques for 'stimulating student-generated theatrical material' devised by Anne Bogart (p. 53). Pendergraft drew on Bogart's techniques to actualize Charles Mee's theatrical aesthetic which is to 'appropriate a classical text, strip it down to its essentials, and reassemble the story in a completely new form' (p. 52). Pendergraft describes how her students took *Tamburlaine Part I*, *The Jew of Malta*, *Doctor Faustus* and *Edward II* as their primary texts and creatively transformed them into powerfully new creative works. She recounts how one group performed Tamburlaine as a puppeteer who theatrically orchestrates Bajazeth's braining via puppet strings (indicative of Tamburlaine holding Fate in chains and turning Fortune's wheel by hand in 1.2.174–5) and Cosroe's death via the cutting of his puppet strings and the pulling of crimson cords from his body (to indicate his life sliding out through his bleeding wounds in 2.7.43). What is so good about these theatrical choices is they are student-produced and textually based: they are, in fact, creative embodiments of close reading.

A rather different model of innovative practice is The Kit Marlowe Project directed by Kristen Abbott Bennett. It describes itself as 'a digital space designed to introduce undergraduates with diverse majors to project-driven, research-based learning, and digital humanities practices' specifically in relation to the study of Marlowe. Most of the content is student-generated and the website 'represents both a work product and a pedagogical resource'. Educators interested in digital pedagogies will find much to ponder when browsing the site because it makes available, for example, course syllabi, an online searching task called the 'Kit Marlowe Scavenger Hunt', navigable Prezi presentations on Marlowe's family tree and social networks, and resources relating to some of his works. The site is rich in digital educational ideas and could be used to inspire students or teachers of Marlowe.

The Shakespeare Theatre Company (Washington, DC) produced a *Teacher Curriculum Guide* to *Tamburlaine* to accompany its 2007–8 production directed by Michael Kahn. The freely downloadable *Guide* includes a biography, synopsis, bibliography, contextual material and activities for students to use before and after the performance.

Astington, John H., 'The "Unrecorded Portrait" of Edward Alleyn', *Shakespeare Quarterly*, 44 (1993), 73–86.

Bamford, Karen, and Alexander Leggatt (eds), *Approaches to Teaching English Renaissance Drama* (New York: Modern Language Association of America, 2002).

Banks, Fiona, *Creative Shakespeare: The Globe Education Guide to Practical Shakespeare* (London: Bloomsbury, 2013).

Bennett, Kristen Abbott (dir.), *The Kit Marlowe Project*, Framingham State University, Framingham, MA. 2017–. https://kitmarlowe.org/

Bowers, Rick, 'Tamburlaine Engraved, 1622 to 1673', *Huntington Library Quarterly*, 59 (1996), 543–49.

Bowman, Ruth Laurion, '"Joking" with the Classics: Using Boal's Joker System in the Performance Classroom', *Theatre Topics*, 7 (1997), 139–51.

Cartelli, Thomas, *Marlowe, Shakespeare, and the Economy of Theatrical Experience* (Philadelphia: University of Pennsylvania Press, 1991).

Conroy, Derval, and Danielle Clarke (eds), *Teaching the Early Modern Period* (Houndmills: Palgrave Macmillan, 2011).

Engle, Lars, and Eric Rasmussen, *Studying Shakespeare's Contemporaries* (Malden, MA: Wiley-Blackwell, 2014).

Gibson, Rex, *Teaching Shakespeare: A Handbook for Teachers* (1998; rev. Cambridge: Cambridge University Press, 2016).

Gieskes, Edward, 'A Survey of Resources: Teaching Edward II', in *Edward II: A Critical Reader*, ed. by Kirk Melnikoff (London: Bloomsbury, 2017), pp. 195–279.

Hackel, Heidi Brayman, and Ian Frederick Moulton (eds), *Teaching Early Modern English Literature from the Archives* (New York: Modern Language Association of America, 2015).

Hiscock, Andrew, and Lisa Hopkins (eds), *Teaching Shakespeare and Early Modern Dramatists* (Basingstoke: Palgrave Macmillan, 2007).

Kahn, Michael (artistic dir.), *Tamburlaine: First Folio Teacher Curriculum Guide* (Washington, DC: The Shakespeare Theatre Company, 2007). http://www.shakespearetheatre.org/education/schools-and-teachers/curriculum-guides/

Logan, Robert A., *Shakespeare's Marlowe: The Influence of Christopher Marlowe on Shakespeare's Artistry* (Aldershot: Ashgate, 2007).

Lunney, Ruth, *Marlowe and the Popular Tradition: Innovation in the English Drama before 1595* (Manchester: Manchester University Press, 2002).

Pendergraft, Stacy, 'Marlowe Mee: Constructing the Marlowe Project', *The Shakespeare Bulletin*, 27 (2009), 51–62.

Scott, Sarah K., 'A Survey of Resources', in *The Jew of Malta: A Critical Reader*, ed. by Robert A. Logan (London, 2013), pp. 169–90.

Scott, Sarah K., 'A Survey of Resources', in *Doctor Faustus: A Critical Reader*, ed. by Sara Munson Deats (London: Continuum, 2010), pp. 159–78.

Semler, Liam E., 'Prosperous Teaching and the Thing of Darkness: Raising a *Tempest* in the Classroom', *Cogent Arts and Humanities*, 3.1 (2016). https://www.tandfonline.com/doi/abs/10.1080/23311983.2016.1235862

Semler, Liam E., *Teaching Shakespeare and Marlowe: Learning versus the System* (London: Bloomsbury, 2013).

Shand, G. B., *Teaching Shakespeare: Passing It On* (Malden, MA: Blackwell, 2009).

Stredder, James, *The North Face of Shakespeare: Activities for Teaching the Plays* (2004; rev. 2007; rpt. Cambridge: Cambridge University Press, 2015).

This Rough Magic: A Peer-Reviewed, Academic, Online Journal Dedicated to the Teaching of Medieval & Renaissance Literature. http://www.thisroughmagic.org

Thompson, Ayanna, and Laura Turchi, *Teaching Shakespeare with Purpose: A Student-Centred Approach* (London: Bloomsbury, 2016).

The Black Tent: Entering the fray

There remains only the Black Tent where scholars are skirmishing over sites of strategic importance to the understanding and appreciation of *Tamburlaine the Great*. The ideas are flying thick and fast as you enter and some excellent bibliographers are recording as much of this intellectual contest as they can. The Marlowe Society of America's open-access Marlowe Bibliography Online, maintained by Allan and McInnis, is a comprehensive, regularly updated and easily searchable database of titles (many with abstracts). A search for 'Tamburlaine' returns over 200 references containing a wealth of scholarship on the play published from about 1910–2019. There are briefer, annotated Oxford Bibliographies on Marlowe by Bevington (2010) and Stapleton (2017) that require subscription. Cheney's bibliography is older (covering 1987–98 and published in 2001), but still valuable and containing three pages on *Tamburlaine* scholarship.

An exciting development is the recent launch of the peer-reviewed, open-access *Journal of Marlowe Studies* edited by Hopkins and Duxfield. This is the online successor to *Marlowe Studies: An Annual* (2011–16), the six issues of which are also freely accessible via an online archive. As the only scholarly journal solely focused on Marlowe Studies, this will be a significant source of reliable research into his work.

Marlowe is honoured by numerous recent collections of essays including: Melnikoff and Knutson's *Christopher Marlowe, Theatrical Commerce and the Book Trade* (2018) in which both *Tamburlaine* plays feature, but it does have a rather technical focus; Bartels and Smith's *Christopher Marlowe in Context* (2013), which is one of the most comprehensive collections; the always interesting collections co-edited by Deats and Logan (2002, 2008, 2015); Cheney's *Cambridge Companion to Christopher Marlowe* (2004), which contains a chapter on *Tamburlaine* and briefer discussions of it throughout; Scott and Stapleton's collection (2010); and Downie and Parnell's *Constructing Christopher Marlowe* (2000). There are older collections too, but these twenty-first-century collections will give teachers more than enough high quality scholarship and ideas to explore. Harraway's thoughtful monograph *Re-citing Marlowe* is of interest to those who are keen to see fresh approaches to the plays (including *Tamburlaine*) married with serious critical reflection on the way scholars have positioned Marlowe and his texts.

As the collections reveal, key topic areas regularly arising in Marlowe scholarship include: language and genre; stagecraft; gender and sexuality; empire, race and religion; and adaptation and performance. Let's address each of these in turn.

Allan, Gayle, and David McInnis (eds), *Marlowe Bibliography Online* (*MBO*), Marlowe Society of America and the University of Melbourne, 2011–. http://www.marlowesocietyofamerica.org/mbo/

Bartels, Emily C., and Emma Smith (eds), *Christopher Marlowe in Context* (Cambridge: Cambridge University Press, 2013).

Bevington, David, 'Christopher Marlowe', *Oxford Bibliographies* (Oxford University Press, 2010).

Cheney, Patrick, 'Recent Studies in Marlowe (1987–1998)', *English Literary Renaissance*, 31 (2001), 288–328.

Cheney, Patrick (ed), *The Cambridge Companion to Christopher Marlowe* (Cambridge: Cambridge University Press, 2004).

Deats, Sara Munson, and Robert A. Logan (eds), *Marlowe's Empery: Expanding his Critical Contexts* (Newark: University of Delaware Press, 2002).

Deats, Sara Munson, and Robert A. Logan (eds), *Placing the Plays of Christopher Marlowe* (Aldershot: Ashgate, 2008).

Deats, Sara Munson, and Robert A. Logan (eds), *Christopher Marlowe at 450* (Burlington, VT: Ashgate, 2015).

Downie, J. A., and J. T. Parnell (eds), *Constructing Christopher Marlowe* (Cambridge: Cambridge University Press, 2000).

Harraway, Clare, *Re-citing Marlowe: Approaches to the Drama* (2000; rpt. New York: Routledge, 2018).

Hopkins, Lisa, and Andrew Duxfield (eds), *Journal of Marlowe Studies*. https://journals.shu.ac.uk/index.php/Marlstud/index

Melnikoff, Kirk, and Roslyn L. Knutson (eds), *Christopher Marlowe, Theatrical Commerce and the Book Trade* (Cambridge: Cambridge University Press, 2018).

Scott, Sarah K., and M. L. Stapleton (eds), *Christopher Marlowe the Craftsman: Lives, Stage and Page* (Farnham: Ashgate, 2010).

Stapleton, M. L., 'Christopher Marlowe', *Oxford Bibliographies* (Oxford University Press, 2017).

1. Language and genre

Tamburlaine is an ideal play for exploring language and genre because Marlowe's 'mighty line' and his manipulation of tragedy, historical romance and comedy are easy for students to sink their teeth into. The result is discussion that touches on large conceptual issues in literary studies as well as detailed close reading of individual lines. Mathew Martin, Grande and Cole devote books to the topic of tragedy in Marlowe and give significant space to the *Tamburlaine* plays. Cheney, looking backwards, contextualizes *Tamburlaine*'s verse in respect to Edmund Spenser in *Marlowe's Counterfeit Profession*, while Logan, looking forwards, contextualizes it in respect to Shakespeare's *Henry V* (as noted above). Frongillo's discussion of comedy in *Tamburlaine* and Richard Martin's discussion of romance are both excellent for enriching classroom discussion of the generic texture of the play.

If we move from generic parameters to the details of the line, there are four works that I have found particularly useful. Brooke, Varn, Levenson and McDonald present analyses of Marlowe's prosody, metrics, syntax and vocabulary that equip students and teachers with linguistic details and techniques to look out for when closely probing the verse. Peet's essay on 'The Rhetoric of *Tamburlaine*' is a good complement to these analyses, and Tarlinskaja's recent book on early modern English versification is fascinating too, but encompasses many authors and is less easily applied to the Marlowe classroom.

An engaging way to focus on poetic detail is to have students discuss the various 'persuasions to love' in the play. You can set the scene by discussing Marlowe's lyric, 'The Passionate Shepherd to his Love', and Walter Ralegh's poetic riposte, 'The Nymph's reply to the Shepherd'. Then consider: Tamburlaine's wooing of Zenocrate (*Part I*, 1.2.82–108); Tamburlaine's wooing of Theridamas (*Part I*, 1.2.165–211); Callapine's wooing of Almeda (*Part II*, 1.3.1–53); and Theridamas's wooing of Olympia and her Ralegh-like reply (*Part II*, 4.2.28–54). This focus makes the *carpe diem* mode visible and it is easily related to the play's larger discourses of desire.

Brooke, C. F. Tucker, 'Marlowe's Versification and Style', *Studies in Philology*, 19 (1922), 186–206.

Cheney, Patrick, *Marlowe's Counterfeit Profession: Ovid, Spenser, Counter-Nationhood* (Toronto: University of Toronto Press, 1997).

Cole, Douglas, *Christopher Marlowe and the Renaissance of Tragedy* (Westport, CT: Greenwood Press, 1995).

Frongillo, John, 'Giving the Tragic Boot to the Comic Sock: The Recoding of Christopher Marlowe's *Tamburlaine* from Low to High Culture', *Popular Entertainment Studies*, 2 (2011), 73–88.

Grande, Troni Y., *Marlovian Tragedy: The Play of Dilation* (Lewisburg, PA: Bucknell University Press, 1999).

Levenson, Jill L., 'Working Words: The Verbal Dynamic of *Tamburlaine*', in *'A Poet and a Filthy Play-maker': New Essays on Christopher Marlowe*, ed. by Kenneth Friedenreich, Roma Gill and Constance B. Kuriyama (New York: AMS Press, 1988), pp. 99–115.

Martin, Mathew R., *Tragedy and Trauma in the Plays of Christopher Marlowe* (Farnham: Ashgate, 2015).

Martin, Richard A., 'Marlowe's *Tamburlaine* and the Language of Romance', *PMLA*, 93 (1978), 248–64.

McDonald, Russ, 'Marlowe and Style', in *The Cambridge Companion to Christopher Marlowe*, ed. by Patrick Cheney (Cambridge: Cambridge University Press, 2004), pp. 55–69.

Pecan, David, 'Dramatic Prologue and the Early Modern Concept of Genre: Understanding Marlowe's *Tamburlaine the Great* in its Critical Context', *This Rough Magic*, 3 (2012), 28–62.

Peet, Donald, 'The Rhetoric of *Tamburlaine*', *ELH*, 26 (1959), 137–55.

Tarlinskaja, Marina, *Shakespeare and the Versification of English Drama, 1561–1642* (2014; rpt. Abingdon: Routledge, 2016).

Varn, Lynn K., 'Marlowe's Muscular Verb: The Answer to his Might', *Language and Style*, 20 (1987), 157–70.

2. Stagecraft

Marlovian stagecraft is regularly discussed by scholars in relation to the power of spectacle. In addition to Lunney's important book noted above (in the Red Tent section), Thurn and Pearson also tackle the impact of *Tamburlaine*'s presentation of spectacular sights on stage. Thomson's survey of Marlowe's stagecraft in all his plays helps students focus on how the stage is used and draws attention to the differing staging requirements of *Parts I* and *II* of *Tamburlaine*. The former amounts to an ever-moving show requiring use of many props carried about on a 'bare platform', while the latter is highly place-conscious and puts 'considerable demands on the tiring-house wall and opening' (27). Thomson emphasizes 'the relatively small and shallow stage' on which all this must happen (28), and in my Marlowe course I bring this alive by taking my class outside to a lawn where we measure out the real size of the Rose Theatre stage and its audience bays with bright yellow cord. With the dimensions of the polygonal theatre fully marked out I can then place students in the stage area and in the audience bays and they are always shocked by how tight the entire space is especially considering how geographically and conceptually expansive the plays are. We then block out a few scenes and explore the sound, sight and space implications of our grassy Rose.

Pearson, Meg, 'The Perils of Political Showmanship: Marlowe's *Tamburlaine the Great*', in *Leadership and Elizabethan Culture*, ed. by Peter I. Kaufman (New York: Palgrave Macmillan, 2013), pp. 175–90.

Thomson, Leslie, 'Marlowe's Staging of Meaning', *Medieval and Renaissance Drama in England*, 18 (2005), 19–36.

Thurn, David H., 'Sights of Power in *Tamburlaine*', *ELR* 19 (1989), 3–21.

3. Gender and sexuality

Teachers seeking a broad introduction to sex, gender and desire across Marlowe's work will find much to consider in the works listed below by White, Tromly, Deats and Goldberg. I explore some resonances of eros in the context of Marlowe pedagogy in *Teaching Shakespeare and Marlowe* (noted above in the Red Tent section). Two powerful ways to open up gender discussions of *Tamburlaine* are via the starting points of Zenocrate (*Parts I* and *II*) and Calyphas (*Part II*), on whom students never fail to have strong opinions. Marlowe's female characters are discussed in Hansen's article and in chapters in Downie and Parnell's *Constructing Christopher Marlowe*, Bartels and Smith's *Christopher Marlowe in Context* and Cheney's *Cambridge Companion*. Evocative pieces on masculinity and *Tamburlaine* are found in work by Shepard, Williams, Turner and Francisco. Discussion of female roles can be expanded by reference to Zabina (*Part I*) and Olympia (*Part II*), and discussion of male roles can be expanded by discussion of Tamburlaine's male friendship bonds with his allies.

Deats, Sara Munson, *Sex, Gender and Desire in the Plays of Christopher Marlowe* (Newark: University of Delaware Press, 1997).

Francisco, Timothy, 'Marlowe's War Horses: Cyborgs, Soldiers and Queer Companions', in *Violent Masculinities: Male Aggression in Early Modern Texts and Culture*, ed. by Jennifer Feather and Catherine E. Thomas (New York: Palgrave Macmillan, 2013), pp. 47–65.

Goldberg, Jonathan, *Sodometries: Renaissance Texts, Modern Sexualities* (1992; rpt. New York: Fordham University Press, 2010).

Hansen, Claire G., '"Who taught thee this?" Female Agency and Experiential Learning in Marlowe's *Tamburlaine, The Jew of Malta* and *Edward the Second*', *Journal of Language, Literature and Culture*, 60 (2013), 157–77.

Shepard, Alan, *Marlowe's Soldiers: Rhetorics of Masculinity in the Age of the Armada* (Burlington, VT: Ashgate, 2002).

Tromly, Frederic B., *Playing with Desire: Christopher Marlowe and the Art of Tantalization* (Toronto: University of Toronto Press, 1998).

Turner, Timothy A., 'Executing Calyphas: Gender, Discipline and Sovereignty in 2 *Tamburlaine*', *Explorations in Renaissance Culture*, 44 (2018), 141–56.

White, Paul Whitfield (ed.), *Marlowe, History and Sexuality: New Critical Essays on Christopher Marlowe* (New York: AMS Press, 1998).

Williams, Carolyn, '"This effeminate brat": Tamburlaine's Unmanly Son', *Medieval and Renaissance Drama in England*, 9 (1997), 56–80.

4. Empire, race and religion

The three most productive pieces of scholarship I have used in class on empire, race and religion are Bartels, Greenblatt and Lindley. These all deal with multiple Marlowe plays including *Tamburlaine* and marry detailed textual reading with theoretical considerations. The first two are classic works of Marlowe scholarship that should not be missed, while the third is a brilliantly engaging piece that my students find accessible and provocative. Three other areas that overlap with these are geography, philosophy and politics. Valuable earlier monographs by Battenhouse and Kocher are now superseded by an enormous body of scholarship incorporating detailed reference to Elizabethan sectarianism and politics, natural philosophy and representations of Islam. The critical collections usually include chapters on these topics and more specialist research connecting with *Tamburlaine* can be found in Gillies, Grogan, Moore, Slotkin, Duxfield, Preedy and Cheney, as listed below.

Bartels, Emily C., *Spectacles of Strangeness: Imperialism, Alienation and Marlowe* (Philadelphia: University of Pennsylvania Press, 1993).

Battenhouse, Roy W., *Marlowe's* Tamburlaine: *A Study on Renaissance Moral Philosophy* (Nashville, TN: Vanderbilt University Press, 1964).

Cheney, Patrick, *Marlowe's Republican Authorship: Lucan, Liberty and the Sublime* (Basingstoke: Palgrave Macmillan, 2009).

Duxfield, Andrew, *Christopher Marlowe and the Failure to Unify* (2015; rpt. Milton Park: Routledge, 2016).

Gillies, John, '*Tamburlaine* and Renaissance Geography', in *Early Modern English Drama: A Critical Companion*, ed. by Garrett A. Sullivan Jr., Patrick Cheney, and Andrew Hadfield (Oxford: Oxford University Press, 2006), pp. 35–49.

Greenblatt, Stephen, *Renaissance Self-Fashioning from More to Shakespeare* (Chicago: University of Chicago Press, 1980).

Grogan, Jane, '"A warre . . . commodious": Dramatizing Islamic Schism in and after *Tamburlaine*', *Texas Studies in Literature and Language*, 54 (2012), 45–78.

Kocher, Paul Harold, *Christopher Marlowe: A Study of his Thought, Learning and Character* (Chapel Hill: University of North Carolina Press, 1946).

Lindley, Arthur, 'The Unbeing of the Overreacher: Proteanism and the Marlovian Hero', *Modern Language Review*, 84 (1989), 1–17.

Moore, Roger E., 'The Spirit and the Letter: Marlowe's *Tamburlaine* and Elizabethan Religious Radicalism', *Studies in Philology*, 99 (2002), 123–51.

Preedy, Chloe Kathleen, *Marlowe's Literary Scepticism: Politic Religion and Post-Reformation Polemic* (London: Bloomsbury, 2012).

Slotkin, Joel Eliot, '"Seeke out another Godhead": Religious Epistemology and Representations of Islam in *Tamburlaine*', *Modern Philology*, 111 (2014), 408–36.

5. Adaptation and performance

Finally, we turn to adaptation and performance of *Tamburlaine*. Some reference has been made above to modern adaptations in teaching contexts. I have found that the idea of sequelization and all it entails in Hollywood movie sequels is a productive way to approach *Part II* with its straining after new material, rehashing of old conceits and relentless escalation of atrocities and provocations. One can add to this the participation of both Marlowe and Edward Alleyn in Elizabethan celebrity culture (on which see Cerasano). Bartels and Smith's collection has a number of helpful chapters on 'Reception' that address Marlowe in the present and in the movies, as does Cheney's *Cambridge Companion*.

Surveys of stage productions may be found in Goeckle's book (pp. 47–78) and Dawson's introduction to his edition of *Tamburlaine* (pp. xxviii–xlii). Three performances that elicit good classroom discussion and have easily findable online material are: Michael Boyd's 'Tamburlaine Parts I and II' for Theatre for a New Audience at the Polonsky Shakespeare Center, New York (2014); Ng Choon Ping's 'Tamburlaine' for the British East Asian Yellow Earth Company at Arcola Theatre, London (2017); and Theodora Skipitares' 'The Rise and Fall of Timur the Lame' which blends dancing, live music and coloured shadow puppets (2002). On these see Brantley, Mazzilli and Stanley for a start.

Something I have theatrical fun with in my Marlowe course, but which also connects with all five key topics in the Black Tent, is a series of exercises focused on *Part I* that I call 'The Crown Package'. It begins by putting students in small groups to workshop and then perform Act 2, Scene 4 in which Tamburlaine and Mycetes discuss the latter's crown. I urge them to milk it for maximum comic effect via caricature, adaptation, props, comic timing, expressions and gestures. This in itself produces highly engaged and hilarious results. Let me suggest, for example, you ask one group to play Mycetes as Gollum/Sméagol and Tamburlaine as Gandalf: you won't be disappointed. After this, I pull out the best performers from each group and challenge them to tone the comedy right down to produce it as a scene without laughs (if they can). We then discuss the scene in terms of Marlowe's wider use of comedy and tragedy in *Tamburlaine*. It is a short step from there to explore the genre and gender texture of two other crown scenes: 3.3, in which Zenocrate and Zabina mind the crowns of Tamburlaine and Bajazeth; and 4.4, in which a banquet boasts a 'course of crowns'. Finally, we end with a full-class discussion of 2.7.12–29 (on Tamburlaine's Jovian and elemental lust for crowns) and reflect on all this via Greenblatt's notion in *Renaissance Self-Fashioning* of Tamburlaine's relentless pursuit of ever elusive goals (pp. 218–21).

Speaking of elusive goals, the moment long deferred has now arrived. Forsake the tents, go forth and follow *Tamburlaine* into that room of eager faces. Your armour is beseeming and your curtle-axe is gleaming (*Part I*, 1.2.42–3): what could possibly go wrong?

Brantley, Ben, 'It's best not to make him angry', *The Guardian*, 18 November 2014.

Cerasano, S. P., 'Edward Alleyn, the New Model Actor, and the Rise of Celebrity in the 1590s', *Medieval and Renaissance Drama in England*, 18 (2005), 47–58.

Goeckle, George L., Tamburlaine *and* Edward II: *Text and Performance* (Atlantic Highlands: Humanities Press International, 1988).

Mazzilli, Mary, 'A New Version of Christopher Marlowe's *Tamburlaine* by Yellow Earth Opens in London', *The Theatre Times,* 15 March 2017.

Stanley, N. T., 'History as Theme Park: Reconfiguring the Human Journey in the Art of Theodora Skipitares', *The Drama Review* 47 (2003), pp. 34–70.

NOTES

Introduction

1 Ben Jonson, 'To the memory of my beloued, The Avthor, Mr. William Shakespeare, And what he hath left vs', in the preface to *Mr. William Shakespeares Comedies, Histories, & Tragedies* (London, 1623).

2 Peter Berek, 'Tamburlaine's Weak Sons: Imitation as Interpretation Before 1593', *Renaissance Drama*, 13 (1982), 55–82.

3 Robert Greene, 'To the Gentlemen readers', *Perimedes the blacke-smith* (London, 1588), sig. A3. A contemporary copy of the Dutch Church Libel, made in Cambridge, survives as Bodleian MS. Don. d. 152, fol. 4v; it is transcribed by Arthur Freeman in 'Marlowe, Kyd, and the Dutch Church Libel', *ELR: English Literary Renaissance*, 3.1 (1973), 44–52 (pp. 50–1).

4 Richard Jones, 'To The Gentlemen Readers', 9–12, preface to *I Tamburlaine* in Anthony B. Dawson, ed. *Tamburlaine, Parts One and Two* (London: A&C Black, 1997).

5 Jones, 'To The Gentleman Readers', 2–3; *A Transcript of the Registers of the Company of Stationers of London, 1554-1640 A.D.*, vol. II, ed. by Edward Arber (London, 1875), p. 558.

6 On the uses of the fourteener, see Scott McMillin and Sally-Beth MacLean, *The Queen's Men and their Plays* (Cambridge: Cambridge University Press, 1998), p. 148.

7 On prospective glasses and *Tamburlaine*, see David McInnis, *Mind-Travelling and Voyage Drama in Early Modern England* (Basingstoke: Palgrave, 2013), pp. 54–7.

8 McMillin and MacLean, p. 166.

9 See, in general terms, Richard Helgerson's *Forms of Nationhood: The Elizabethan Writing of England* (Chicago: University of Chicago Press, 1992).

10 McMillin and MacLean, p. 167.

11 Wagner, 'Towards a Racialized *Tamburlaine*', p. 137.

12 R. A. Foakes, ed. *Henslowe's Diary* (2nd edn) (Cambridge: Cambridge University Press, 2002), pp. 321–2.

13 Ibid.

14 See E. K. Chambers, *The Elizabethan Stage*, vol. II (Oxford: Clarendon Press, 1923), p. 135.

15 See Foakes, ed., pp. 23–9, 31 and 33.

16 Michael J. Hirrel, '*Alcazar*, The Lord Admiral's, and Aspects of Performance', *Review of English Studies*, 66 (2014), 40–59.

17 A counterpoint is the handling of the lost 'Hercules' plays, which premiered so closely together that they must have been conceived as a pair from the outset; they were, however, 'self-contained enough to be seen independently of the other' (Martin Wiggins, in association with Catherine Richardson, *British Drama, 1533–1642: A Catalogue*, 11 vols [Oxford: Oxford University Press, 2012–], #999).

18 Wiggins does not list a lost second part in his *Catalogue*.

19 *The First part of the Tragicall raigne of Selimus, sometime Emperour of the Turkes* (London, 1594), sig. K3r.

20 Foakes, ed., p. 23.

21 Roslyn L. Knutson, 'Marlowe Reruns: Repertorial Commerce and Marlowe's Plays in Revival', in *Marlowe's Empery: Expanding His Critical Contexts*, ed. by Sara Munson Deats and Robert A. Logan (London: Associated University Presses, 2002), pp. 25–42 (pp. 25–6).

22 Matthew Steggle, *Digital Humanities and the Lost Drama of Early Modern England* (Farnham: Ashgate, 2015), p. 77.

23 See the entry for 'Mahomet' in the *Lost Plays Database*, ed. by Roslyn L. Knutson, David McInnis, and Matthew Steggle (Washington, DC: Folger Shakespeare Library, 2009–), https://lostplays.folger.edu/Mahomet

24 Foakes, ed., p. 26. Lawrence Manley and Sally-Beth MacLean note that 'Regular back-to-back performance of the two "tamberlen" plays in December or January 1594/95 is the first such arrangement to be found in the diary'; *The Lord Strange's*

Men and Their Plays (New Haven: Yale University Press, 2014), p. 139.

25 Foakes, ed., pp. 36 and 47.

26 On the 'Tamar Cham' plays replacing the *Tamburlaine* plays in the Admiral's repertory, see McInnis, *Mind-Travelling*, p. 72.

27 'The Plotte of the First Parte of the Tamar Cam' in *The plays of William Shakspeare: in twenty-one volumes: with the corrections and illustrations of various commentators, to which are added notes / by Samuel Johnson and George Steevens* (1803), foldout after leaf 2D8 verso (p. 414). See the *Lost Plays Database* entry for the 'Tamar Cham' plays for a digitization of Steevens' transcription of the plot.

28 See Manley and MacLean, pp. 138–43; McInnis, *Mind-Travelling*, pp. 71–2.

29 Berek, p. 82.

30 Roslyn L. Knutson, 'Marlowe in Repertory, 1587–1593', in *Christopher Marlowe, Theatrical Commerce, and the Book Trade*, ed. by Kirk Melnikoff and Roslyn L. Knutson (Cambridge: Cambridge University Press, 2018), p. 28.

31 See the *Lost Plays Database* entries for 'Cutlack', 'George Scanderbeg', and 'Charlemagne'; Steggle's chapter 'Cutlack (1594)' in *Digital Humanities*, pp. 61–76; and McInnis, 'Marlowe's Influence and "The True History of George Scanderbeg"', *Marlowe Studies: An Annual*, 2 (2012), 71–85.

32 McMillin and MacLean, p. 145.

33 *The Famous Victories of Henry the Fifth* (Queen's Men Editions), ed. by Mathew Martin (Victoria, BC: University of Victoria, n.d.), 6.534: https://qme.internetshakespeare.uvic.ca/doc/FV_M/scene/6/index.html

34 As Pascale Aebischer suggests (personal communication, email, 3 October 2019), it is possible that rather than Tamburlaine wearing armour beneath shepherd's weeds as I describe, he might receive the armour as a gift from Zenocrate as part of her dowry, along with the treasure that her followers carry on stage in the first stage direction of the scene; on late-medieval and early modern gifts of weapons and armours see Brigitte Buettner, 'Past Presents: New Year's Gifts at the Valois Courts, ca. 1400',

The Art Bulletin, 83 (2001), 598–625. According to Aebischer's reading then, Tamburlaine audaciously makes himself a 'lord' through the spoils of war that he wins with Zenocrate, and thus literally takes on the shape of her future husband.

35 Wagner, 'New Directions: Towards a Racialized *Tamburlaine*', p. 144.

36 Tom Rutter, *The Cambridge Introduction to Christopher Marlowe* (Cambridge: Cambridge University Press, 2012), p. 32.

37 McMillin and MacLean, p. 130.

38 See Rutter, *Introduction*, p. 29.

39 McMillin and MacLean, p. 142.

40 See McInnis, 'Booking Marlowe's Plays' in *Christopher Marlowe, Theatrical Commerce, and the Book Trade*, ed. by Kirk Melnikoff and Roslyn L. Knutson (Cambridge: Cambridge University Press, 2018), pp. 228–42.

41 Ben Jonson, *Discoveries* (1641), ed. by Lorna Hutson, ll. 562–4 in *The Cambridge Edition of the Works of Ben Jonson*, gen. eds. David Bevington, Martin Butler and Ian Donaldson (Cambridge: Cambridge University Press, 2012); Jones, ll. 13–14.

42 Charles Saunders, *Tamerlaine the Great* (London, 1681), sig. a1ᵛ.

43 Richard Wilson, 'Specters of Marlowe: The State of the Debt and the Work of Mourning' in *Christopher Marlowe at 450*, ed. by Sara Munson Deats and Robert A. Logan (Farnham: Ashgate, 2015), pp. 227–56.

44 Peter Kirwan, 'The Performance History: "High Astounding Terms" – Tamburlaine and *Tamburlaine* on stage', p. 44.

45 Robert Darnton, 'What is the History of Books?', *Daedalus*, 111.3 (1982), 65–83.

46 Robert Darnton, '"What is the History of Books?" Revisited', *Modern Intellectual History*, 4.3 (2007), 495–508 (pp. 502–4); see Thomas R. Adams and Nicholas Barker, 'A New Model for the Study of the Book' in *A Potencie of Life: Books in Society*, ed. by Nicholas Barker (London: British Library, 1993), pp. 5–43.

47 Claire M. L. Bourne, 'New Directions: Mending *Tamburlaine*', p. 86.

48 Matthew Dimmock, 'New Directions: Retooling Timür', p. 147.
49 Ibid., p. 164.
50 Sydnee Wagner, 'New Directions: Towards a Racialized *Tamburlaine*', pp. 130–1.
51 Ibid., p. 133.
52 Tom Rutter, 'New Directions: Tamburlaine the Weather Man', p. 109.

Chapter 1

1 Greene, *Perimedes the Blacksmith* (John Wolfe, 1588), sig. A3; Marlowe, *Tamburlaine the Great* (London: Richard Jones, 1590), sig. A2; *Henslowe's Diary*, ed. by R. A. Foakes and R. T. Rickert (Cambridge: Cambridge University Press, 1961), pp. 23, 320–2, 217.

2 Dekker, *The Wonderful Year* (London: Thomas Creede, 1603), sig. D; Dekker, *Old Fortunatus* (London: S. S. for William Aspley, 1600), sig. E; Shakespeare, *The second part of Henrie the fourth* (London: Printed by V S for Andrew Wise, and William Aspley, 1600), sig. D4; Anon., *Histrio-Mastix* (Printed for Th: Thorp, 1610), sig. G.

3 Hall, *Virgidemiarum: Six Bookes* (London: T. Creede for R. Dexter, 1597), p.6.

4 Heywood, Prologue to *The Jew of Malta* (Nicholas Vavasour, 1633), sig. A4v.

5 Phillips, *Theatrum Poetarum* (London: Charles Smith, 1675), p. 82.

6 Langbaine, *An Account of the English Dramatick Poets* (London: Printed by L. L. for George West and Henry Clements, 1691), pp. 344–5. For other references, see C. F. Tucker Brooke, 'The Reputation of Christopher Marlowe', *Transactions of the Connecticut Academy of Arts and Sciences*, 25 (1921–2), pp. 20–1, notes 16–17.

7 Respectively, *Ben Jonson*, 11 vols., eds. C. H. Herford, Percy Simpson, and Evelyn Simpson (Oxford: Clarendon, 1925–53), VIII, 587; Gayton, *Pleasant Notes upon Don Quixot* (London:

William Hunt, 1654), pp. 271, 286. For other references, see Brooke, 'Reputation', pp. 382–4.

8   Lamb, *Specimens of English Dramatic Poets Who Lived about the Time of Shakspeare*, 2 vols (London: E. Moxon, 1835), I, 17; Collier, 'On the Early English Dramatists who Preceded Shakespeare', pt. 1, *Edinburgh Review*, 6 (June 1820), p. 517.

9   *The Works of Christopher Marlowe*, 3 vols, ed. Dyce (London: Pickering, 1850); the 'Pickering edition' was *The Works of Christopher Marlowe*, 3 vols [ed. by George Robinson] (London: Pickering, 1826); for Broughton, see Dorothy U. Seyler, 'James Broughton, Editor of Marlowe's Plays', *PBSA*, 69 (1975), p. 315; Hallam, *Introduction to the Literature of Europe*, 4 vols (London: Murray, 1837–39), II, 233; Hunt, *Imagination and Fancy* (London: Smith, Elder, 1844), pp. 138–40.

10   'Christopher Marlowe', *Fortnightly Review*, 37 n.s. (1 Jan 1870), p. 75.

11   Dabbs, *Reforming Marlowe* (Lewisburg: Bucknell University Press, 1991), p. 15; Bradley, 'Christopher Marlowe', in *The English Poets, Selections*, 4 vols, ed. by Thomas Humphry Ward (London: Macmillan, 1880), I, 412–13; *The Works of Christopher Marlowe*, ed. Bullen (London: Nimmo, 1884), I, xviii–xix.

12   *Christopher Marlowe*, ed. by Ellis, intro. by J. A. Symonds (London: Vizetelly, 1887), pp. xxxii, xxxiv; Symonds, *Shakspere's Predecessors in the English Drama* (London: Smith, Elder, and Co., 1884), pp. 624–6.

13   *The Works of Christopher Marlowe*, ed. by Brooke (Oxford: Clarendon, 1910); *The Tudor Drama:* (Boston: Houghton Mifflin, 1911); and 'Reputation', pp. 235, 302, 245, 302, respectively.

14   Swinburne, *The Age of Shakespeare* (London: Chatto and Windus, 1908), pp. 1–2.

15   Crawford, *The Marlowe Concordance*, 3 vols (Louvain: Librarie Universitaire, 1911–32); Seaton, 'Marlowe's Map', *Essays and Studies by Members of the English Association*, 10 (1924), pp. 13–35 and 'Fresh Sources for Marlowe', *Review of English Studies*, 5 (1929), pp. 385–401; Spence, 'The Influence of Marlowe's Sources on *Tamburlaine I*', *Modern Philology*, 24

(1926), pp. 181–99, and 'Tamburlaine and Marlowe', *PMLA*, 42 (1927), pp. 604–22; Camden, 'Tamburlaine: The Choleric Man', *Modern Language Notes*, 44 (1929), pp. 430–5; and Thorp, 'The Ethical Problem in Marlowe's Tamburlaine', *JEGP*, 29 (1930), pp. 385–9.

16 Eliot, 'Christopher Marlowe' [1918], in *The Sacred Wood: Essays on Poetry and Criticism* (New York: Knopf, 1921), pp. 82–3; Chambers, *The Elizabethan Stage*, 4 vols (Oxford: Clarendon, 1923), II, 135; *Tamburlaine the Great*, ed. by Ellis-Fermor (London: Methuen, 1930); *Christopher Marlowe* (London: Methuen, 1927), pp. 24–60.

17 Battenhouse, *Marlowe's 'Tamburlaine': A Study in Renaissance Moral Philosophy* (Nashville, TN: Vanderbilt University Press, 1941), p. 258; Bakeless, *The Tragicall History of Christopher Marlowe*, 2 vols (Cambridge, MA: Harvard University Press, 1942), II, 176, I, 238–73.

18 Kocher, 'Marlowe's Art of War', *Studies in Philology*, 39 (1942), pp. 207–25; *Christopher Marlowe: A Study of His Thought, Learning and Character* (Chapel Hill: University of North Carolina Press, 1946), p. 188; Wilson, *Marlowe and the Early Shakespeare* (Clarendon: Oxford, 1953), pp. 19, 48.

19 Levin, *The Overreacher: A Study of Christopher Marlowe* (Boston: Beacon Press, 1952), p. 48.

20 Ribner, 'The Idea of History in Marlowe's *Tamburlaine*', *English Literary History*, 20 (1953), pp. 251–66; 'Machiavelli and Marlowe', *Comparative Literature*, 6 (1954), pp. 349–56; 'Greene's Attack on Marlowe: Some Light on *Alphonsus* and *Selimus*', *Studies in Philology*, 52 (1955), pp. 161, 166, 163.

21 Waith, *The Herculean Hero in Marlowe, Chapman, Shakespeare, and Dryden* (London: Chatto and Windus, 1962); Cole, *Suffering and Evil in the Plays of Christopher Marlowe* (Princeton, NJ: Princeton University Press, 1962), pp. 113, 250; Bevington, *From 'Mankind' to Marlowe: Growth of Structure in the Drama of Tudor England* (Cambridge, MA: Harvard University Press, 1962), p. 216.

22 Leech, ed., *Marlowe: A Collection of Critical Essays* (Englewood Cliffs, NJ: Prentice Hall, 1964); Morris, *Christopher Marlowe* (London: Ernest Benn, 1968); *Tulane Drama Review*, Marlowe

Issue, 8 (1964); Steane, *Marlowe: A Critical Study* (Cambridge: Cambridge University Press, 1964); Steane, ed., *Christopher Marlowe: The Complete Plays* (Harmondsworth: Penguin, 1969).

23 'Introduction', in *The Cambridge Companion to Christopher Marlowe*, ed. by Patrick Cheney (Cambridge: Cambridge University Press, 2004), pp. 1–23; Leech, ed., *Marlowe*, p. 9.

24 Barber, 'The Death of Zenocrate: "Conceiving and subduing both" in Marlowe's *Tamburlaine*', *Literature and Psychology*, 16 (1966), p. 18; Sanders, *The Dramatist and the Received Idea* (Cambridge: Cambridge University Press, 1968), p. 35; Fanta, *Marlowe's 'Agonists': An Approach to the Ambiguity of His Plays* (Cambridge, MA: Harvard University Press, 1970), p. 7; *The Plays of Christopher Marlowe*, ed. by Gill (Oxford: Oxford University Press, 1971), p. xii.

25 Cutts, 'Tamburlaine "as fierce Achilles was"', *Comparative Drama*, 1 (1967), p. 108; Armstrong, *Marlowe's 'Tamburlaine': The Image and the Stage* (Hull: Hull University Press, 1966), p. 9; Cockcroft, 'Emblematic Irony: Some Possible Significances of Tamburlaine's Chariot', *Renaissance and Modern Studies*, 12 (1968), p. 33.

26 Merchant, 'Marlowe the Orthodox', and Hattaway, 'Marlowe and Brecht', in *Christopher Marlowe*, ed. by Morris (London: Ernest Benn, 1968), pp. 177–92 and 95–112.

27 Morris, 'Marlowe's Poetry', *Tulane Drama Review*, Marlowe Issue, 8 (1964), p. 139; Brown, 'Marlowe and the Actors', *Tulane Drama Review*, Marlowe Issue, 8 (1964), pp. 158–60; Richards, 'Marlowe's *Tamburlaine II*: A Drama of Death', *Modern Language Quarterly*, 26 (1965), p. 204.

28 Steane, *Marlowe: A Critical Study* (Cambridge: Cambridge University Press, pp. 82–3, 69, 73, 87, 82–3; Godshalk, *The Marlovian World Picture* (Mouton: The Hague, 1974), p. 13.

29 Barber, 'The Death of Zenocrate', pp. 19, 16; Kuriyama, *Hammer or Anvil* (New Brunswick, NJ: Rutgers University Press, 1980), pp. 13, 23, 26–8. For reviews, see Claude Summers in *Journal of English and Germanic Philology*, 81 (1982),

pp. 254–8; and T. McAlindon, *Review of English Studies*, 34 n.s. (1983), pp. 210–12.

30 Greenblatt, *Renaissance Self-Fashioning from More to Shakespeare* (Chicago: University of Chicago Press, 1980), p. 194; Garber, '"Here's Nothing Writ": Scribe, Script, and Circumscription in Marlowe's Plays', *Theatre Journal*, 36 (1984), p. 302; Dollimore, *Radical Tragedy: Religion, Ideology, and Power in the Drama of Shakespeare and His Contemporaries* (Chicago: University of Chicago Press, 1984), p. 112; Shepherd, *Marlowe and the Politics of Elizabethan Theatre* (Brighton: Harvester Press, 1986), p. 120.

31 *Tamburlaine the Great Parts I and II*, ed. by John Jump (Lincoln: University of Nebraska Press, 1967);*Tamburlaine the Great Parts 1 and 2*, ed. by J. W. Harper (London: Benn, 1971); *The Complete Works of Christopher Marlowe*, ed. by Fredson Bowers (Cambridge: Cambridge University Press, 1973); *Tamburlaine the Great*, ed. by J. S. Cunningham (Manchester: Manchester University Press, 1981).

32 Brooks, 'Marlowe and Early Shakespeare', in *Christopher Marlowe*, ed. by Brian Morris (New York: Hill and Wang, 1969), p. 92; Altman, *The Tudor Play of Mind: Rhetorical Inquiry and the Development of Elizabethan Drama* (Berkeley, CA: University of California Press, 1978), p. 323.

33 Ribner, 'Marlowe and the Critics', *Tulane Drama Review*, Marlowe Issue, 8 (1964), pp. 211–24; Friedenreich, 'Directions in *Tamburlaine* Criticism', in *Christopher Marlowe's 'Tamburlaine Part I and Part II': Text and Major Criticism,* ed. by Irving Ribner (Indianapolis, IN: Bobbs-Merrill, 1974), pp. 341–52; Maclure, *Christopher Marlowe: The Critical Heritage 1588-1896* (Routledge and Kegan Paul, 1979); Fehrenbach et al, eds, *A Concordance to the Plays, Poems, and Translations of Christopher Marlowe* (Ithaca, NY: Cornell University Press, 1979).

34 Rose, *The Expense of Spirit* (Ithaca, NY: Cornell University Press, 1988), pp. 96, 149–52; Sinfield, *Faultlines: Cultural Materialism and the Politics of Dissident Reading* (Berkeley, CA: University of California Press, 1992), pp. 237–8, 241; Bartels, 'The Double Vision of the East: Imperialist Self-Construction in Marlowe's *Tamburlaine, Part One*', *Renaissance Drama*, n.s., 23

(1992), p. 24; see also *Spectacles of Strangeness: Imperialism, Alienation, and Marlowe* (Philadelphia: University of Pennsylvania Press, 1993); Hopkins, '"And shall I die, and this unconquered?": Marlowe's Inverted Colonialism', *Early Modern Literary Studies*, 2.2 (1996), pp. 1–23; Shepard, 'Endless Sacks: Soldiers' Desire in *Tamburlaine*', *Renaissance Quarterly*, 46 (1993), pp. 739–40, 735–6.

35 Deats, *Sex, Gender, and Desire in the Plays of Christopher Marlowe* (Newark, DE: University of Delaware Press, 1997); Starks, '"Won with thy words and conquered with thy looks": Sadism, Masochism, and the Masochistic Gaze in *1 Tamburlaine*', in *Marlowe, History, and Sexuality: New Critical Essays on Christopher Marlowe*, ed. by Paul Whitfield White (New York: AMS Press, 1998), p. 179; Emsley, '"I Cannot Love, to be an Emperess": Women and Honour in *Tamburlaine*', *Dalhousie Review*, 80 (2000), p. 186.

36 Cheney, *Marlowe's Counterfeit Profession: Ovid, Spenser, Counter-Nationhood* (Toronto: University of Toronto Press, 1997), p. 118. For Burnett, see '*Tamburlaine the Great, Parts One and Two*', in *The Cambridge Companion to Christopher Marlowe*, ed. by Patrick Cheney (Cambridge: Cambridge University Press, 2004), p. 127; 'Tamburlaine: An Elizabethan Vagabond', *Studies in Philology*, 84 (1987), pp. 308–23; '*Tamburlaine* and the Renaissance Concept of Honour', *Studia Neophilologica*, 59 (1987), pp. 201–6; '*Tamburlaine* and the Body', *Criticism*, 33 (1991), pp. 31–47; *Marlowe, History and Sexuality: New Critical Essays on Christopher Marlowe* (New York: AMS Press, 1998); *Christopher Marlowe: The Complete Plays* (London: Everyman, 1999).

37 Wilson, 'Visible Bullets: *Tamburlaine the Great* and Ivan the Terrible', in *Christopher Marlowe*, ed. by Richard Wilson (London: Longman, 1999), pp. 120–39; *Tamburlaine the Great, Parts 1 and 2*, ed. by David Fuller (Oxford: Clarendon Press, 1998).

Chapter 2

1 Benedict Nightingale, 'Amphitheatre of War', *New Statesman*, 8 October 1976.

2   Lyn Gardner, 'Tamburlaine review – stylish take on Marlowe's tale of toxic masculinity', *Guardian*, 21 March 2017.

3   Michael Boyd, 'Q&A with *Tamburlaine* Director Michael Boyd', *RSC*, n.d., 2009. https://web.archive.org/web/20180611201516/https://www.rsc.org.uk/news/q-a-with-tamburlaine-director-michael-boyd [accessed 17 January 2020].

4   Christopher Marlowe, *The famous tragedy of the rich Ievv of Malta* (London, 1633), A4v.

5   Ibid.

6   Robert Greene, *Perimedes the blacke-smith* (London, 1588), A3r.

7   Tom Rutter, '*Tamburlaine*: Parts One and Two' in *Christopher Marlowe at 450*, ed. by Sara Munson Deats and Robert A. Logan (Farnham: Ashgate, 2015), pp. 51–70 (p. 51).

8   Holger Schott Syme, 'Marlowe in his Moment' in *Christopher Marlowe in Context*, ed. by Emily C. Bartels and Emma Smith (Cambridge: Cambridge University Press, 2013), pp. 275–84.

9   Qtd in Richard Wilson, 'Visible Bullets: Tamburlaine the Great and Ivan the Terrible', *ELH* 62.1 (1995), 47–68 (p. 59).

10 Ben Jonson, *Discoveries*, ed. by Lorna Hutson, in *The Cambridge Edition of the Works of Ben Jonson*, ed. by David Bevington, Martin Butler and Ian Donaldson (Cambridge: Cambridge University Press, 2012), 562–4.

11 Christopher Matusiak, 'Marlowe and Theatre History' in *Christopher Marlowe at 450*, ed. by Sara Munson Deats and Robert A. Logan (Farnham: Ashgate, 2015), pp. 281–308 (p. 289).

12 See Peter Kirwan, 'Marlowe's Early Books: The *Contention* and a "Marlowe Effect"' in *Christopher Marlowe, Theatrical Commerce, and the Book Trade*, ed. by Kirk Melnikoff and Roslyn L. Knutson (Cambridge: Cambridge University Press, 2018), pp. 134–48.

13 Anthony B. Dawson, ed., *Tamburlaine*, 2nd edn. (London: New Mermaids, 1997), p. xxx.

14 R. A. Foakes, ed. *Henslowe's Diary*, 2nd edn (Cambridge: Cambridge University Press, 2002), p. 322.

15 Heather J. Violanti, '*Tamburlaine the Great*, Cannon's Mouth Productions', *Research Opportunities in Medieval and Renaissance Drama*, 43 (2004), 123–4 (p. 123).

16 Lyn Gardner, 'Tamburlaine the Great', *Guardian*, 15 September 2003.

17 Violanti, pp. 123–4.

18 Paul Menzer (private communication, email, 30 May 2019).

19 Charles Saunders, *Tamerlane the Great* (London, 1681), preface.

20 Nancy T. Leslie, '*Tamburlaine* in the Theater: Tartar Grand Guignol or Janus?', *Renaissance Drama*, 4 (1971), 105–20 (p. 106).

21 Linda McJannet, 'Timür's Theatrical Journey: Or, when Did Tamburlaine Become Black?', *Sederi* 26 (2016), 31–66 (p. 35).

22 Saunders, E4v.

23 Donald B. Clark, 'The Source and Characterization of Nicholas Rowe's *Tamerlane*', *Modern Language Notes* 65.3 (1950), 145–52 (p. 145).

24 McJannet, p. 38.

25 Ibid.

26 Clark, p. 151.

27 McJannet, p. 39.

28 McJannet, p. 41.

29 Leslie, p. 110.

30 Ibid.

31 Leslie, p. 112.

32 Ervin Beck, '"Tamburlaine" for the Modern Stage', *Educational Theatre Journal* 23.1 (1971), 62–74 (p. 62).

33 Beck, p. 64.

34 Beck, p. 68.

35 Tyrone Guthrie, qtd in Beck, p. 71.

36 Leslie, p. 113.

37 Richard Hayes, 'Kings and Desperate Men', *Commonweal*, 9 March 1956.

38 Jane W. Stedman, '*Tamburlaine the Great* by Christopher Marlowe', *Educational Theatre Journal* 25.1 (1973), p. 106.

39 David Bevington, 'Marlowe's Plays in Performance: A Brief History' in *Christopher Marlowe at 450*, ed. by Sara

Munson Deats and Robert A. Logan (Farnham: Ashgate, 2015), pp. 257–80 (p. 266).

40 John Heilpern, 'Play it with chutzpah!', *Observer*, 19 December 1976, pp. 12–16 (p.15).

41 The National Theatre Archive file RNT/PO/3/1/1 contains a diagrammatic breakdown of the blocking through plans and cartoons.

42 Ibid.

43 John Elsom, 'Gore and Trinkets', *Listener*, 14 October 1976.

44 Ibid.

45 Michael Billington, 'Tamburlaine', *Guardian*, 5 October 1976.

46 Irving Wardle, 'Tamburlaine the Great: Olivier', *The Times*, 5 October 1976.

47 Heilpern, p. 14.

48 Wardle, 'Tamburlaine the Great: Olivier'.

49 Ibid.

50 Billington, 'Tamburlaine'.

51 Elsom; John Walker, 'An Excellent Opener for the Olivier', *Herald Tribune*, 9 October 1976.

52 Irving Wardle, 'Theatre / Marlowe's Rambo triumphant: Tamburlaine – Swan; Merry Wives of Windsor – Royal Shakespeare, Stratford; Amphibians – Pit', *Independent*, 6 September 1992.

53 Martin Wiggins, 'Review, *Tamburlaine the Great*', *Cahiers Élisabéthains* 44.1 (1993), 81–4 (p. 81).

54 J. S. Cunningham and Eithne Henson, eds, *Tamburlaine* (Manchester: Manchester University Press, 1998), p. 29.

55 Bevington, p. 274.

56 Michael Billington, 'In the Court of A Monster', *Guardian*, 3 September 1992.

57 Terry Hands, interviewed in Brian G. Myers, 'Terry Hands on "Tamburlaine": Humanity with Teeth Bared', *Shakespeare Bulletin* 11.2 (1993), 21–2 (p. 21).

58 Margaret Loftus Ranald, '*Tamburlaine the Great*', *Shakespeare Bulletin* 11.2 (1993), 20–1 (p. 20).

59 Wardle, 'Theatre / Marlowe's Rambo triumphant'.

60 Lyn Gardner, '*Tamburlaine*', *Guardian*, 15 October 2005.

61 Ibid.

62 Skip Shand, '*Tamburlaine*', *Shakespeare Bulletin* 24.2 (2006), 49–54 (p. 49).

63 David Farr, 'Tamburlaine wasn't censored', *Guardian*, 25 November 2005.

64 Kevin Quarmby, '*Tamburlaine*, Young Genius', *Research Opportunities in Medieval and Renaissance Drama* 45 (2006), 143–5 (pp. 143–4).

65 Sam Marlowe, 'Theatre – *Tamburlaine*', *The Times*, 11 November 2005; Shand, p. 50.

66 McJannet, pp. 51ff.

67 Laura G. Godwin, '*Tamburlaine* and *Edward II*', *Shakespeare Bulletin* 27.1 (2009), 122–31 (pp. 124–5).

68 McJannet, p. 52.

69 Anita M. Hagerman, '*Tamburlaine*, Shakespeare Theatre Company', *Research Opportunities in Medieval and Renaissance Drama* 47 (2008), 144–7 (p. 145).

70 Paul Harris, 'Marlowe Festival: *Tamburlaine*, *Edward II*', *Variety*, 13 November 2007.

71 Godwin, p. 126.

72 McJannet, pp. 53–4, quoting Godwin, p. 125.

73 Hagerman, p. 146.

74 Charles Isherwood, 'Shakespeare's New House Makes Room for Marlowe', *New York Times*, 15 November 2007.

75 Maryam Philpott, 'Tamburlaine the Great: Part 2 – Jackson's Lane, London', *The Reviews Hub*, 19 March 2015. https://www.thereviewshub.com/tamburlaine-the-great-part-2-jacksons-lane-london/ [accessed 24 March 2019].

76 Neil Cheesman, 'Tamburlaine the Great at Tristan Bates Theatre – Review', *London Theatre 1*, 5 July 2015. https://www.londontheatre1.com/reviews/tamburlaine-the-great-at-tristan-bates-theatre-review/ [accessed 24 March 2019].

77 Philpott.

78 Yellow Earth, '*Tamburlaine*', https://yellowearth.org/tamburlaine/ [accessed 16 March 2019].

79 Gardner, 'Tamburlaine review'.

80 Peter Malin, '*Tamburlaine* by Christopher Marlowe', *Blogging Shakespeare*, 13 April 2017. http://bloggingshakespeare.com/reviewing-shakespeare/tamburlaine-christopher-marlowe-adapted-dir-ng-choon-ping-yellow-earth-theatre-old-fire-station-oxford-april-2017/ [accessed 24 March 2019].

81 Boyd.

82 Claire M. L. Bourne, '*Tamburlaine the Great, Parts I and II*' (review), *Shakespeare Bulletin* 33.2 (2015), 347–50 (pp. 347–8).

83 Pascale Aebischer, '*Tamburlaine*, presented by the Royal Shakespeare Company' (review), *Shakespeare Bulletin* 37.1 (2019), 115–19 (p. 117).

84 Dan Venning, '*Tamburlaine, Parts I and II*' (review), *Theatre Journal* 67.4 (2015), 727–9 (p. 728).

85 Bourne, p. 350.

86 Aebischer, p. 116.

87 McJannet, p. 55.

88 Eric Minton, 'Who Had *It*, Who Lost It, and Who Won', *Shakespeareances*, 12 October 2011. http://www.shakespeareances.com/willpower/nonshakespeare/Tamburlaine-01-ASC11.html [accessed 24 March 2019].

89 Wardle, 'Theatre / Marlowe's Rambo triumphant'.

Chapter 3

1 Tom Rutter, '*Tamburlaine*: Parts One and Two', in *Christopher Marlowe at 450*, ed. by Sara Munson Deats and Robert A. Logan (Farnham: Ashgate, 2015), pp. 51–70 (p. 55).

2 See Nabil Matar, *Islam in Britain, 1558–1685* (Cambridge: Cambridge University Press, 1998) and *Britain and Barbary, 1589–1689* (Gainesville: University Press of Florida, 2005).

3   Richmond Barbour, *Before Orientalism: London's Theatre of the East, 1576–1626* (Cambridge: Cambridge University Press, 2003), p. 3.

4   Jonathan Burton, 'Anglo-Ottoman Relations and the Image of the Turk in *Tamburlaine*', *Journal of Medieval and Early Modern Studies* 30.1 (2000), 125–56 (p. 127).

5   Burton, p. 138.

6   Matthew Dimmock, *New Turkes: Dramatizing Islam and the Ottomans in Early Modern England* (Aldershot: Ashgate, 2005; rpt. Abingdon: Routledge, 2016), p. 159.

7   Linda McJannet, *The Sultan Speaks: Dialogue in English Plays and Histories about the Ottoman Turks* (Basingstoke: Palgrave, 2006), pp. 72–89. For more on the *Tamburlaine* plays' portrayal of the Islamic world and what they reveal about early modern English attitudes to 'Turks' and other Muslim peoples, see Jane Grogan, '"A Warre . . . commodious": Dramatizing Islamic Schism in and after *Tamburlaine*', *Texas Studies in Literature and Language* 54.1 (2012), 45–78; Daniel Vitkus, *Turning Turk: English Theatre and the Multicultural Mediterranean, 1570–1630* (Basingstoke: Palgrave Macmillan, 2003); and others.

8   Jonathan Gil Harris, 'Tamburlaine in Hindustan' in *Theatre Cultures within Globalising Empires: Looking at Early Modern England and Spain*, ed. by Joachim Küpper and Leonie Pawlita (Berlin: De Gruyter, 2018), pp. 188–204 (pp. 198, 203).

9   Vin Nardizzi, 'Environ', in *Veer Ecology: A Companion for Environmental Thinking*, ed. by Jeffrey Jerome Cohen and Lowell Duckert (Minneapolis: University of Minnesota Press, 2017), pp. 183–95 (p. 187).

10 Nardizzi, p. 192.

11 Nardizzi, p. 193.

12 Zümre Gizem Yilmaz, 'The Sweet Fruition of an Earthly Crown': Elemental Mastery and Eophobia in *Tamburlaine the Great* and *Doctor Faustus*', *SEDERI: Journal of the Spanish Society for English Renaissance Studies*, 28 (2018), 79–96 (pp. 95–6).

13 John Parker, *The Aesthetics of Antichrist: From Christian Drama to Christopher Marlowe* (Ithaca: Cornell University Press, 2007), pp. 219–20.

14 Joel Elliot Slotkin '"Seeke out another Godhead": Religious Epistemology and Representations of Islam in *Tamburlaine*', *Modern Philology*, 111.3 (2014), 408–36 (p. 416).

15 Slotkin, p. 435.

16 Leila Watkins, 'Justice *Is* a Mirage: Failures of Religious Order in Marlowe's *Tamburlaine* Plays', *Comparative Drama* 46.2 (2012), 163–85.

17 Foundational to late-twentieth and twenty-first century scholarship on the history of material texts has been Leah S. Marcus, *Unediting the Renaissance: Shakespeare, Marlowe, Milton* (London: Routledge, 1996).

18 Mathew R. Martin, 'Inferior Readings: The Transmigration of "Material" in *Tamburlaine the Great*', *Early Theatre*, 17.2 (2014), 57–75 (p. 57).

19 Kirk Melnikoff, 'Jones's Pen and Marlowe's Socks: Richard Jones, Print Culture, and the Beginnings of English Dramatic Literature', *Studies in Philology*, 102.2 (2005), 184–209.

20 Melnikoff, 'Jones's Pen', pp. 206, 190–1.

21 Kirk Melnikoff and Roslyn L. Knutson, eds, *Christopher Marlowe, Theatrical Commerce, and the Book Trade* (Cambridge: Cambridge University Press, 2018), p. xviii.

22 Adam G. Hooks, 'Making Marlowe', in *Christopher Marlowe, Theatrical Commerce, and the Book Trade*, ed. by Melnikoff and Knutson (Cambridge: Cambridge University Press, 2018), pp. 97–114.

23 Claire M. L. Bourne, 'Making a Scene; or *Tamburlaine the Great* in Print' in *Christopher Marlowe, Theatrical Commerce, and the Book Trade*, ed. by Melnikoff and Knutson (Cambridge: Cambridge University Press, 2018), pp. 115–33.

24 Peter Kirwan, 'Marlowe's Early Books: The *Contention* and a "Marlowe Effect"', in *Christopher Marlowe, Theatrical Commerce, and the Book Trade*, ed. by Melnikoff and Knutson (Cambridge: Cambridge University Press, 2018), pp. 134–48.

25 Tara L. Lyons, 'Richard Jones, *Tamburlaine the Great*, and the Making (and Remaking) of a Serial Play Collection in the 1590s', in *Christopher Marlowe, Theatrical Commerce, and the*

Book Trade, ed. by Melnikoff and Knutson (Cambridge: Cambridge University Press, 2018), pp. 149–64 (p. 150).

26 See Wall-Randell, 'What is a Staged Book? Books as "Actors" in the Early Modern English Theatre', in *Rethinking Theatrical Documents in Shakespeare's England*, ed. by Tiffany Stern (London: Bloomsbury, 2019) pp. 128–51.

27 See Lisa Hopkins, *A Christopher Marlowe Chronology* (Basingstoke: Palgrave Macmillan, 2005), pp. 178, 182; see also M. L. Stapleton's chapter in this volume.

28 Hooks, 'Making Marlowe', pp. 107–8.

29 On the Greene preface, see Tom Rutter, 'Marlowe, the "Mad Priest of the Sun," and Heliogabalus', *Early Theatre*, 13.1 (2010), 109–19 (pp. 109–10).

30 See Melnikoff, 'Jones's Pen', pp. 185–8 for a discussion of the history of critical responses to Jones's account of his cuts.

31 Another critical approach to *Tamburlaine* that remains underdeveloped in recent years, relative to its visibility in the wider field of early modern literary study, is a feminist or gender-focused reading. Future scholars may continue on the path charted by Mary Beth Rose in *Gender and Heroism in Early Modern English Literature* (Chicago: University of Chicago Press, 2002). Calling Tamburlaine 'perhaps the case in point' for 'the privileging of active male agency in defining and achieving heroic dominance' (p. 3), Rose focuses not just on the problematically 'static and decorative' Zenocrate but also on 'the fluctuating interchange of gendered positions that constitute Tamburlaine's heroic identity' (pp. 4–5).

32 Peter Gibbard, 'Breaking Up the Line: The Sententious Style in Elizabethan Blank Verse', *Modern Philology*, 112.2 (2014), 312–35 (pp. 328–32).

33 Bryan Lowrance, 'Marlowe's Wit: Power, Language, and the Literary in *Tamburlaine* and *Doctor Faustus*', *Modern Philology*, 111.4 (2014), 711–33 (p. 712).

34 Lowrance, p. 714.

35 Lowrance, p. 722.

36 Catherine Nicholson, *Uncommon Tongues: Eloquence and Eccentricity in the English Renaissance* (Philadelphia: University of Pennsylvania Press, 2013), pp. 150, 18.

37 Andrew Duxfield, *Christopher Marlowe and the Failure to Unify* (Farnham: Ashgate, 2015), p. 39

38 Duxfield, p. 63.

39 Jacques Lezra, 'Geography and Marlowe' in *Christopher Marlowe in Context*, ed. by Emily C. Bartels and Emma Smith (Cambridge: Cambridge University Press, 2013), pp. 125–37 (p. 126).

40 Patrick Cheney, *Marlowe's Republican Authorship: Lucan, Liberty, and the Sublime* (Basingstoke: Palgrave Macmillan, 2009), p. 9.

41 Cheney, *Marlowe's Republican Authorship*, p. 81.

42 Cheney, *Marlowe's Republican Authorship*, pp. 110, 96, 112.

43 Patrick Cheney, *English Authorship and the Early Modern Sublime: Fictions of Transport in Spenser, Marlowe, Jonson, and Shakespeare* (Cambridge: Cambridge University Press, 2018), p. 137.

44 Cheney, *English Authorship*, p. 16.

45 Lisa Hopkins, *Christopher Marlowe: A Literary Life* (Basingstoke: Palgrave Macmillan, 2000), pp. 43–64.

46 Hopkins, *Christopher Marlowe: A Literary Life*, p. 57.

47 David Riggs, *The World of Christopher Marlowe* (New York: Henry Holt and Company, 2004), pp. 159–73.

48 Riggs, pp. 166–7, citing *I Tam* 2.7.21.

49 Riggs, pp. 170–2.

50 Riggs, pp. 213–16.

51 Park Honan, *Christopher Marlowe: Poet and Spy* (Oxford: Oxford University Press, 2005), p. 167.

52 Honan, p. 167.

53 Charles Whitney, *Early Responses to Renaissance Drama* (Cambridge: Cambridge University Press, 2008), p. 20.

Chapter 4

1 Gill Partington and Adam Smyth, introduction to *Book Destruction from the Medieval to the Contemporary* (New York and Basingstoke: Palgrave Macmillan, 2014), p. 4.

2   *Tamburlaine the Great* (London: Richard Jones, 1590), sig. K5r.

3   On the genre debate surrounding *Tamburlaine*, see Sara Munson Deats, 'Marlowe's Interrogative Drama: *Dido, Tamburlaine, Doctor Faustus,* and *Edward II*', in *Marlowe's Empery: Expanding His Critical Contexts*, ed. by Deats and Robert A. Logan (Newark: University of Delaware Press, 2002), pp. 107–30; Joel Altman, *The Tudor Play of the Mind: Rhetorical Inquiry and the Development of Elizabethan Drama* (Berkeley CA: University of California Press, 1978), p. 71; and Tara L. Lyons, 'Richard Jones, *Tamburlaine the Great*, and the Making (and Remaking) of Serial Play Collections in the 1590s', in *Christopher Marlowe, Theatrical Commerce, and the Book Trade*, ed. by Kirk Melnikoff and Roslyn L. Knutson (Cambridge: Cambridge University Press, 2018), pp. 149–64.

4   See Sonia Massai, *Shakespeare and the Rise of the Editor* (Cambridge: Cambridge University Press, 2009).

5   *Tamburlaine the greate . . . The second part* (London: Edward White, 1606), sig. L2r, 1977 2594, Beinecke Rare Book and Manuscript Library.

6   See note 3. Arber, Edward. *A Transcript of the Registers of the Company of Stationers of London, 1554–1640*, 5 vols. (London: [n.p.], 1875–1877), II (1875), p. 558; and *Tamburlaine* (1590), sigs. A1r and A2r.

7   'Daunted' is not a variant that appears in any earlier edition.

8   Indeed, David McInnis has pointed out that there is no known evidence of the *Tamburlaine* plays ever being commonplaced ('Booking Marlowe's Plays', *Christopher Marlowe, Theatrical Commerce, and the Book Trade*, pp. 130–2). On the general difficulty of 'proving' how early modern readers read their books, see William H. Sherman, *Used Books: Marking Readers in Renaissance England* (Philadelphia: University of Pennsylvania Press, 2007), p. xvi; and Heidi Brayman, 'Consuming Readers: Ladies, Lapdogs, and Libraries', in *Reading Material in Early Modern England* (Cambridge: Cambridge University Press, 2005), pp. 196–255.

9   See Zachary Lesser and Peter Stallybrass, 'The First Literary *Hamlet* and the Commonplacing of Professional Plays', *Shakespeare Quarterly*, 59.4 (2008), 371–420; and Claire M. L.

Bourne, 'This Play I Red and Other Marginal Notes on Reading', *The Collation: Research and Exploration at the Folger* (blog), 5 March 2015, https://collation.folger.edu/2015/03/this-play-i-red-and-other-marginal-notes-on-reading/

10 See Aaron T. Pratt, 'Stab-Stitching and the Status of Early English Playbooks as Literature', *The Library*, 7th series, 16.3 (2015), 304–28.

11 On Jones's agency in bringing the plays to press, see Kirk Melnikoff, 'Jones's Pen and Marlowe's Socks: Richard Jones, Print Culture, and the Beginnings of English Dramatic Literature', *Studies in Philology*, 102.2 (2005), 184–209; and Claire M. L. Bourne, 'Making a Scene: *Tamburlaine the Great* in Print', in *Christopher Marlowe, Theatrical Commerce, and the Book Trade*, pp. 115–33.

12 See Lyons, 'Serial Play Collections', pp. 149–64.

13 There is no entry in the *Stationers' Register* recording this transfer. See Kirk Melnikoff, 'Jones, Richard (fl. 1564–1613), bookseller and printer', *Oxford Dictionary of National Biography*. https://doi.org/10.1093/ref:odnb/15070

14 William Oxberry, ed. *Tamburlaine the Great: a tragedy* (London, [n.p.], 1820).

15 Charles Whitney, *Early Responses to Renaissance Drama* (Cambridge: Cambridge University Press, 2006), p. 18.

16 Christopher Marlowe, *The Famous Tragedy of the Rich Iew of Malta* (London: Nicholas Vavasour, 1633), sig. A4v.

17 William Prynne, *Histrio-Mastix. The Players Scovrge* (London: Michael Sparke, 1633), sig. Ddd2r.

18 Lucy Munro, 'Marlowe on the Caroline Stage', *Shakespeare Bulletin*, 27.1 (2009), 39–50 (pp. 43–7).

19 Munro, p. 39.

20 Alan B. Farmer and Zachary Lesser, 'Canons and Classics: Publishing Drama in Caroline England', in *Localizing Caroline Drama: Politics and Economics of the Early Modern English Stage, 1625-1642*, ed. by Adam Zucker and Alan B. Farmer (New York and Basingstoke: Palgrave Macmillan, 2006), pp. 31–2.

21 Farmer and Lesser, 'Canons and Classics', p. 40.

22 See Adam G. Hooks, 'Making Plays: Booksellers and the Bio-bibliography of Shakespeare', in *Selling Shakespeare: Bibliography, Biography, and the Book Trade* (Cambridge: Cambridge University Press, 2016), pp. 136–77; and Aaron T. Pratt, 'The Status of Playbooks in Early Modern England' (unpublished doctoral dissertation, Yale University, 2016), pp. 132–3.

23 *The Careles Shepherdess . . . With an Alphebeticall Catologue of all such Plays that ever were Printed* (London: Richard Rogers and William Lee, 1656).

24 Pratt, 'Status of Playbooks', p. 133. Here, Pratt suggests that this inventory probably included both playbooks that Rogers and Lee had purchased wholesale from other stationers *and* used copies of plays they had acquired from readers and collectors.

25 Unlike Rogers and Lee's catalogue, Archer's was bibliographically independent and thus could have been easily circulated with other quartos or by itself.

26 *The Excellent Comedy, called The Old Law: OR A new way to please you. . . . Together with an exact and perfect Catalogue of all the Playes, with the Authors Names, and what are Comedies, Tragedies, Histories, Pastoralls, Masks, Interludes, more exactly Printed then ever before* (London: Edward Archer, 1656).

27 *Tamburlaine* (1590), sig. A2r.

28 The two-play octavo published in 1597 (STC 17427), the quarto of *I Tamburlaine* published in 1605 (STC 17428), and the quarto of *II Tamburlaine* published in 1606 (STC 17428a) do not label the play a 'tragedy'.

29 *A True, perfect, and exact Catalogue of all the Comedies, Tragedies, Tragi-Comedies, Pastorals, Masques and Interludes, that were ever yet printed and published, till this present year 1661* (London: Francis Kirkman, 1661), sig. A1r.

30 See W. W. Greg, *A Bibliography of the English Printed Drama to 1660*, 4 vols. (London: The Bibliographical Society, 1939-59), III (1957), p. 1328; and Hooks, 'Making Plays', p. 147.

31 *The Unlucky Citizen* (London: Francis Kirkman, 1673), sig. S1v–S3r.

32 Edward Phillips, *Theatrum Poetarum* (London: Charles Smith, 1675), sig. Hh7v. Newton translated *Thebais* for the 1581

edition of Seneca's tragedies. See Hooks, 'Making Marlowe', in *Christopher Marlowe, Theatrical Commerce, and the Book Trade*, p. 109.

33 *A true, perfect, and exact catalogue of all the Comedies, Tragedies, Tragi-comedies, Pastorals, Masques and Interludes, that were ever yet printed and published, till this present year 1671* (London: Francis Kirkman, 1671), sig. B3v.

34 Gerard Langbaine, *A New Catalogue of English Plays : Containing All The Comedies, Tragedies, Tragi-comedies, Opera's, Masques, Pastorals, Interludes, Farces, &c. Both Ancient and Modern, that have ever yet been Printed, to this present Year, 1688* (London: Nicholas Cox, 1688 [i.e., 1687]).

35 Gerard Langbaine, *An Account of the English Dramatick Poets* (London: George West and Henry Clements, 1691), sig. Y4v.

36 William Van Lennep, ed. *The London Stage, 1660-1800*, 3 vols. (Carbondale, IL: Southern Illinois University Press, 1965–8), I (1965), p. 295.

37 George Saunders, *Tamerlane the Great* (London: Richard Bentley and James Magnes, 1681), sig. a1v.

38 Saunders explained that he 'drew the design' of his *Tamerlane* 'from a late *Novell*, call'd *Tamerlane* and *Asteria,* which I'm sure bears not half the Age of the Tragedy before mention'd, and I am confident the Characters are quite different' (*Tamerlane*, sig. a1v). See Emma Depledge, *Shakespeare's Rise to Cultural Prominence* (Cambridge: Cambridge University Press, 2018), p. 74.

39 Charles Gildon, rev. *The Lives and Characters of the English Dramatick Poets* (London: Thomas Leigh and William Turner, 1699), sig. G6v.

40 STC 17428a, Folger Shakespeare Library.

41 *Doctor Faustus* seems to have been the only play by Marlowe to be performed in the Restoration (Munro, p. 40).

42 For publishers as astute readers of the plays they saw to market, see Zachary Lesser, *Renaissance Drama and the Politics of Publication* (Cambridge: Cambridge University Press, 2004), esp. pp. 20–2.

43 On the potential difficulties of mediating comic material factoring into Jones's decision to omit the 'Iestures', see Bourne, 'Making a Scene', pp. 132–3.
44 Philip Sidney, *An Apologie for Poetrie* (London: Henry Olney, 1595), sig. K1v.
45 For Jones's attempt to manage the patchiness of *II Tamburlaine*, see Bourne, 'Making a Scene', p. 131.
46 John D. Jump, ed. *Tamburlaine the Great: Parts 1 and 2* (Lincoln: University of Nebraska Press, 1967), p. xiv.
47 These episodes have been explicitly described as Marlowe's attempt to 'fill in the gaps' of the Tamburlaine story (Roma Gill, ed. *The Plays of Christopher Marlowe*, vol 5 [Oxford: Oxford University Press, 1971], p. xvii).
48 *Tamburlaine the Great* (1606), sig. B2v, PR2669.A1 1606, Eberly Family Special Collections Library, Penn State.
49 *Tamburlaine the Great* (1606), sig. F3r, PR2669.A1 1606, Eberly Family Special Collections Library, Penn State.
50 *Tamburlaine the Great* (1606), sig. C2v, PR2669.A1 1606, Eberly Family Special Collections Library, Penn State.
51 *Tamburlaine the Great* (1606), sig. E2v and E3r, PR2669.A1 1606, Eberly Family Special Collections Library, Penn State.
52 *Tamburlaine the Great* (1606), sig. H1r and H1v, PR2669.A1 1606, Eberly Family Special Collections Library, Penn State.
53 *Tamburlaine the Great* (1606), sig. H4r, PR2669.A1 1606, Eberly Family Special Collections Library, Penn State.
54 *Tamburlaine the Great* (1606), sig. A2r.
55 *Tamburlaine the Great* (1606), sig. E3v, PR2669.A1 1606, Eberly Family Special Collections Library, Penn State.
56 *Tamburlaine the Great* (1606), sig. E4r, PR2669.A1 1606, Eberly Family Special Collections Library, Penn State.
57 *Tamburlaine the Great* (1606), sig. F2r, PR2669.A1 1606, Eberly Family Special Collections Library, Penn State.
58 *Tamburlaine the Great* (1606), sig. D4r, PR2669.A1 1606, Eberly Family Special Collections Library, Penn State.
59 *Tamburlaine the Great* (1606), sig. E1r, PR2669.A1 1606, Eberly Family Special Collections Library, Penn State.

60 *Tamburlaine the Great* (1606), sigs. E3r and F1v, PR2669.A1 1606, Eberly Family Special Collections Library, Penn State.

61 Copies of *Tamburlaine* with damaged, inlaid, or missing title pages include: STC 17425 (Malone 267[1], Bodleian Library; PR2669.A1 1590, Rare and Manuscript Collections, Cornell University Library; and RB 136105, Huntington Library); STC 17427 (RB 12954, Huntington Library); STC 17428 (1977 2594 [pt I], Beinecke Rare Book and Manuscript Library; Case 34 628, Newberry Library; and STC 17428, Folger Shakespeare Library); and STC 17428a (STC 17428a, Folger Shakespeare Library; Plays 2.9, Worcester College Library; 1977 2594 [pt II], Beinecke Rare Book and Manuscript Library).

Chapter 5

1 All references to *Tamburlaine* use Christopher Marlowe, *Tamburlaine Parts One and Two*, ed. by Anthony B. Dawson, 2nd edn. (London: A & C Black, 1997).

2 William Shakespeare, *King Richard II*, ed. by Charles R. Forker (London: Arden Shakespeare, 2002).

3 Howard Marchitello and Evelyn Tribble, 'Introduction', in *The Palgrave Handbook of Early Modern Literature and Science*, ed. by Howard Marchitello and Evelyn Tribble (London: Palgrave, 2017), pp. xxv–xlvi (p. xxvi).

4 Juliet Cummins and David Burchell, 'Introduction', in *Science, Literature and Rhetoric in Early Modern England*, ed. by Juliet Cummins and David Burchell (Aldershot: Ashgate, 2007), pp. 1–12 (pp. 6, 8). '"Natural philosophy" is often used by historians of science as an umbrella term to designate the study of nature before it could easily be identified with what we call "science" today': Ann Blair, 'Natural Philosophy', in *The Cambridge History of Science*, vol. 3: *Early Modern Science*, ed. by Katharine Park and Lorraine Daston (Cambridge: Cambridge University Press, 2006), pp. 365–406 (p. 365).

5 Mary Thomas Crane, *Losing Touch with Nature: Literature and the New Science in Sixteenth-Century England* (Baltimore: Johns Hopkins University Press, 2014), p. 2.

6   Chloe Kathleen Preedy, *Marlowe's Literary Scepticism: Politic Religion and Post-Reformation Polemic* (London: Arden Shakespeare, 2012), p. 192.

7   Steve Mentz, 'Tongues in the Storm: Shakespeare, Ecological Crisis, and the Resources of Genre', in *Ecocritical Shakespeare*, ed. by Lynne Bruckner and Dan Brayton (Farnham: Ashgate, 2011), pp. 155–71 (p. 164). See also Todd Borlik, *Ecocriticism and Early Modern English Literature: Green Pastures* (Abingdon: Routledge, 2011) and Gabriel Egan, *Green Shakespeare: From Ecopolitics to Ecocriticism* (London: Routledge, 2006), especially chapter 4, 'Supernature and the Weather: *King Lear* and *The Tempest*'.

8   Sophie Chiari, *Shakespeare's Representation of Weather, Climate and Environment: The Early Modern 'Fated Sky'* (Edinburgh: Edinburgh University Press, 2019), p. 15.

9   Craig Martin, *Renaissance Meteorology: Pomponazzi to Descartes* (Baltimore: Johns Hopkins University Press, 2011), pp. 2, 15.

10 Blair, pp. 367–8.

11 S. K. Heninger, Jr, *A Handbook of Renaissance Meteorology* (Durham, NC: Duke University Press, 1960), pp. 12, 20.

12 In the seventh scene of *Doctor Faustus*, Mephistopheles offers Faustus an account of the cosmos broadly in line with this summary.

13 Aristotle, *Meteorologica*, tr. by H. D. P. Lee, Loeb Classical Library 397 (Cambridge, MA: Harvard University Press, 1952), 1.3. My account of Aristotelian meteorological theory is also indebted to the texts by Heninger and Martin cited in these notes.

14 Aristotle, 1.2.

15 Aristotle, 1.4.

16 Heninger, p. 38.

17 *Luther's Works*, vol. 1: *Lectures on Genesis Chapters 1-5*, ed. by Jaroslav Pelikan (Saint Louis: Concordia, 1958), p. 53; Martin, p. 40.

18 Heninger, p. 133. There has been some critical discussion of whether the Nurse's observation in Shakespeare's *Romeo and*

Juliet, "'Tis since the earthquake now eleven years' (1.3.24), alludes to that of 1580, but the Arden editor René Weis argues that if any specific earthquake is intended, a later one of 1585 is more likely. See William Shakespeare, *Romeo and Juliet*, ed. by René Weis (London: Arden Shakespeare, 2012), pp. 36–7.

19 Arthur Golding, *A Discourse vpon the Earthquake that Hapned throughe this Realme of Englande, and Other Places of Christendom, the Sixt of Aprill. 1580* (London, 1580), A2r, A4r–B1r. For an account of comparable responses to the earthquake by Thomas Churchyard and the actor/writer Richard Tarlton, see Lily B. Campbell, 'Richard Tarlton and the Earthquake of 1580', *Huntington Library Quarterly* 4 (1941), 293–301.

20 [Gabriel Harvey and Edmund Spenser], *Three Proper, and Wittie, Familiar Letters: Lately Passed Betvveene Tvvo Vniuersitie Men: Touching the Earthquake in Aprill Last, and Our English Refourmed Versifying* (London, 1580), pp. 16–17, 19.

21 Harvey and Spenser, pp. 10–11.

22 Heninger, pp. 38–9. See for example Bartholomaeus Anglicus, *De proprietatibus rerum*, tr. by John Trevisa, rev. by Stephen Batman as *Batman vppon Bartholome* (London, 1582), fol. 163v: 'And sometime mist is corrupt by vapours, of the which it is gendered, and is ful greeuous and corrupteth veynes that burgen, and breedeth in beasts diuerse sicknesses and euilles.'

23 Thomas Lodge and Robert Greene, *A Looking Glasse for London and England* (London, 1594), sig. G2r (stage direction).

24 Harvey and Spenser, p. 18.

25 See also Lisa Hopkins, 'Playing with Matches: Christopher Marlowe's Incendiary Imagination', *Marlowe Studies: An Annual*, 1 (2011), 125–40. Hopkins writes that 'Tamburlaine himself is little short of a spirit of fire' (132).

26 In classical mythology, Danaë, imprisoned in a tower, was impregnated by the god Jupiter, who came to her in the form of a shower of gold.

27 Christopher Marlowe, *The Jew of Malta*, ed. by James R. Siemon, 3rd edn. (London: Methuen Drama, 2009), 5.5.122–3.

28 Niccolò Machiavelli, *Discourses on Livy*, tr. by Harvey C. Mansfield and Nathan Tarcov (Chicago: University of Chicago

Press, 1996), pp. 34–5. On this aspect of Machiavelli's thinking, see also Preedy, pp. 10–11.

29 *Letter Book of Gabriel Harvey, A. D. 1573-1580*, ed. by Edward John Long Scott (London: Camden Society, 1884), p. 79.

30 Letter to Sir John Puckering repr. in Arthur Freeman, *Thomas Kyd: Facts and Problems* (Oxford: Clarendon Press, 1967), p. 183.

31 For a somewhat different view of Tamburlaine's use of astrology, see Vanessa Ivette Corredera, 'Faces and Figures of Fortune: Astrological Physiognomy in *Tamburlaine Part 1*', *Early Modern Literary Studies*, 18 (2015), 1–26, which stresses Tamburlaine's ability to read astrological signs as indications of future events.

32 William Fulke, *A Goodly Gallery . . . to Beholde the Naturall Causes of All Kind of Meteors* (London, 1563), fol. 52r.

33 Crane, p. 152.

34 Fulke, fols. 15v–16r.

35 Crane, p. 22.

36 Francis Shakelton, *A Blazyng Starre or Burnyng Beacon, Seene the 10. of October Laste (and Yet Continewyng)* (London, 1580), sigs D3r–D3v, D6r.

37 The suggestion is made by Lisa Hopkins in *Christopher Marlowe, Renaissance Dramatist* (Edinburgh: Edinburgh University Press, 2008), p. 103.

38 Crane, pp. 148–9.

39 Crane, p. 153.

40 William Shakespeare, *Titus Andronicus*, ed. by Jonathan Bate (London: Routledge, 1995).

41 Gwilym Jones, *Shakespeare's Storms* (Manchester: Manchester University Press, 2015), pp. 31–49 (pp. 39, 46); William Shakespeare, *Julius Caesar*, ed. by David Daniell (London: Arden Shakespeare, 1998, rpt. 2002).

42 George Peele, *The Battle of Alcazar*, Act 5 Prologue. 5 SD–6, 14 SD–15, in *The Stukeley Plays*, ed. by Charles Edelman (Manchester: Manchester University Press, 2005).

43 3.2.0 SD 4 (note). Conceivably, such visual effects might have been among the 'fond and frivolous gestures' that the play's

printer Richard Jones said he '(purposely) omitted' ('To the gentlemen readers', lines 9–10).

44 Lisa Hopkins, *A Christopher Marlowe Chronology* (Basingstoke: Palgrave Macmillan, 2005), p. 135.

45 Shakelton, sig. D5v.

46 Golding, sig. A2r.

47 Golding, sigs C3r–C3v.

Chapter 6

1 All quotations of Shakespeare's *Othello* from the revised Arden 3 series *Othello*, ed. by E. A. J. Honigmann with a new introduction by Ayanna Thompson (London: Bloomsbury, rpt. 2019).

2 Notably, reluctance on discussing race or racial ideologies in early modern studies is not limited to scholarship on *Tamburlaine* or Marlowe more broadly. For a thorough discussion of this phenomenon, see Peter Erickson and Kim F. Hall, '"A New Scholarly Song": Re-Reading Early Modern Race', *Shakespeare Quarterly*, 67.1 (2016), 1–13.

3 Jonathan Burton, 'Anglo-Ottoman Relations and the Image of the Turk in *Tamburlaine*', *Journal of Medieval and Early Modern Studies*, 30.1 (2000), 125–57 (p. 125).

4 Emily C. Bartels, 'The Double Vision of the East: Imperialist Self-Construction in Marlowe's *Tamburlaine, Part One*', *Renaissance Drama*, 23 (1992), 3–24 (p. 7).

5 Mark Thornton Burnett, 'Tamburlaine: An Elizabethan Vagabond', *Studies in Philology*, 84.3 (1987), 308–23 (p. 310).

6 Garrett A. Sullivan, Jr., 'Geography and Identity in Marlowe', in *The Cambridge Companion to Christopher Marlowe*, ed. by Patrick Cheney (Cambridge: Cambridge University Press, 2004), pp. 231–44 (p. 231).

7 Mary Floyd-Wilson, *English Ethnicity and Race in Early Modern Drama* (Cambridge, Cambridge University Press, 2003), p. 89.

8   Judith Haber, *Desire and Dramatic Form in Early Modern England* (Cambridge: Cambridge University Press, 2009).

9   Stephen Greenblatt, *Will in the World: How Shakespeare Became Shakespeare* (New York: W.W. Norton & Company, 2004), pp. 189–249.

10 See Laura Bovilsky's *Barbarous Play* (Minneapolis: University of Minnesota Press, 2008), particularly the chapter 'Exemplary Jews and the Logic of Gentility', pp. 67–102.

11 For scholarship on early modern English representations of Jewishness and *Merchant of Venice*, see Emma Smith, 'Was Shylock Jewish?' *Shakespeare Quarterly*, 64.2 (2013), 188–219.

12 Ian Smith, *Race and Rhetoric in the Renaissance: Barbarian Errors* (New York: Palgrave Macmillan, 2009), p. 3.

13 Geraldine Heng, *The Invention of Race in the European Middle Ages* (Cambridge: Cambridge University Press, 2018), p. 3. The quotation appears in italics in Heng but is here given in roman.

14 Alexander G. Weheliye, *Habeas Viscus: Racializing Assemblages, Biopolitics, and Black Feminist Theory of the Human* (Durham: Duke University Press, 2014), p. 3.

15 Sianne Ngai, *Ugly Feelings* (Cambridge, MA: Harvard University Press, 2005), p. 7.

16 Ngai, *Ugly Feelings*, pp. 2–3.

17 See Surekha Davies, *Renaissance Ethnography and the Invention of the Human: New Worlds, Maps and Monsters* (Cambridge: Cambridge University Press, 2016).

18 This rebuttal of recent geo-humoral scholarship is not to suggest geo-humoral theory is not an important facet to early modern racial ideologies, but to encourage future scholarship to not use early modern humoralism as a rationalization for a burgeoning system of white nationalism.

19 Robert M. Young, 'Racist society, racist science' in *Racism and Education: Structures and Strategies*, ed. by Dawn Gill, Barbara Mayor and Maud Blair (London: SAGE, rpt. 1995), pp. 303–19 (p. 304).

20 The concept of race being a product of racism, or racism preceding race, is a concept coming from critical race theory, particularly black feminist thought. For more see Karen E. Fields

and Barbara J. Fields, *Racecraft: The Soul of Inequality in American Life* (New York: Verso Books, 2014).

21 See Sylvia Wynter, '1492: A New World View' in *Race, Discourse, and the Origin of the Americas: A New World View*, ed. by Vera Lawrence Hyatt and Rex Nettleford (Washington, DC: Smithsonian Institution Press, 1995), pp. 5–57; Weheliye, *Habeas Viscus*, p. 3.

22 For more on early modern English representations of the Ottomans, see Jonathan Burton's *Traffic and Turning: Islam and English Drama, 1579-1624* (Cranbury, NJ: University of Delaware Press, 2005); Matthew Dimmock, *New Turkes: Dramatizing Islam and the Ottomans in Early Modern England* (Burlington, VT: Ashgate, 2005); and Anders Ingram, *Writing the Ottomans: Turkish History in Early Modern England* (Basingstoke: Palgrave Macmillan, 2015).

23 Emily C. Bartels, 'Too Many Blackamoors: Deportation, Discrimination, and Elizabeth I', *SEL: Studies in English Literature, 1500-1900*, 46.2 (2006), 305–22. For more on the expulsion of the English Jewish population and early modern reception of Jews, see Eva Johanna Holmberg's *Jews in the Early Modern English Imagination: A Scattered Nation* (Farnham: Ashgate, 2011); Anthony Julius's *Trials of the Diaspora: A History of Anti-Semitism in England* (Oxford: Oxford University Press, 2010); and Jeffrey S. Shoulson's *Fictions of Conversion: Jews, Christians, and Cultures of Changes in Early Modern England* (Philadelphia: University of Pennsylvania Press, 2013). For more on early modern English Egyptian Acts and the expulsion of Romani people, see David Cressy, 'Trouble With Gypsies', *The Historical Journal*, 59.1 (2016), 45–70.

24 All citations of *Tamburlaine the Great* from Christopher Marlowe, *Tamburlaine, Parts One and Two*, ed. by Anthony B. Dawson (2nd edn) (London: A & C Black, 1997).

25 Floyd-Wilson, *English Ethnicity and Race in Early Modern Drama*, p. 1.

26 For more information on Scythians, see Ellis Hovell Minns, *Scythians and Greeks: A Survey of Ancient History and Archaeology on the North Coast of the Euxine from the Danube to the Caucasus* (Cambridge: Cambridge University Press, 2011).

27 Hippocrates, *On Airs, Waters, Places* (400 BCE), in *Race in Early Modern England*, ed. by Ania Loomba and Jonathan Burton (New York: Palgrave Macmillan, 2007), p. 43.

28 Claudius Ptolemaeus, *Tetrabiblos* (2nd Century CE), in *Race in Early Modern England*, p. 48.

29 Jean Bodin, *Method for the Easy Comprehension of History* (1566), in *Race in Early Modern England*, pp. 95–6.

30 Barnabe Rich, *A new description of Ireland* (1610), in *Race in Early Modern England*, p. 185.

31 Fynes Moryson, *An itinerary . . . containing his ten yeeres travel (1617)*, in *Race in Early Modern England*, p. 200.

32 Edmund Spenser, *A Veue of the present state of Irelande* (1633), in *Race in Early Modern England*, p. 223. Spenser notably was heavily involved in the English colonization of Ireland, and served as private secretary to the Lord Deputy. For more on Spenser and Ireland, read Walter S. H. Lim, *The Arts of Empire: The Poetics of Colonialism from Raleigh to Milton* (Newark: University of Delaware, 1998).

33 For more on the racialization of Petrarchan 'fairness,' see Kim F. Hall's *Things of Darkness: Economies of Race and Gender in Early Modern England* (Ithaca: Cornell University Press, 1995).

34 Gail Kern Paster posits that red, black, and white are 'the key colors and thermal markers of early modern humoralism. For more, see Paster, *Humoring the Body: Emotions and the Shakespearean Stage* (Chicago: University of Chicago, 2004), pp. 29–30.

35 Miscegenation, and the anxieties around mixed-race children, also features in *Titus Andronicus*, in which Aaron the Moor's relationship with Tamora produces a 'coal-black' child. For more on this theme through *Titus Andronicus*, see Francesca T. Royster, 'White-Limed Walls: Whiteness and Gothic Extremism in Shakespeare's *Titus Andronicus*', *Shakespeare Quarterly*, 51.4 (2000), 432–55. For scholarship on race and pregnancy in the early modern period, see Jennifer L. Morgan's *Laboring Women* (Philadelphia: University of Pennsylvania Press, 2004).

36 Ian Smith, 'Othello's Black Handkerchief', *Shakespeare Quarterly*, 64.1 (2013), 1–25 (p. 4).

37 For scholarship on Tamburlaine and modern performance, including the Royal Shakespeare Company's 1992 production, see David Fuller, '*Tamburlaine The Great* in Performance', in *Marlowe's Empery: Expanding his Critical Contexts*, ed. by Sara Munson Deats and Robert A. Logan (Newark: University of Delaware Press, 2002), pp. 61–84, and Peter Kirwan's chapter in this volume.

38 For more information on the use of early modern blackface cosmetics, see Farah Karim-Cooper's *Cosmetics in Shakespearean and Renaissance Drama* (Edinburgh: Edinburgh University Press, 2006); Andrea Stevens, *Inventions of the Skin: The Painted Body in Early English Drama* (Edinburgh: Edinburgh University Press, 2013); and Virginia Mason Vaughan's *Performing Blackness on English Stages, 1580–1800* (Cambridge: Cambridge University Press, 2005).

39 In early modern England, ink was used, both rhetorically and materially, to reify the blackness of racialized figures. In his scholarship on inked bodies, Miles Parks Grier uncovers the concept of 'inkface', a 'concept [which] enables a rich account of performances of literacy as rituals that invented an elastic racial category of illiterate, legible blacks'. Grier continues with his discussion of racialized ink, surmising, 'Inkface, the metonymic play that represents "blacks" as marked signifiers in a European characterology, was crucial to an early modern English imperial project. Specifically, it reconfigured the imagined geography of race and slavery so that England appeared not as a homeland of Rome's barbaric slaves but rather as the seat of the ethnos that would replicate Rome's empire in the Atlantic arena.' Though Grier is looking specifically at print culture, I believe this rendering of black bodies through ink has extended itself to textiles, with the use of black dyes conscripting 'legible' black figures for the purposes of reconfiguring English whiteness to mirror classical models of empire. See Miles Parks Grier, 'Inkface: The Slave Stigma in England's Early Imperial Imagination', in *Scripturalizing the Human: The Written as the Political*, ed. by Vincent L. Wimbush (New York: Routledge, 2015), pp. 193–220 (pp. 195–6).

Chapter 7

1 Frederick S. Boas, *Christopher Marlowe: A Biographical and Critical Study* (Oxford: Clarendon Press, 1940), p. 73.

2 John Bakeless, *Christopher Marlowe* (London: Jonathan Cape, 1938), p. 108.

3 Boas, p. 73.

4 Una Ellis-Fermor, 'Introduction' in Christopher Marlowe, *Tamburlaine the Great, in Two Parts*, ed. by Ellis-Fermor (London: Methuen, 1930), pp. 1–62 (p. 52).

5 See for example Rick Bowers's work on the reception of the two parts of *Tamburlaine*, 'Tamburlaine in Ludlow', *Notes & Queries*, 243 (1998), 361–3 and 'Tamburlaine Engraved', *Huntington Library Quarterly* 59.4 (1996), 542–9; and Richard Levin, 'The Contemporary Perception of Marlowe's Tamburlaine', *Medieval and Renaissance Drama in England* 1 (1984), 51–70.

6 On the 'timelessness' of the orient, see Edward Said, *Orientalism* (London: Routledge and Kegan Paul, 1978), p. 94; Ellis-Fermor, 'Introduction', p. 4.

7 Michel Poirier, *Christopher Marlowe* (London: Chatto and Windus, 1951), p. 92.

8 The interrelationship of archaeology and empire in later periods is detailed in Susan Lawrence, 'Exporting Culture: Archaeology and the Nineteenth-Century British Empire', *Historical Archaeology* 37.1 (2003), pp. 20–33, and Shawn Malley, 'Layard Enterprise: Victorian Archaeology and Informal Imperialism in Mesopotamia', *International Journal of Middle East Studies* 40.4 (2008), pp. 623–46.

9 Poirier, p. 92.

10 For instance Robert Weimann, *Shakespeare and the Popular Tradition in the Theater: Studies in the Social Dimension of Dramatic Form and Function* (Baltimore: Johns Hopkins University Press, 1978), p. 182.

11 This question resonates with Liam Semler's recognition of the usefulness of bringing elements of Timür's biography into the teaching of Marlowe's *Tamburlaine* plays in Chapter 8 of this

volume: 'Three Tents for Tamburlaine: Resources and Approaches for Teaching the Play'.

12 Asfar Moin, *The Millennial Sovereign: Sacred Kingship & Sainthood in Islam* (New York: Columbia University Press, 2012); Jonathan Gil Harris, 'Tamburlaine in Hindustan' in *Theatre Cultures within Globalising Empires: Looking at Early Modern England and Spain*, ed. by Joachim Küpper and Leonie Pawlita (Berlin: De Gruyter, 2018), pp. 188–204.

13 Harris, p. 191.

14 All references to the two parts of *Tamburlaine* come from Christopher Marlowe, *Tamburlaine, Parts One and Two* (2nd edn, New Mermaids), ed. by Anthony B. Dawson (London: A & C Black, 1997).

15 Moin, p. 25.

16 Moin, p. 35.

17 Sanjay Subrahmanyam, 'Connected Histories: Notes Towards a Reconfiguration of Early Modern Eurasia', *Modern Asian Studies* 31.3, Special Issue: 'The Eurasian Context of the Early Modern History of Mainland South-East Asia, 1400-1800' (1997), pp. 735–62 (p. 739).

18 The relevant elements of both of these texts and a number of other potential sources for the two parts of *Tamburlaine* are edited and reproduced in Vivien Thomas and William Tydeman, eds, *Christopher Marlowe: The Plays and their Sources* (London and New York: Routledge, 1994). See particularly pp. 90–6 and 97–122.

19 The shape, origins and circulation of narratives of the life of 'Mahomet' in early modern England are extensively discussed in Matthew Dimmock, *Mythologies of the Prophet Muhammad in Early Modern English Culture* (Cambridge: Cambridge University Press, 2013).

20 Malcolm Kelsall, *Christopher Marlowe* (Leiden: Brill, 1981), p. 82. There is an extensive body of critical work focused on Tamburlaine's self-declared role as the 'scourge of God'. See for example Roy Battenhouse's influential discussion in *Marlowe's Tamburlaine* (Nashville: Vanderbilt University Press, 1964); C. A. Patrides, '"The Bloody and Cruell Turke": The Background of a Renaissance Commonplace', *Studies in the Renaissance*, 10

(1963), 126–35; and the discussion in Matthew Dimmock, *New Turkes: Dramatizing Islam and the Ottomans in Early Modern England* (Aldershot: Ashgate, 2005), pp. 135–61.

21 Moin, p. 56.

22 Moin, p. 91.

23 Subrahmanyam, p. 752.

24 On the anticipation of this year and associated prognostications, see Subrahmanyam, pp. 751–4 and Moin, pp. 132–69, 179.

25 On these anachronisms see Ladan Niayesh, 'Shakespeare's Persians', *Shakespeare* 4 (2008), pp. 127–36, 130; Dimmock, *New Turkes*, pp. 137–42; Jane Grogan, *The Persian Empire in English Renaissance Writing, 1549-1622* (Basingstoke: Palgrave Macmillan, 2014), pp. 135–49; Harris, p. 195.

26 Mexia, quoted in Thomas and Tydeman, pp. 89–90.

27 Whetstone quoted in Hafiz Abid Masood, 'From Cyrus to Abbas: Staging Persia in Early Modern England' (Unpublished doctoral thesis: University of Sussex, 2011), p. 63.

28 John Foxe, *Actes and monuments of matters most special and memorable, happening in the Church* (London, 1583), p. 743; Masood, p. 64.

29 Tamburlaine's role as reliever of Constantinople may well have been explicitly celebrated later in what seems to be a lost play, 'The Tartarian Cripple, Emperor of Constantinople' (*c.*1600). However there is a great deal of uncertainty about the status of this text: see https://lostplays.folger.edu/Tartarian_Cripple,_The_(Emperor_of_Constantinople).

30 This episode in discussed in detail in Dimmock, *Mythologies of the Prophet Muhammad*, pp. 118–23, and in Masood, pp. 65–7.

31 Mexia, quoted in Thomas and Tydeman, p. 85.

32 Perondinus, quoted in Thomas and Tydeman, pp. 101–2.

33 The success of Marlowe's presentation of Tamburlaine on the English stage is evident in his production of a sequel, and in the numerous 'Turk plays' that appeared in subsequent years attempting to emulate the initial success – see Mark Hutchings, 'The 'Turk Phenomenon' and the Repertory of the Late Elizabethan Playhouse', *Early Modern Literary Studies*, Special

Issue 16 (2007), paras. 1–39 – as well as in ballads and libels of the period, such as the controversial 'Dutch Church Libel' signed by a provocateur under the pseudonym 'Tamburlaine'.

34 Stephen Greenblatt, *Renaissance Self-Fashioning: From More to Shakespeare* (Chicago: University of Chicago Press, 1980), p. 194; Joan Thirsk, 'England's Provinces: Did They Serve or Drive Material London?' in *Material London ca. 1600*, ed. by Lena Cowen Orlin (Philadelphia: University of Pennsylvania Press, 2000), pp. 97–108 (p. 97). On the influence of Chinggissid and later Timürid conquests on trade routes, see Thomas T. Allsen, *Commodity and Exchange in the Mongol Empire: A Cultural History of Islamic Textiles* (Cambridge: Cambridge University Press, 1997).

35 Thomas Healy, *Christopher Marlowe* (Plymouth: Northcote House, 1994), p. 46; Greenblatt, p. 220.

36 Healy, pp. 47, 50.

37 Kelsall, p. 134.

38 Poirier, p. 112.

39 Mexia, quoted in Thomas and Tydeman, p. 89.

40 Perondinus, quoted in Thomas and Tydeman, pp. 97, 99.

41 Ibid., p. 111.

42 Cambinus, quoted in Thomas and Tydeman, p. 130.

43 As recorded in Jane A. Lawson, ed., *The Elizabethan New Year's Gift Exchanges 1559-1603* (Oxford: Oxford University Press for The British Academy, 2013), p. 405 (89.406).

44 Quotation from Ben Jonson, George Chapman and John Marston, *Eastward Ho!*, ed. by C. G. Petter (London: A & C Black [New Mermaids], 1973).

45 As extensively discussed in Robert Batchelor, *London: The Selden Map and the Making of a Global City, 1549-1689* (Chicago: University of Chicago Press, 2014), pp. 23–6, 61–3.

46 Pietro Martire d'Anghiera, *The decades of the new worlde or west India*, trans. by Richard Eden (London, 1555), sig. 233^r–234^v.

47 Matthew Dimmock, *Elizabethan Globalism: England, China and the Rainbow Portrait* (London: Paul Mellon Centre for Studies in British Art, 2019), pp. 219–50.

48 Jane Schneider, 'Fantastical Colors in Foggy London: The New Fashion Potential of the Late Sixteenth Century' in Orlin, pp. 109–27, 112.

49 Philip Henslowe, *Henslowe Papers: Being Documents Supplementary to Henslowe's Diary*, ed. by Walter W. Greg (London: A. H. Bullen, 1907), pp. 119–20.

50 Jean MacIntyre, *Costumes and Scripts in the Elizabethan Theatres* (Edmonton: University of Alberta Press, 1992), p. 100.

51 William Cecil, Lord Burghley, 'Notes on towns and commodities of the Levant' (1582?) from BL Lansdowne MS 34, ff. 178–9, reproduced in S. A. Skilliter, *William Harborne and the Trade with Turkey 1578-1582: A Documentary Study of the First Anglo-Ottoman Relations* (Oxford: Oxford University Press for The British Academy, 1977), pp. 177–8.

52 Ibid., p. 178.

53 As discussed in detail in Matthew Dimmock, 'Guns and Gawds: Elizabethan England's Infidel Trade' in *A Companion to the Global Renaissance: English Literature and Culture in the Era of Expansion*, ed. by Jyotsna G. Singh (Oxford: Wiley-Blackwell, 2009), pp. 207–22.

54 See Dimmock, *Elizabethan Globalism*, pp. 219–24.

55 Thomas Roe, *The Embassy of Sir Thomas Roe to the Court of the Great Mogul, 1615-19, as Narrated in His Journal and Correspondence*, ed. by William Foster, 2 vols (London: Hakluyt Society, 1894), II, p. 334. This episode is also discussed in Harris, pp. 199–201.

56 Roe, p. 334.

57 Moin, p. 211.

58 See Harris, p. 200.

59 For example, the letter from Roe in Istanbul to Elizabeth Stuart, Queen of Bohemia (20 March 1622) in which he talks of an Ottoman galley cruising 'in tryumph through Persepolis'. Elizabeth Stuart, *The Correspondence of Elizabeth Stuart, Queen of Bohemia, Vol. I: 1603-1631*, ed. by Nadine Akkerman (Oxford: Oxford University Press, 2015), no. 1816.

60 Marcia Pointon, *Brilliant Effects: Gems and Jewellery as Agency in History, Literature and the Visual Arts* (New Haven, CT: Yale University Press, 2009), p. 111.

61 Pointon, p. 17.

62 Ethel Seaton, 'Marlowe's Map' in *Marlowe: A Collection of Critical Essays*, ed. by Clifford Leech (Englewood Cliffs, NJ: Prentice-Hall, 1964), pp. 36–56 (p. 55).

63 See the discussion of this term in Daniel Carey, 'Questioning Incommensurability in Early Modern Cultural Exchange', *Common Knowledge* 6.3 (1997), pp. 32–50, and the relevant sections in Sanjay Subrahmanyam, *Courtly Encounters: Translating Courtliness and Violence in Early Modern Eurasia* (Cambridge, MA: Harvard University Press, 2012).

Chapter 8

1 All play references are to Anthony B. Dawson (ed), *Tamburlaine, Parts One and Two* (1997; rpt. London: Bloomsbury, 2018). I want to thank David McInnis for excellent guidance as I wrote this essay.

WORKS CITED AND SELECTED FURTHER READING

Altman, Joel, *The Tudor Play of Mind: Rhetorical Inquiry and the Development of Elizabethan Drama* (Berkeley, CA: University of California Press, 1978).
Armstrong, William A., *Marlowe's 'Tamburlaine': The Image and the Stage* (Hull: Hull University Press, 1966).
Astington, John H., 'The "Unrecorded Portrait" of Edward Alleyn', *Shakespeare Quarterly*, 44 (1993), 73–86.
Bakeless, John, *The Tragicall History of Christopher Marlowe*, 2 vols. (Cambridge, MA: Harvard University Press, 1942).
Bamford, Karen, and Alexander Leggatt, eds, *Approaches to Teaching English Renaissance Drama* (New York: Modern Language Association of America, 2002).
Barber, C. L., 'The Death of Zenocrate: "Conceiving and subduing both" in Marlowe's *Tamburlaine*', *Literature and Psychology*, 16 (1966), 15–24.
Barbour, Richmond, *Before Orientalism: London's Theatre of the East, 1576–1626* (Cambridge: Cambridge University Press, 2003).
Bartels, Emily C., 'The Double Vision of the East: Imperialist Self-Construction in Marlowe's *Tamburlaine, Part One*', *Renaissance Drama*, 23 (1992), 3–24.
Bartels, Emily C., *Spectacles of Strangeness: Imperialism, Alienation, and Marlowe* (Philadelphia: University of Pennsylvania Press, 1993).
Bartels, Emily C., 'Too Many Blackamoors: Deportation, Discrimination, and Elizabeth I', *SEL: Studies in English Literature, 1500–1900*, 46.2 (2006), 305–22.
Bartels, Emily C., and Emma Smith, eds, *Christopher Marlowe in Context* (Cambridge: Cambridge University Press, 2013).

Battenhouse, Roy W., *Marlowe's 'Tamburlaine': A Study in Renaissance Moral Philosophy* (Nashville, TN: Vanderbilt University Press, 1941).

Beck, Ervin, '*Tamburlaine* for the Modern Stage', *Educational Theatre Journal*, 23 (1971), 62–74.

Bennett, Kristen Abbott, dir., *The Kit Marlowe Project*, Stonehill College, Easton, MA. 2017–. https://kitmarlowe.org/

Berek, Peter, 'Tamburlaine's Weak Sons: Imitation as Interpretation Before 1593', *Renaissance Drama*, 13 (1982), 55–82.

Bevington, David, *From 'Mankind' to Marlowe: Growth of Structure in the Drama of Tudor England* (Cambridge, MA: Harvard University Press, 1962).

Bevington, David, 'Christopher Marlowe', *Oxford Bibliographies* (Oxford University Press, 2010).

Bevington, David, 'Marlowe's Plays in Performance: A Brief History' in *Christopher Marlowe at 450*, ed. by Sara Munson Deats and Robert A. Logan (Farnham: Ashgate, 2015), pp. 257–80.

Boas, Frederick S., *Christopher Marlowe: A Biographical and Critical Study* (Oxford: Clarendon Press, 1940).

Bourne, Claire M. L., 'Making a Scene; or *Tamburlaine the Great* in Print', in *Christopher Marlowe, Theatrical Commerce, and the Book Trade*, ed. by Kirk Melnikoff and Roslyn L. Knutson (Cambridge: Cambridge University Press, 2018), pp. 115–33.

Bovilsky, Lara, *Barbarous Play: Race on the English Renaissance Stage*. Minneapolis: University of Minnesota Press, 2008.

Bowers, Rick, 'Tamburlaine Engraved, 1622 to 1673', *Huntington Library Quarterly*, 59 (1996), 542–9.

Bowers, Rick, 'Tamburlaine in Ludlow', *Notes & Queries*, 243 (1998), 361–3.

Bradley, A. C., 'Christopher Marlowe', in *The English Poets, Selections*, 4 vols, ed. by Thomas Humphry Ward (London: Macmillan, 1880), I.411–17.

Brooke, C. F. Tucker, *The Tudor Drama: A History of English National Drama to the Retirement of Shakespeare* (Boston: Houghton Mifflin, 1911).

Brooke, C. F. Tucker, 'The Reputation of Christopher Marlowe', *Transactions of the Connecticut Academy of Arts and Sciences*, 25 (1921–22), 347–408.

Brooks, Charles, 'Tamburlaine and Attitudes toward Women', *English Literary History*, 24 (1957), 1–11.

Brooks, Harold F., 'Marlowe and Early Shakespeare', in *Christopher Marlowe*, ed. by Brian Morris (New York: Hill and Wang, 1969), pp. 65–94.

Brown, John Russell, 'Marlowe and the Actors', *Tulane Drama Review*, Marlowe Issue, 8 (1964), 155–73.

Burnett, Mark Thornton, 'Tamburlaine: An Elizabethan Vagabond', *Studies in Philology*, 84.3 (1987), 308–23.

Burnett, Mark Thornton, '*Tamburlaine* and the Renaissance Concept of Honour', *Studia Neophilologica*, 59 (1987), 201–6.

Burnett, Mark Thornton, '*Tamburlaine* and the Body', *Criticism*, 33 (1991), 31–47.

Burnett, Mark Thornton, ed., *Marlowe, History and Sexuality: New Critical Essays on Christopher Marlowe* (New York: AMS Press, 1998).

Burnett, Mark Thornton, '*Tamburlaine the Great, Parts One and Two*', in *The Cambridge Companion to Christopher Marlowe*, ed. by Patrick Cheney (Cambridge: Cambridge University Press, 2004), pp. 127–43.

Burton, Jonathan, 'Anglo-Ottoman Relations and the Image of the Turk in *Tamburlaine*', *Journal of Medieval and Early Modern Studies*, 30.1 (2000), 125–56.

Burton, Jonathan, *Traffic and Turning: Islam and English Drama, 1579–1624* (Cranbury, NJ: University of Delaware Press, 2005).

Camden, Carroll, 'Tamburlaine: The Choleric Man', *Modern Language Notes*, 44 (1929), 430–5.

Cartelli, Thomas, *Marlowe, Shakespeare, and the Economy of Theatrical Experience* (Philadelphia: University of Pennsylvania Press, 1991).

Cerasano, S. P., 'Edward Alleyn, the New Model Actor, and the Rise of Celebrity in the 1590s', *Medieval and Renaissance Drama in England*, 18 (2005), 47–58.

Chambers, E. K., *The Elizabethan Stage*, 4 vols (Oxford: Clarendon, 1923).

Charney, Maurice, 'The Voice of Marlowe's Tamburlaine in Early Shakespeare', *Comparative Drama*, 31 (1997), 213–23.

Cheney, Patrick, *Marlowe's Counterfeit Profession: Ovid, Spenser, Counter-Nationhood* (Toronto, ON: University of Toronto Press, 1997).

Cheney, Patrick, 'Recent Studies in Marlowe', *English Literary Renaissance*, 31 (2001), 288–328.

Cheney, Patrick, 'Introduction', in *The Cambridge Companion to Christopher Marlowe*, ed. by Patrick Cheney (Cambridge: Cambridge University Press, 2004), pp. 1–23.

Cheney, Patrick, *Marlowe's Republican Authorship: Lucan, Liberty, and the Sublime* (Basingstoke: Palgrave Macmillan, 2009).

Cheney, Patrick, *English Authorship and the Early Modern Sublime: Fictions of Transport in Spenser, Marlowe, Jonson, and Shakespeare* (Cambridge: Cambridge University Press, 2018).

Chew, Samuel C., 'The Allegorical Chariot in English Literature of the Renaissance', in *De Artibus Opuscula XL: Essays in Honor of Erwin Panofsky*, 2 vols., ed. by Millard Meiss (New York: New York University Press, 1961), I.37–54.

Cockcroft, Robert, 'Emblematic Irony: Some Possible Significances of Tamburlaine's Chariot', *Renaissance and Modern Studies*, 12 (1968), 33–55.

Cole, Douglas, *Suffering and Evil in the Plays of Christopher Marlowe* (Princeton, NJ: Princeton University Press, 1962).

Collier, John Payne, 'On the Early English Dramatists who Preceded Shakespeare', pt. 1, *Edinburgh Review*, 6 (June 1820), p. 517.

Conroy, Derval, and Danielle Clarke, eds, *Teaching the Early Modern Period* (Houndmills: Palgrave Macmillan, 2011).

Corredera, Vanessa Ivette, 'Faces and Figures of Fortune: Astrological Physiognomy in *Tamburlaine Part 1*', *Early Modern Literary Studies*, 18 (2015), 1–26.

Crawford, Charles, *The Marlowe Concordance*, 3 vols. (Louvain: Librarie Universitaire, 1911–32).

Cutts, John, 'Tamburlaine "as fierce Achilles was"', *Comparative Drama*, 1 (1967), 105–9.

Dabbs, Thomas, *Reforming Marlowe: The Nineteenth-Century Canonization of a Renaissance Dramatist* (Lewisburg, PA: Bucknell University Press, 1991).

Daiches, David, 'Language and Action in Marlowe's *Tamburlaine*', in *More Literary Essays* (Edinburgh: Oliver and Boyd, 1968), pp. 42–69.

Davies, Surekha, *Renaissance Ethnography and the Invention of the Human* (Cambridge: Cambridge University Press, 2016).

Dawson, Anthony B., ed., *Tamburlaine, Parts One and Two* (London: A&C Black, 1997).

Deats, Sara Munson, *Sex, Gender, and Desire in the Plays of Christopher Marlowe* (Newark: University of Delaware Press, 1997).

Deats, Sara Munson, and Robert A. Logan, eds, *Marlowe's Empery: Expanding His Critical Contexts* (Newark: University of Delaware Press, 2002).

Deats, Sara Munson, 'Marlowe's Interrogative Drama: *Dido, Tamburlaine, Doctor Faustus,* and *Edward II*', in *Marlowe's Empery: Expanding His Critical Contexts*, ed. by Deats and Robert A. Logan (Newark: University of Delaware Press, 2002), pp. 107–30.

Deats, Sara Munson, *Placing the Plays of Christopher Marlowe* (Aldershot: Ashgate, 2008).

Deats, Sara Munson, *Christopher Marlowe at 450* (Burlington, VT: Ashgate, 2015).

Dimmock, Matthew, *New Turkes: Dramatizing Islam and the Ottomans in Early Modern England* (Aldershot: Ashgate, 2005).

Dimmock, Matthew, *Mythologies of the Prophet Muhammad in Early Modern English Culture* (Cambridge: Cambridge University Press, 2013).

Dodsley, Robert, ed., *A Select Collection of Old Plays*, 12 vols (London: R. Dodsley, 1744).

Dodsley, Robert, ed., *A Select Collection of Old Plays*, 2nd edn., 12 vols (London: Printed by J. Nichols for J. Dodsley, 1780).

Dollimore, Jonathan, *Radical Tragedy: Religion, Ideology, and Power in the Drama of Shakespeare and His Contemporaries* (Chicago: University of Chicago Press, 1984).

Dowden, Edward, 'Christopher Marlowe', *Fortnightly Review* 37 n.s. (1 Jan 1870), 69–81.

Downie, J. A., and J. T. Parnell, eds, *Constructing Christopher Marlowe* (Cambridge: Cambridge University Press, 2000).

Duxfield, Andrew, *Christopher Marlowe and the Failure to Unify* (Farnham: Ashgate, 2015).

Eliot, T. S., "Christopher Marlowe" [1918], in *The Sacred Wood: Essays on Poetry and Criticism* (New York: Knopf, 1921).

Ellis-Fermor, Una Mary, *Christopher Marlowe* (London: Methuen, 1927).

Emsley, Sarah, '"I Cannot Love, to be an Emperess": Women and Honour in *Tamburlaine*', *Dalhousie Review*, 80 (2000), 169–86.

Engle, Lars, and Eric Rasmussen, *Studying Shakespeare's Contemporaries* (Malden, MA: Wiley-Blackwell, 2014).

Erickson, Peter, and Kim F. Hall, '"A New Scholarly Song": Rereading Early Modern Race', *Shakespeare Quarterly*, 67.1 (2016), 1–13.

Fanta, Christopher G., *Marlowe's 'Againsts': An Approach to the Ambiguity of His Plays* (Cambridge, MA: Harvard University Press, 1970).

Farey, Peter, ed., Marlowe Page. http://www.rey.prestel.co.uk/

Fehrenbach, Robert J., et al., *A Concordance to the Plays, Poems, and Translations of Christopher Marlowe* (Ithaca, NY: Cornell University Press, 1979).

Floyd-Wilson, Mary, *English Ethnicity and Race in Early Modern Drama* (Cambridge: Cambridge University Press, 2003).

Foakes, R. A., and R. T. Rickert, eds, *Henslowe's Diary* (Cambridge: Cambridge University Press, 1961).

Francisco, Timothy, 'Marlowe's War Horses: Cyborgs, Soldiers and Queer Companions', in *Violent Masculinities: Male Aggression in Early Modern Texts and Culture*, ed. by Jennifer Feather and Catherine E. Thomas (New York: Palgrave Macmillan, 2013), pp. 47–65.

Freeman, Arthur, 'Marlowe, Kyd, and the Dutch Church Libel', *ELR: English Literary Renaissance*, 3.1 (1973), 44–52.

Friedenreich, Kenneth, 'Directions in *Tamburlaine* Criticism', in *Christopher Marlowe's 'Tamburlaine Part I and Part II": Text and Major Criticism,* ed. by Iriving Ribner (Indianapolis, IN: Bobbs-Merrill, 1974), pp. 341–52.

Friedenreich, Kenneth, Roma Gill, and Constance Kuriyama, eds, *A Poet and a Filthy Play-Maker: New Essays on Christopher Marlowe* (New York: AMS Press, 1988).

Frongillo, John, 'Giving the Tragic Boot to the Comic Sock: The Recoding of Christopher Marlowe's *Tamburlaine* from Low to High Culture', *Popular Entertainment Studies*, 2 (2011), 73–88.

Fuller, David. '*Tamburlaine The Great* in Performance' in *Marlowe's Empery: Expanding his Critical Contexts*, ed. by Sara Munson Deats and Robert A. Logan (Newark: University of Delaware Press, 2002), pp. 61–84.

Garber, Marjorie, '"Here's Nothing Writ": Scribe, Script, and Circumscription in Marlowe's Plays', *Theatre Journal*, 36 (1984), pp. 301–20.

Gardner, Helen L., 'The Second Part of *Tamburlaine the Great*', *Modern Language Review*, 37 (1942), 18–24.

Ganzel, Dewey, *Fortune and Men's Eyes: The Career of John Payne Collier* (Oxford: Oxford University Press, 1982).

Geckle, George L., ed., *'Tamburlaine' and 'Edward II': Text and Performance* (London: Macmillan, 1988).

Gibbard, Peter, 'Breaking Up the Line: The Sententious Style in Elizabethan Blank Verse', *Modern Philology*, 112.2 (2014), 312–35.

Gibson, Rex, *Teaching Shakespeare: A Handbook for Teachers* (1998; rev. Cambridge: Cambridge University Press, 2016).

Gillies, John, '*Tamburlaine* and Renaissance Geography', in Garrett A. Sullivan Jr., Patrick Cheney, and Andrew Hadfield, eds, *Early Modern English Drama: A Critical Companion* (Oxford: Oxford University Press, 2006), pp. 35–49.

Godshalk, W. L., *The Marlovian World Picture* (Mouton: The Hague, 1974).

Goeckle, George L., Tamburlaine *and* Edward II: *Text and Performance* (Atlantic Highlands: Humanities Press International, 1988).

Greenblatt, Stephen J., *Renaissance Self-Fashioning from More to Shakespeare* (Chicago: University of Chicago Press, 1980).

Greene, Robert, *Perimedes the Blacksmith: A Golden Method How to Use the Mind in Pleasant and Profitable Exercise* (London: Printed by John Wolfe for Edward White, 1588).

Grier, Miles Parks, 'Inkface: The Slave Stigma in England's Early Imperial Imagination' in *Scripturalizing the Human: The Written as the Political*, ed. by Vincent L. Wimbush (New York: Routledge, 2015).

Grogan, Jane, '"A warre . . . commodious": Dramatizing Islamic Schism in and after *Tamburlaine*', *Texas Studies in Literature and Language*, 54 (2012), 45–78.

Grogan, Jane, *The Persian Empire in English Renaissance Writing, 1549–1622* (Basingstoke: Palgrave Macmillan, 2014).

Gurr, Andrew, *Shakespeare's Opposites: The Admiral's Company 1594–1625* (Cambridge: Cambridge University Press, 2009).

Hall, Joseph, *Virgidemiarum: Six Bookes* (London: T. Creede for R. Dexter, 1597).

Hall, Kim F., *Things of Darkness: Economies of Race and Gender in Early Modern England* (Ithaca: Cornell University Press, 1995).

Hallam, Henry, *Introduction to the Literature of Europe in the Fifteenth, Sixteenth, and Seventeenth Centuries*, 4 vols (London: John Murray, 1837–39).

Hansen, Claire G., '"Who taught thee this?" Female Agency and Experiential Learning in Marlowe's *Tamburlaine, The Jew of Malta* and *Edward the Second*', *Journal of Language, Literature and Culture*, 60 (2013), 157–77.

Harraway, Clare, *Re-citing Marlowe: Approaches to the Drama* (2000; rpt. New York: Routledge, 2018).

Harris, Jonathan Gil, 'Tamburlaine in Hindustan' in *Theatre Cultures within Globalising Empires: Looking at Early Modern England and Spain*, ed. by Joachim Küpper and Leonie Pawlita (Berlin: De Gruyter, 2018), pp. 188–204.

Hattaway, Michael, 'Marlowe and Brecht', in *Christopher Marlowe*, ed. by Brian Morris (New York: Hill and Wang, 1969), pp. 95–112.

Hiscock, Andrew, and Lisa Hopkins, eds, *Teaching Shakespeare and Early Modern Dramatists* (Basingstoke: Palgrave Macmillan, 2007).

Honan, Park, *Christopher Marlowe: Poet and Spy* (Oxford: Oxford University Press, 2005).

Hopkins, Lisa, '"And shall I die, and this unconquered?": Marlowe's Inverted Colonialism', *Early Modern Literary Studies* 2.2 (1996), paras. 1–23.

Hopkins, Lisa, *Christopher Marlowe: A Literary Life* (Houndmills: Palgrave Macmillan, 2000).

Hopkins, Lisa, *A Christopher Marlowe Chronology* (Basingstoke: Palgrave Macmillan, 2005).

Hopkins, Lisa, 'Playing with Matches: Christopher Marlowe's Incendiary Imagination', *Marlowe Studies: An Annual*, 1 (2011), 125–40.

Hunter, G. K., 'The Beginnings of Elizabethan Drama: Revolution and Continuity', *Renaissance Drama*, 17 (1986), 29–62.

Hutchings, Mark, 'The 'Turk Phenomenon' and the Repertory of the Late Elizabethan Playhouse', *Early Modern Literary Studies*, Special Issue 16 (2007), paras. 1–39.

Ingram, Anders, *Writing the Ottomans: Turkish History in Early Modern England* (Basingstoke: Palgrave Macmillan, 2015).

Kahn, Michael, artistic dir., *Tamburlaine: First Folio Teacher Curriculum Guide* (Washington, DC: The Shakespeare Theatre Company, 2007). http://www.shakespearetheatre.org/education/schools-and-teachers/curriculum-guides/

Karim-Cooper, Farah, *Cosmetics in Shakespearean and Renaissance Drama* (Edinburgh: Edinburgh University Press, 2006).

Kendall, Roy, *Christopher Marlowe and Richard Baines: Journeys through the Elizabethan Underground* (Madison: Fairleigh Dickinson University Press, 2003).

Kimbrough, Robert, '*1 Tamburlaine*: A Speaking Picture in a Tragic Glass', *Renaissance Drama*, 7 (1964), 20–34.

Knutson, Roslyn L., 'Marlowe Reruns: Repertorial Commerce and Marlowe's Plays in Revival' in *Marlowe's Empery: Expanding His Critical Contexts*, ed. by Sara Munson Deats and Robert A. Logan (London: Associated University Presses, 2002), pp. 25–42.

Knutson, Roslyn L., 'Marlowe in Repertory, 1587–1593', in *Christopher Marlowe, Theatrical Commerce, and the Book Trade*, ed. by Kirk Melnikoff and Roslyn L. Knutson (Cambridge: Cambridge University Press, 2018), pp. 26–40.

Kocher, Paul H., 'Marlowe's Art of War', *Studies in Philology*, 39 (1942), 207–25.

Kocher, Paul H., *Christopher Marlowe: A Study of His Thought, Learning and Character* (Chapel Hill: University of North Carolina Press, 1946).

Kozuka, Takashi, and J. R. Mulryne, eds, *Shakespeare, Marlowe, Jonson: New Directions in Biography* (2006; rpt. New York and London: Routledge, 2016).

Kuriyama, Constance B., *Hammer or Anvil: Psychological Patterns in Christopher Marlowe's Plays* (New Brunswick, NJ: Rutgers University Press, 1980).

Kuriyama, Constance B., *Christopher Marlowe: A Renaissance Life* (Ithaca: Cornell University Press, 2002).

Langbaine, Gerard. *An Account of the English Dramatick Poets* (London: Printed by L. L. for George West and Henry Clements, 1691).

Leech, Clifford, 'The Structure of *Tamburlaine*', *Tulane Drama Review*, Marlowe Issue, 8 (1964), 32–46.

Leech, Clifford, ed., *Marlowe: A Collection of Critical Essays* (Englewood Cliffs, NJ: Prentice Hall, 1964).

Leggatt, Alexander, 'Tamburlaine's Sufferings', *Yearbook of English Studies*, 3 (1973), 28–38.

Leslie, Nancy T., '*Tamburlaine* in the Theater: Tartar Grand Guignol or Janus?', *Renaissance Drama*, 4 (1971), 105–20.

Levenson, Jill L., 'Working Words: The Verbal Dynamic of *Tamburlaine*', in *'A Poet and a Filthy Play-maker': New Essays on Christopher Marlowe*, ed. by Kenneth Friedenreich, Roma Gill and Constance B. Kuriyama (New York: AMS Press, 1988), pp. 99–115.

Levin, Harry, *The Overreacher: A Study of Christopher Marlowe* (Boston: Beacon Press, 1952).

Levin, Harry, 'Marlowe Today', *Tulane Drama Review*, Marlowe Issue, 8 (1964), 22–31.

Levin, Richard, 'The Contemporary Perception of Marlowe's *Tamburlaine*', *Medieval and Renaissance Drama in England*, 1 (1984), 51–70.

Lezra, Jacques, 'Geography and Marlowe' in *Christopher Marlowe in Context*, ed. by Emily C. Bartels and Emma Smith (Cambridge: Cambridge University Press, 2013), pp. 125–37.

Lim, Walter S. H., *The Arts of Empire: The Poetics of Colonialism from Raleigh to Milton*. Newark: University of Delaware, 1998.

Logan, Robert A., *Shakespeare's Marlowe: The Influence of Christopher Marlowe on Shakespeare's Artistry* (Aldershot: Ashgate, 2007).

Loomba, Ania and Jonathan Burton, eds, *Race in Early Modern England* (New York: Palgrave Macmillan, 2007).

Lost Plays Database, ed. by Roslyn L. Knutson, David McInnis, and Matthew Steggle (Washington, DC: Folger Shakespeare Library, 2009–), https://lostplays.folger.edu

Lowrance, Bryan, 'Marlowe's Wit: Power, Language, and the Literary in *Tamburlaine* and *Doctor Faustus*', *Modern Philology*, 111.4 (2014), 711–33.

Lunney, Ruth, *Marlowe and the Popular Tradition: Innovation in the English Drama before 1595* (Manchester: Manchester University Press, 2002).

Lyons, Tara L. 'Richard Jones, *Tamburlaine the Great*, and the Making (and Remaking) of a Serial Play Collection in the 1590s', in *Christopher Marlowe, Theatrical Commerce, and the Book*

Trade, ed. by Kirk Melnikoff and Roslyn L. Knutson (Cambridge: Cambridge University Press, 2018), pp. 149–64.

Maclure, Millar, ed., *Christopher Marlowe: The Critical Heritage 1588–1896* (Routledge and Kegan Paul, 1979).

Mahood, M. M., *Poetry and Humanism* (London: Jonathan Cape, 1950).

Manley, Lawrence and Sally-Beth MacLean, *The Lord Strange's Men and Their Plays* (New Haven: Yale University Press, 2014).

Marlowe, Christopher, *Tamburlaine the Great. Who, from a Scythian Shepheard by his rare and wonderfull Conquestes, became a most puissant and mightie Monarch. And (for his tyrannie, and terrour in warre) was tearmed, The Scourge of God. The first part of the two Tragicall discourses* (London: Richard Jones, 1592).

Marlowe, Christopher, *Tamburlaine the Great*, ed. by William Oxberry (London: W. Simpkin, R. Marshall, and C. Chappel, 1820).

Marlowe, Christopher, *The Works of Christopher Marlowe*, 3 vols, ed. by George Robinson (London: Pickering, 1826).

Marlowe, Christopher, *The Dramatic Works of Christopher Marlowe, with Prefatory Remarks, Notes Critical and Explanatory, by W. Oxberry* (London: W. Simpkin, R. Marshall, and C. Chappel, 1827).

Marlowe, Christopher, *The Works of Christopher Marlowe*, 3 vols, ed. by Alexander Dyce (London: Pickering, 1850).

Marlowe, Christopher, *The Works of Christopher Marlowe*, 3 vols ed. by A. H. Bullen (London: John C. Nimmo, 1884).

Marlowe, Christopher, *Christopher Marlowe*, ed. by Havelock Ellis, intro J. A. Symonds (London: Vizetelly, 1887).

Marlowe, Christopher, *The Works of Christopher Marlowe*, ed. by C. F. Tucker Brooke (Oxford: Clarendon, 1910).

Marlowe, Christopher, *Tamburlaine the Great in Two Parts*, ed. by Una M. Ellis-Fermor (London: Methuen, 1930).

Marlowe, Christopher, *Tamburlaine the Great Parts I and II*, ed. by John Jump (Lincoln: University of Nebraska Press, 1967).

Marlowe, Christopher, *Christopher Marlowe: The Complete Plays*, ed. by J. B. Steane (Harmondsworth: Penguin, 1969).

Marlowe, Christopher, *The Plays of Christopher Marlowe*, ed. by Roma Gill (Oxford: Oxford University Press, 1971).

Marlowe, Christopher, *Tamburlaine the Great Parts 1 and 2*, ed. by J. W. Harper (London: Benn, 1971).

Marlowe, Christopher, *The Complete Works of Christopher Marlowe*, ed. by Fredson Bowers (Cambridge: Cambridge University Press, 1973).

Marlowe, Christopher, *Christopher Marlowe's 'Tamburlaine', Part One and Part Two: Text and Major Criticism*, ed. by Irving Ribner (Indianapolis, IN: Bobbs-Merrill, 1974).

Marlowe, Christopher, *Tamburlaine the Great*, ed. by J. S. Cunningham (Manchester: Manchester University Press, 1981).

Marlowe, Christopher, *Tamburlaine, Parts One and Two*, 2nd ed. by Anthony B. Dawson (London: A & C Black, 1997).

Marlowe, Christopher, *Tamburlaine the Great, Parts 1 and 2*, ed. by David Fuller, in *The Complete Works of Christopher Marlowe*, Vol V., gen. ed. Roma Gill (Oxford: Clarendon Press, 1998).

Marlowe, Christopher, *Tamburlaine the Great, Part One and Part Two*, ed. by Mathew R. Martin (Toronto: Broadview, 2014).

Martin, Mathew R., 'Inferior Readings: The Transmigration of "Material" in *Tamburlaine the Great*', *Early Theatre*, 17.2 (2014), 57–75.

Martin, Mathew R., *Tragedy and Trauma in the Plays of Christopher Marlowe* (Farnham: Ashgate, 2015).

Martin, Richard A., 'Marlowe's Tamburlaine and the Language of Romance', *PMLA*, 93 (1978), 248–64.

Matar, Nabil, *Islam in Britain, 1558–1685* (Cambridge: Cambridge University Press, 1998).

Matar, Nabil, *Britain and Barbary, 1589–1689* (Gainesville: University Press of Florida, 2005).

Matusiak, Christopher, 'Marlowe and Theatre History' in *Christopher Marlowe at 450*, ed. by Sara Munson Deats and Robert A. Logan (Farnham: Ashgate, 2015), pp. 281–308.

McAlindon, T., Review of *Hammer or Anvil: Psychological Patterns in Christopher Marlowe's Plays* (1980), *Review of English Studies*, 34 (1983), 210–12.

McDonald, Russ, 'Marlowe and Style', in Patrick Cheney, ed., *The Cambridge Companion to Christopher Marlowe* (Cambridge: Cambridge University Press, 2004), pp. 55–69.

McInnis, David, 'Marlowe's Influence and "The True History of George Scanderbeg"', *Marlowe Studies: An Annual*, 2 (2012), 71–85.

McInnis, David, *Mind-Travelling and Voyage Drama in Early Modern England* (Basingstoke: Palgrave Macmillan, 2013).

McInnis, David, 'Booking Marlowe's Plays', in *Christopher Marlowe, Theatrical Commerce, and the Book Trade*, ed. by Kirk Melnikoff and Roslyn L. Knutson (Cambridge: Cambridge University Press, 2018), pp. 228–42.

McJannet, Linda, *The Sultan Speaks: Dialogue in English Plays and Histories about the Ottoman Turks* (Basingstoke: Palgrave Macmillan, 2006).

McJannet, Linda, 'Timur's Theatrical Journey: Or, when Did Tamburlaine Become Black?', *Sederi*, 26 (2016), 31–66.

McMillin, Scott and Sally-Beth MacLean, *The Queen's Men and their Plays* (Cambridge: Cambridge University Press, 1998).

Melnikoff, Kirk, 'Jones's Pen and Marlowe's Socks: Richard Jones' *Tamburlaine the Great* (1590), and the Beginnings of English Dramatic Literature', *Studies in Philology*, 102.3 (2005), 184–209.

Melnikoff, Kirk, 'Jones, Richard (fl. 1564–1613), bookseller and printer', *Oxford Dictionary of National Biography*. https://doi.org/10.1093/ref:odnb/15070

Melnikoff, Kirk, and Roslyn L. Knutson, eds, *Christopher Marlowe, Theatrical Commerce, and the Book Trade* (Cambridge: Cambridge University Press, 2018).

Merchant, W. Moelwyn, 'Marlowe the Orthodox', in *Christopher Marlowe*, ed. by Brian Morris (New York: Hill and Wang, 1969), pp. 177–92.

Moore, Roger E., 'The Spirit and the Letter: Marlowe's *Tamburlaine* and Elizabethan Religious Radicalism', *Studies in Philology*, 99 (2002), 123–51.

Morris, Brian, ed., *Christopher Marlowe* (London: Ernest Benn, 1968).

Morris, Harry, 'Marlowe's Poetry', *Tulane Drama Review*, Marlowe Issue, 8 (1964), 134–54.

Mulryne, J. R., and Stephen Fender, 'Marlowe and the "Comic Distance"', in *Christopher Marlowe*, ed. by Brian Morris (New York: Hill and Wang, 1969), pp. 47–64.

Munro, Lucy, 'Marlowe on the Caroline Stage', *Shakespeare Bulletin*, 27.1 (2009), 39–50.

Nardizzi, Vin, 'Environ', in *Veer Ecology: A Companion for Environmental Thinking*, ed. by Jeffrey Jerome Cohen and Lowell Duckert (Minneapolis: University of Minnesota Press, 2017), pp. 183–95.

Ngai, Sianne, *Ugly Feelings* (Cambridge, MA: Harvard University Press, 2005).

Niayesh, Ladan, 'Shakespeare's Persians', *Shakespeare*, 4 (2008), 127–36.

Nicholl, Charles, *The Reckoning: The Murder of Christopher Marlowe* (1992; rev. London: Vintage, 2002).

Nicholson, Catherine, *Uncommon Tongues: Eloquence and Eccentricity in the English Renaissance* (Philadelphia: University of Pennsylvania Press, 2013).

Palmer, D. J., 'Marlowe's Naturalism', in *Christopher Marlowe*, ed. by Brian Morris (New York: Hill and Wang, 1969), pp. 151–76.

Parker, John, *The Aesthetics of Antichrist: From Christian Drama to Christopher Marlowe* (Ithaca: Cornell University Press, 2007).

Parr, Johnstone. *Tamburlaine's Malady and Other Essays on Astrology in Elizabethan Drama* (University, AL; University of Alabama Press, 1953).

Paster, Gail Kern. *Humoring the Body: Emotions and the Shakespearean Stage* (Chicago: University of Chicago Press, 2004).

Patrides, C. A., '"The Bloody and Cruell Turke": The Background of a Renaissance Commonplace', *Studies in the Renaissance*, 10 (1963), 126–35.

Pearson, Meg, 'The Perils of Political Showmanship: Marlowe's *Tamburlaine the Great*', in *Leadership and Elizabethan Culture*, ed. by Peter Iver Kaufman (New York: Palgrave Macmillan, 2013), pp. 175–90.

Pecan, David, 'Dramatic Prologue and the Early Modern Concept of Genre: Understanding Marlowe's *Tamburlaine the Great* in its Critical Context', *This Rough Magic*, 3 (2012), 28–62.

Peet, Donald, 'The Rhetoric of Tamburlaine', *ELH*, 26 (1959), 137–55.

Pendergraft, Stacy, 'Marlowe Mee: Constructing the Marlowe Project', *Shakespeare Bulletin*, 27 (2009), 51–62.

Phillips, Edward, *Theatrum Poetarum, or a Compleat Collection of the Poets, Especially The most Eminent, of all Ages* (London: Charles Smith, 1675).

[Poe, Edgar Allan], *Tamerlane and Other Poems*, by a Bostonian (Boston: Calvin F. S. Thomas, 1827).

Poirier, Michel, *Christopher Marlowe* (London: Chatto and Windus, 1951).

Powell, Jocelyn, 'Marlowe's Spectacle', *Tulane Drama Review*, Marlowe Issue, 8 (1964), 195–210.

Preedy, Chloe Kathleen, *Marlowe's Literary Scepticism: Politic Religion and Post-Reformation Polemic* (London: Arden Shakespeare, 2012).

Reiss, Timothy J., *Tragedy and Truth: Studies in the Development of a Renaissance and Neoclassical Discourse* (New Haven, CT: Yale University Press, 1980).

Ribner, Irving, 'The Idea of History in Marlowe's *Tamburlaine*', *ELH*, 20 (1953), 251–66.

Ribner, Irving, 'Machiavelli and Marlowe', *Comparative Literature*, 6 (1954), 349–56.

Ribner, Irving, 'Greene's Attack on Marlowe: Some Light on *Alphonsus* and *Selimus*', *Studies in Philology*, 52 (1955), 162–71.

Ribner, Irving, 'Marlowe and the Critics', *Tulane Drama Review*, Marlowe Issue, 8 (1964), 211–24.

Richards, Susan, 'Marlowe's *Tamburlaine II*: A Drama of Death', *Modern Language Quarterly*, 26 (1965), 375–87.

Riggs, David, *The World of Christopher Marlowe* (New York: Henry Holt and Company, 2004).

Rose, Mary Beth, *The Expense of Spirit: Love and Sexuality in Renaissance Drama* (Ithaca: Cornell University Press, 1988).

Rowe, Nicholas, *Tamerlane: A Tragedy, As it is Acted at the New Theater in Little Lincoln's-Inn-Fields* (London: Jacob Tonson, 1702).

Rowe, Stephen D., and Richard A. Martin, *'Tambulaine'*, *PMLA*, 93 (1978), 1014–16.

Rutter, Tom, *The Cambridge Introduction to Christopher Marlowe* (Cambridge: Cambridge University Press, 2012).

Rutter, Tom, *'Tamburlaine*: Parts One and Two', in *Christopher Marlowe at 450*, ed. by Sara Munson Deats and Robert A. Logan (Farnham: Ashgate, 2015), pp. 51–70.

Rutter, Tom, 'Allusions to Marlowe in Printed Plays, 1594', in *Christopher Marlowe, Theatrical Commerce, and the Book Trade*, ed. by Kirk Melnikoff and Roslyn L. Knutson (Cambridge: Cambridge University Press, 2018), pp. 199–213.

Sanders, Wilbur, *The Dramatist and the Received Idea: Studies in the Plays of Marlowe and Shakespeare* (Cambridge: Cambridge University Press, 1968).

Saunders, C[harles], *Tamerlane the Great, A Tragedy As it is Acted by their Majesties Servants at the Theatre Royal* (London: Printed for Richard Bentley and M. Magnes, 1681).

Schuman, Samuel, 'Minor Characters and the Thematic Structure of Marlowe's *Tamburlaine II*', *Modern Language Studies*, 8 (1978), 27–33.

Scott, Sarah K., and M. L. Stapleton, eds, *Christopher Marlowe the Craftsman: Lives, Stage and Page* (Farnham: Ashgate, 2010).

Seaton, Ethel, 'Marlowe's Map', *Essays and Studies by Members of the English Association* 10 (1924), 13–35.

Seaton, Ethel, 'Fresh Sources for Marlowe', *Review of English Studies*, 5 (1929), 385–401.

Semler, Liam E., *Teaching Shakespeare and Marlowe: Learning Versus the System* (London: Bloomsbury Arden Shakespeare, 2013).

Seyler, Dorothy U., 'James Broughton, Editor of Marlowe's Plays', *PBSA* 69 (1975), 311–22.

Shepard, Alan, 'Endless Sacks: Soldiers' Desire in *Tamburlaine*', *Renaissance Quarterly* 46 (1993), 734–53.

Shepard, Alan, *Marlowe's Soldiers: Rhetorics of Masculinity in the Age of the Armada* (Burlington, VT: Ashgate, 2002).

Shepherd, Simon, *Marlowe and the Politics of Elizabethan Theatre* (Brighton: Harvester Press, 1986).

Sinfield, Alan, *Faultlines: Cultural Materialism and the Politics of Dissident Reading* (Berkeley, CA: University of California Press, 1992).

Slotkin, Joel Eliot, '"Seeke out another Godhead": Religious Epistemology and Representations of Islam in *Tamburlaine*', *Modern Philology*, 111 (2014), 408–36.

Smith, Ian, *Race and Rhetoric in the Renaissance: Barbarian Errors* (New York: Palgrave MacMillan, 2009).

Smith, Ian, 'Othello's Black Handkerchief', *Shakespeare Quarterly*, 64.1 (2013), 1–25.

Spence, Leslie, 'The Influence of Marlowe's Sources on *Tamburlaine I*', *Modern Philology*, 24 (1926), 181–99.

Spence, Leslie, 'Tamburlaine and Marlowe', *PMLA*, 42 (1927), 604–22.

Stapleton, M. L., 'Christopher Marlowe', *Oxford Bibliographies* (Oxford University Press, 2017).

Starks, Lisa, '"Won with thy words and conquered with thy looks": Sadism, Masochism, and the Masochistic Gaze in *1 Tamburlaine*', in *Marlowe, History, and Sexuality: New Critical Essays on Christopher Marlowe*, ed. by Paul Whitfield White (New York: AMS Press, 1998), pp. 179–93.

Steane, J. B., *Marlowe: A Critical Study* (Cambridge: Cambridge University Press, 1964).

Stedman, Jane W., '*Tamburlaine the Great* by Christopher Marlowe', *Educational Theatre Journal* 25.1 (1973), 106–8.

Stevens, Andrea, *Inventions of the Skin: The Painted Body in Early English Drama* (Edinburgh: Edinburgh University Press, 2014).

Sullivan, Garrett A., Jr. 'Geography and Identity in Marlowe' in *The Cambridge Companion to Christopher Marlowe*, ed. by Patrick Cheney (Cambridge: Cambridge University Press, 2004), pp. 231–44.

Syme, Holger Schott, 'Marlowe in his Moment' in *Christopher Marlowe in Context*, ed. by Emily C. Bartels and Emma Smith (Cambridge: Cambridge University Press, 2013), pp. 275–84.

Symonds, John Addington, *Shakspere's Predecessors in the English Drama* (London: Smith, Elder, and Co., 1884).

Tarlinskaja, Marina, *Shakespeare and the Versification of English Drama, 1561–1642* (2014; rpt. Abingdon: Routledge, 2016).

Thomas, Vivien, and William Tydeman, eds, *Christopher Marlowe: The Plays and Their Sources* (1994; rpt. London: Routledge, 2011).

Thomson, Leslie, 'Marlowe's Staging of Meaning', *Medieval and Renaissance Drama in England*, 18 (2005), 19–36.

Thorp, Willard, "The Ethical Problem in Marlowe's Tamburlaine', *JEGP*, 29 (1930), 385–9.

Thurn, David H., 'Sights of Power in *'Tamburlaine'*, *English Literary Renaissance,* 19 (1989), 3–21.

Toynbee, Arnold J., *A Study of History* (Oxford: Oxford University Press, 1946).

Tromly, Frederic B., *Playing with Desire: Christopher Marlowe and the Art of Tantalization* (Toronto: University of Toronto Press, 1998).

Turner, Timothy A., 'Executing Calyphas: Gender, Discipline and Sovereignty in *2 Tamburlaine*', *Explorations in Renaissance Culture*, 44 (2018), 141–56.

Vaughan, Virginia Mason. *Performing Blackness on English Stages, 1500–1800*. Cambridge: Cambridge University Press, 2009.

Violanti, Heather J., '*Tamburlaine the Great*, Cannon's Mouth Productions', *Research Opportunities in Medieval and Renaissance Drama*, 43 (2004), 123–4.

Vitkus, Daniel, *Turning Turk: English Theatre and the Multicultural Mediterranean, 1570–1630* (Basingstoke: Palgrave Macmillan, 2003).

Waith, Eugene, *The Herculean Hero in Marlowe, Chapman, Shakespeare, and Dryden* (London: Chatto and Windus, 1962).

Weil, Judith, *Christopher Marlowe: Merlin's Prophet* (Cambridge: Cambridge University Press, 1977).

Wiggins, Martin, in association with Catherine Richardson, *British Drama, 1533–1642: A Catalogue*, 11 vols (Oxford: Oxford University Press, 2012–).

Williams, Carolyn, '"This Effeminate Brat": Tamburlaine's Unmanly Son', *Medieval and Renaissance Drama in England* 9 (1997), 56–80.

Wilson, F. P., *Marlowe and the Early Shakespeare* (Clarendon: Oxford, 1953).

Wilson, Richard, 'Introduction', in *Christopher Marlowe*, ed. by Richard Wilson (London: Longman, 1999), pp. 1–29.

Wilson, Richard, 'Visible Bullets: *Tamburlaine the Great* and Ivan the Terrible', in *Christopher Marlowe*, ed. by Richard Wilson (London: Longman, 1999), pp. 120–39.

Wilson, Richard, 'Specters of Marlowe: The State of the Debt and the Work of Mourning' in *Christopher Marlowe at 450*, ed. by Sara Munson Deats and Robert A. Logan (Farnham: Ashgate, 2015), pp. 227–56.

Wraight, A. D. and Virginia F. Stern, *In Search of Christopher Marlowe: A Pictorial Biography* (1965; rpt. Chichester: Adam Hart, 1993).

Yilmaz, Zümre Gizem, 'The sweet fruition of an earthly crown': Elemental Mastery and Ecophobia in *Tamburlaine the Great* and *Doctor Faustus*', *SEDERI: Journal of the Spanish Society for English Renaissance Studies*, 28 (2018), 79–96.

INDEX

Note: Endnotes are not included in the index.

Adams, Thomas R. 17
Admiral's Men 5, 7–10, 76, 169
Aebischer, Pascale 64–5
Alleyn, Edward 20, 21, 34, 44–6, 47, 89–90, 189
Altman, Joel 37
American Shakespeare Center 47–8, 66
Archer, Edward 91–3
Aristotle 110–13
Armstrong, William A. 33
Arya, Sagar I M 65
Astington, John H. 176, 180

Bakeless, John 29, 147–8
Baines, Richard 73, 126, 169, 170, 171, 173
Bamford, Karen 174, 180
Banks, Fiona 174, 180
Barber, C. L. 32, 35
Barbour, Richmond 68–9
Barker, Nicholas 17
Bartels, Emily C. 38–9, 79, 131, 182–3, 187, 188, 189
Battenhouse, Roy W. 27, 28–30, 32, 33, 188
Beck, Ervin 51
Beinecke Library 86–7, 97
Benét, Vincent 50

Bennett, Kristen Abbott
　The Kit Marlowe Project 179–80
Berek, Peter 1, 11
Bevington, David 31, 37, 52, 56, 171, 172, 182–3
Billington, Michael 55
Boal, Augusto 177–8
Boas, Frederick 147–8
Bodin, Jean 141
Bogart, Anne 179
Borlik, Todd, 109
Boston Public Library 172
Bourne, Claire M. L. 64, 75
Bowers, Fredson 37, 40, 176
Bowman, Ruth Laurion 177, 180
Boyd, Michael 44, 63–5, 144–5, 190
Bradley, A. C. 25
Brantley, Ben 190, 191
British Library 173
Brook, Nathaniel 92
Brooke, C. F. Tucker 26, 184, 185
Brooks, Avery 59–60
Brooks, Harold F. 37
Broughton, James A. 23, 76
Brown, John Russell 34
Bullen, A. H. 25
Burchell, David 108–9

Burnett, Mark Thornton 39–40, 131
Burton, Jonathan 68, 69, 131

Camden, Carrol 27, 29
Cannon's Mouth 47, 61
Cartelli, Thomas 177, 180
Case, R. H. 28
Case, Sarah 60–1
Cecil, William (Lord Burghley) 161
Cerasano, S. P. 189, 191
Chambers, E. K. 28, 37
Chapman, George
  Eastward Ho! 158–9
Cheesman, Neil 61
Cheney, Patrick 32, 39–40, 79–80, 82, 182–3, 184, 185, 187, 188, 189
Chiari, Sophie 110
Clarke, Danielle 174, 180
Clarke, Donald B. 49
Cockcroft, Robert 33
Cole, Douglas 31, 184, 185
Collier, John Payne 22, 26, 76
Conroy, Derval 174, 180
Coryate, Thomas 70–1
Crane, Gregory R. 172
Crane, Mary Thomas 18, 109, 122–4
Crawford, Charles 27, 38
Cummins, Juliet 108–9
Cunningham, J. S. 37, 56, 170, 172
Cutts, John 33

Dabbs, Thomas 24, 40
Daniel, Samuel 78
Darnton, Robert 17
Davenant, William
  A Playhouse to Be Let 21–2
Davies, Surekha 134
Dawson, Anthony 46, 170, 172, 189
Deats, Sara Munson 39, 182–3, 186, 187
Dekker, Thomas 70
  Old Fortunatus 20
  The Wonderful Year 20
Digges, Thomas 123
Dimmock, Matthew 70
Dionisotti, Paola 52
Dollimore, Jonathan 36
Dowden, Edward 24, 25
Downie, J. A. 182–3, 187
Drama Online 172
Dryden, John
  The Conquest of Granada 22
Dukes, Ricky 61
Dutch Church Libel 2
Duxfield, Andrew 78, 182–3, 188
Dyce, Alexander 23, 24, 25

Early English Books Online (EEBO) 172, 174, 176
Eberly Family Special Collections Library 87, 97–104
Egan, Gabriel 109
Ellis, Havelock 16, 25
Ellis-Fermor, Una 28, 32, 33, 148
Eliot, T. S. 28, 34, 52
EMED: A Digital Anthology of Early Modern English Drama 172
Emsley, Sarah 39
Engle, Lars 175, 180

Faberes, Lourdes 61–2
Famous Victories of Henry the Fifth 11–15
Fanta, Christopher 32
Farey, Peter 172
Farmer, Alan B. 90
Farmer, Richard 21
Farr, David 57–8
Fehrenbach, Robert J. 38
Finney, Albert 53, 55
Floyd-Wilson, Mary 131, 134, 136
Fortescue, Thomas 27, 153, 157
Fourth Monkey 60–1
Foxe, John 153
Francisco, Timothy 187
Frazer, Rupert 52
Friedenreich, Kenneth 38
Frongillo, John 184, 185
Fulgosius, Baptista 154
Fulke, William 111, 121, 122
Fuller, David 40

Garber, Marjorie 36
Gardner, Lyn 43, 47, 57
Gawdy, Philip 8, 28, 37, 46
Gayton, Edmund 22
Gibbard, Peter 77
Gibson, Rex 174, 180
Gildon, Charles 94
Gill, Roma 32
Gillies, John 188
Giovio, Paulo 157
Glasgow Citizens' Company 52–3
Godshalk, W. L. 35, 37
Godwin, Laura G. 59, 60
Goeckle, George L. 189, 191
Goldberg, Jonathan 186, 187
Golding, Arthur 112–13, 126–7

Grande, Troni Y. 184, 185
Green, Steve 60–1
Greenblatt, Stephen 36, 131, 156, 188, 189, 190
Greene, Robert 7, 70
  Alphonsus of Arragon 30
  A Looking-Glass for London and England 114
  Perimedes 1–2, 19, 30, 45, 73, 76
  Selimus 8, 10, 30
Grogan, Jane 188, 189
Guthrie, Tyrone 51–2
Gwilym, Mike 52

Haber, Judith 131
Hack, Keith 52–3
Hackel, Heidi Brayman 174, 180
Hagerman, Anita M. 59, 60
Hakluyt, Richard 156
Hall, Joseph 20, 46
Hall, Peter 53–5, 58
Hallam, Arthur 23, 24
Handel, George Frideric
  Tamerlano 50
Hands, Terry 56–7
Hansen, Claire G. 187
Harper, J. W. 37
Harraway, Clare 182–3
Harrington-Odedra, Gavin 61
Harris, Jonathan Gil 70–1, 155
Harvey, Gabriel 113–14, 116, 119
Hattaway, Michael 33
Hayes, Richard 52
Healy, Thomas 156, 157
Heilpern, John 53, 55
Heng, Geraldine 133
Heninger, S. K. 111–12, 116

Henslowe, Philip 5, 8–9, 20, 22, 46, 160
Henson, Eithne 56, 170, 172
Heywood, Thomas 2, 20, 45, 76, 89–90, 93
Hicks, Greg 57
Hippocrates 141
Hirrel, Michael J. 8
Hiscock, Andrew 175, 181
Honan, Park 81, 82–3, 169, 170, 173
Hooks, Adam G. 75, 76
Hopkins, Lisa 38–9, 81, 169, 170, 175, 181, 182–3
Hunt, Leigh 23–4

Internet Archive 172
Isherwood, Charles 60
Iwuji, Chuk 65

Janson, Merritt 64, 145
Johnson, Lawrence 176
Johnson, Thomas 92
Jokinen, Anniina 172, 173
Jones, Gwilym 125
Jones, Richard 2, 3, 4, 15, 19–20, 27, 74, 75, 76, 86, 87, 89–90, 92, 95–6, 101, 176–7
Jonson, Ben 1
  Eastward Ho! 158–9
  Timber 15, 21, 46
Journal of Marlowe Studies 182–3
Jump, John D. 36–7

Kahn, Michael 58–60
Kelsall, Malcolm 156
Kemble, John Philip 94
Kendall, Roy 169–70, 173

Kent, Jonathan 52
King's Men 7
Kirkman, Francis 21, 92–6
Kirwan, Peter 75
Kissoon, Jeffery 52
Knutson, Roslyn L. 9, 11, 74–6, 169, 170, 182–3
Kocher, Paul H. 29–30, 32, 188, 189
Kozuka, Takashi 169–70
Kuriyama, Constance Brown 35–6, 81, 169, 170, 173
Kyd, Thomas 70, 73, 119–20, 171
  Spanish Tragedy 5, 6

Lamb, Charles 22, 26
Langbaine, Gerard 93–4
Lazarus Theatre 61
Lee, William 91
Leech, Clifford 31–2, 33, 34
Leggat, Alexander 174, 180
Leslie, Nancy 49, 50–1, 52
Lesser, Zachary 90
Levenson, Jill L. 184, 185
Levin, Harry 30
Lezra, Jacques 79
LibriVox 271
Lindley, Arthur 188, 189
Lindsey, Robert 171, 173
Lodge, Thomas 7
  A Looking-Glass for London and England 114
Logan, Robert A. 175, 181, 182–3, 184
lost plays
  'Belin Dun' 9
  'Charlemagne' 11
  'Cutlack' 11
  'Godfrey of Boulogne' 9

'Hercules, parts 1 and 2' 10
'Mahomet' 9
'Scanderbeg' 11
'Tamar Cham, parts 1 and 2' 10, 15
'The Turkish Mahomet and Hiren the Fair Greek' 9
Lowrance, Bryan 77
Lukacs, Peter 172, 173
Lunney, Ruth 177, 181, 185
Luther, Martin 112
Lyly, John 7, 77
Lyons, Tara L. 75

McDiarmid, Ian 52
McDonald, Russ 184, 185
Machiavelli, Niccolò 33, 37, 119
MacIntyre, Jean 160
McJannet, Linda 49, 56, 59, 60, 65, 70
MacLean, Sally-Beth 4, 6–7
MacLure, Millar 38
McMillin, Scott 4, 6–7
Malin, Peter 62
Malone, Edmond 21, 76
Marchitello, Howard 108
Marlowe, Christopher 7, 90, 111, 114, 119, 123
  attribution of *Henry VI* plays to 27
  attribution of *Locrine* to 27
  attribution of *Lust's Dominion* to 22, 27
  biographies of 168–70
  Doctor Faustus 2, 9, 10, 44, 67, 91, 94, 131, 171, 174, 179
  Edward II 22, 44, 171, 174, 179
  Hero and Leander 25
  Jew of Malta 2, 9, 10, 20, 44, 45, 76, 89–90, 93, 119, 131, 156, 171, 174, 175, 179
  'mighty line' 1, 3, 77–8, 184
  'Passionate Shepherd to his Love' 171, 184
  Tamburlaine, see separate entry
Marlowe, Sam 58
Marlowe Bibliography Online 182
Marlowe Studies: An Annual 182
Marsh, Henry 92
Marston, John
  Eastward Ho! 158–9
Martin, Craig 110–12
Martin, Mathew R. 74, 170, 173, 184, 185
Martin, Richard A. 184, 185
Martire, Pietro 159
Masood, Abid 153
Matar, Nabil 68, 81
Matusiak, Christopher 46
Mazzilli, Mary 190, 191
Mee, Charles 179
Melnikoff, Kirk 74–6, 169, 170, 182–3
Mentz, Steve 109–10
Menzer, Paul 48
Merchant, W. Moelwyn 33
Mexia, Pedro 151, 153, 154, 155, 157
Middleton, Thomas 76
Mills, Amy 61
Minton, Eric 66
Moin, Asfar 150, 152
Moore, Roger E. 188, 189
Morris, Harry 34

Moryson, Fynes 141
Moulton, Ian Frederick 174, 180
Mulryne, J. R. 169, 170

Nardizzi, Vin 71–2
Nashe, Thomas 7, 171
National Theatre 16, 53–5
Naylor, Ben 47, 58
Newton, Thomas 21, 93
Ngain, Sianne 134
Nicholl, Charles 81, 169, 170
Nicholson, Catherine 77–8
Nightingale, Benedict 43–4, 66

Olivier Theatre 53–5
Online Library of Liberty 172, 173
Owusu, Jude 63, 145
Oxberry, William 23, 76, 89
Oxford Bibliographies Online 182

Parker, John 72–3
Parnell, J. T. 182–3, 187
Partington, Gill 85, 104
Pearson, Meg 186
Pecan, David 174, 185
Peele, George 7
    Battle of Alcazar 9, 10, 125
    Titus Andronicus 124, 131
Peet, Donald 184, 185
Pendergraft, Stacy 178, 181
Perondinus, Petrus 151, 154, 155, 157–8
Perseus Digital Library 172
Phillips, Edward 20, 76, 93
Philpott, Maryam 60–1
Piper, Tom 65
Pliny 111

Plockey, Prince 61
Pointon, Marcia 163
Poirier, Michel 156–7, 161
Pollard, Richard 92
Powell, Jocelyn 34–5
Power, Ben 47
Pratt, Aaron T. 91
Preedy, Chloe Kathleen 18, 109, 188, 189
Project Gutenberg, 172, 173
Prynne, William 90
Ptolemy (Claudius Ptolemaeus) 141
Puttenham, George 78

Quayle, Anthony 51
Queen's Men 3–6, 11–15
Quilley, Denis 54

Ralegh, Walter 184
Ranald, Margaret Loftus 57
Rasmussen, Eric 171–2, 175, 180
Red Bull 90
Renascence Editions 172, 173
Ribner, Irving 30–1, 32, 38
Rich, Barnabe 141
Richards, Susan 34
Riggs, David 81–2, 169, 170
Roe, Sir Thomas 70–1, 162–5
Rogers, Richard 91
Romany, Frank 171, 173
Rose, Mary Beth 38
Rose playhouse 5, 8, 20, 45, 46, 47, 186
Rowe, Nicholas
    Tamerlane 49–50, 51
Royal Shakespeare Company 56–7, 60, 63–5, 66, 145
Rutter, Tom 12, 45, 68, 169, 170

Said, Edward 68, 148
Sanders, Wilbur 32
Saunders, Charles
    Tamerlaine the Great
        15, 48–9, 93–5
Schneider, Jane 160
Scott, Sarah K. 182–3
Scythians 140–2
Seaton, Ethel 27, 29, 164
Semler, Liam E. 177–8, 181, 186–7
Shadwell, Thomas
    The Humourists 22
Shakelton, Francis 123, 126
Shakespeare, William 1, 3, 174
    First Part of the Contention... 75
    Hamlet 5, 143–4
    Henry IV, Parts 1 and 2 11, 20, 45, 132
    Henry V 6–7, 11, 132, 175, 184
    Julius Caesar 125
    King Lear 14, 49, 110
    Merchant of Venice 132
    Othello 129–30, 144
    Richard II 108, 132
    The Tempest 139
    Titus Andronicus 124, 131
Shakespeare Theatre Company (Washington, DC) 58–60, 180
Shand, G. B. 174, 180
Shand, Skip 57, 58
Shepard, Alan 38–9, 187
Shepherd, Simon 36
Sher, Anthony 56–7, 145
Sidney Harman Hall 59
Sidney, Philip 95
Sinfield, Alan 38

Sir Clyomon and Clamydes 3
Skipitares, Theodora
    'The Rise and Fall of Timur the Lame' 190
Slotkin, Joel Elliot 73, 188, 189
Smith, Emma 79, 182–3, 187, 189
Smith, Ian 132–3, 144
Smyth, Adam 85, 104
Spence, Leslie 27
Spenser, Edmund 28, 77, 82, 113, 141–2, 184
Stanley, N. T. 190, 191
Stapleton, M. L. 182–3
Starks, Lisa 39
Stationers' Register 86
Steane, J. B. 32, 35
Stedman, Jane 52
Steevens, George 10
Steggle, Matthew 9
Stern, Tiffany 75–6
Stern, Virginia F. 169, 170, 173
Storry, Malcolm 56
Strange's Men 10
Stredder, James 174, 181
Suckling, John
    The Goblins 21
Sullivan, Garrett A., Jr 131
Swan Theatre (RSC) 56–7
Swinburne, A. C. 26–7, 28
Syme, Holger Schott 45–6
Symonds, John Addington 25

Tamburlaine
    Anglo-Ottoman studies and 68–71, 135–6
    authorship of 20–3, 76, 93–4
    critical editions of 23, 25–6, 27, 32, 36–7, 40, 170–3
    dramaturgy of 11–15, 185–6

early publication of 2, 19, 73–6, 85–105
environmentalism and 71–2
gender and sexuality in 186–8
genre of 2–4, 86, 92, 96, 101, 104, 184–5
form of 6–7, 8, 24, 95–6
influence of 1, 6, 8
literary influences on 79–80
Marlowe biography and 80–3
meteorology in 107–28
morality of 1, 5–6, 28–9, 95, 97
new philology and 77–9
novelty of 1, 3
performance history, 7–11, 19–20, 43–66, 73–6, 189–91
race and 71, 129–46, 188–9
religion and 72–3, 188–9
repertorial context 7–11
scholarship on 19–41, 67–83
sources of 147–65, 173–4
teaching 167–91
Tarlinskaja, Marina 184, 185
Tarlton, Richard 1
Theatre for a New Audience 63–5, 144–5, 190
Thirsk, Joan 156
Thomas, Vivien 173–4
Thompson, Ayanna 174, 181
Thompson, John Douglas 63, 64, 144–5
Thomson, Leslie 186
Thorp, Willard 27
Thurn, David H. 185–6
Tilney, Edmund 4

Timür (Amir Timür Gurgan) 17, 49, 70–1, 147–65, 169, 175
Tribble, Evelyn 108
Tromly, Frederic B. 186, 187
Turchi, Laura 174, 181
Turner, Timothy A. 187
Tydeman, William 173–4

Varn, Lynn K. 184, 185
Vaughan, Robert 176
Venning, Dan 64
Violanti, Heather J. 47
Vivaldi, Antonio
  Bajazet 50

Waith, Eugene 31
Walsingham, Sir Francis 4, 161
Wan, Leo 61
Wardle, Irving 55, 56, 57, 66
Watkins, Leila 73
Weheliye, Alexander 133–4, 144
Whetstone, George 151, 153
White, Edward 89–90, 92, 96
White, Paul Whitfield 186, 187
Whitney, Charles 83
Wiggins, Martin 56
Williams, Carolyn 187, 188
Wilson, F. P. 30
Wilson, Richard 15, 40
Wolfit, Donald 51
Woolley, Edgar Montillion 50
Wraight, A. D. 169–70, 173

Yale University (1919 production) 50–1
Yellow Earth 61–3, 190
Yilmaz, Zümre Gizem 72
Young Genius 57–8
Young, Robert 135

www.ingramcontent.com/pod-product-compliance
Lightning Source LLC
Chambersburg PA
CBHW062124300426
44115CB00012BA/1796